ISLANDS IN TIME

ISLANDS IN TIME
A Natural and Human History of the Islands of Maine

by Philip W. Conkling

Drawings by Katherine Hall Fitzgerald

Photographs by: George Putz, Jim Kosinski, and Rick Perry

Down East Books   CAMDEN, MAINE

Copyright © 1981 by Philip Conkling
Photographs copyright © 1981 by George Putz, Jim Kosinski, and Rick Perry
Photograph on p. 195 © 1985 by Peter M. Ralston
ISBN 0-89272-224-X
Library of Congress Catalog Card Number 80-70610

Text design by Ingrid Beckman
Cover design by Dawn Peterson
Cover photograph used courtesy of Hurricane Island Outward Bound
School. Photo by Rick Perry.
Maps by Katherine Hall Fitzgerald

5

Printed at Capital City Press, Inc., Montpelier, Vermont

DOWN EAST BOOKS / Camden, Maine

For Jamien

Contents

Acknowledgments

THE WORLD SEEMS to have an amused tolerance of book writing, even though it usually involves a great deal of inconvenience for those whose lives touch its edges. I owe the first debt of gratitude to those who were not simply tolerant of the questions and requests scattered before them, but were positively cheerful in answering them.

I do not know how to properly thank the artists whose works contribute most of the attractions this book has to offer. Rick Perry volunteered his small boat on short notice for photographic assignments across large stretches of water. Jim Kosinski worked so many nights in the darkroom to make sure that all of our (as well as his) prints would achieve their best effect that the rest of us worried over his health. Kate Fitzgerald was consistently patient with requests to rework small details of her already fine and detailed drawings. Finally, George Putz not only contributed his favorite photographs, but he read the entire manuscript twice and generally browbeat me into shoring up its weaknesses.

One other friend and colleague had a large and unseen hand in the book. Ray Leonard of the United States Forest Service Lab in Durham, New Hampshire, hired me to collect baseline ecological data on Maine islands and was generous enough to put up with the chaotic work schedule that too often borrowed from his time.

Hurricane Island Outward Bound School, with which I have enjoyed the last half decade of a working life on the Maine islands, took me to literally hundreds of islands, often under difficult conditions, and has wholeheartedly supported the research efforts upon which this book is based. Without the likes of Ed Dietrich, Chip Bauer, and Carol Rohl of Hurricane's waterfront; and Peter Willauer and Bob Rheault up front (to name only a few of the staff members who have contributed their time and intimate knowledge of the islands), this book would have remained only a gleam in my eye.

Many of the others who provided help probably had no idea they were doing anything unusual; they're just nice people. Professor Bill Drury of the College of the Atlantic discussed dozens of topics while we were under-way to one island or another, and these helped shape important sections of the book. Cap deRochemont found me the perfect place to write the manuscript. Peter and Raquel Boehmer housed George Putz and myself on Monhegan, as did Jonathan Nolan and his mother on Cushing Island. Charles Mclane of Dartmouth College shared historical information and sources he collected over the years. Joe Johanssen of Medomak provided valuable information on the early National Audubon Preserves. Robert Dow of the Maine Department of Marine Resources made available to me volumes of information on the Gulf of Maine. Barbara Richardson read the chapter on fish and offered suggestions and encouragement. Sandy Sawyer came for a winter visit and typed (and retyped) two long chapters. Kerry O'Brien and Carol Rohl typed the others on short notice.

Finally, my editor, Kathleen Brandes, went out of her way to check facts and correct errors that are more appropriately my responsibility. I, for one, hope she found most of them, because the rest belong to me.

Introduction: Apart and Between

OUT THERE, between the point where you can take your last dry step and the faint horizon of your mind's eye, lies another world, apart. A world of islands—part sea, part rock; part wild, part subdued; part fish, part man; and with winged birds between. From the tip of Cape Elizabeth or Cape Wash, from Cape Small or Cape Split, from the ends of Schoodic Point or Pemaquid Point, from Newbury Neck or Linekin Neck, from Owl's Head or Schooner Head, you can see them out there like sequins—small and shining objects in the water. Islands. Not just a few islands, but countless multitudes of great and little wave-washed rocks. A lifetime's worth of islands, apart and between.

How many islands are there out there? Maybe we should know, but we don't. Can't even count them. The number changes too often with storms, history, and the tides—but mostly with the tides—to make the effort seem worthwhile. If you count them at high water, for instance, you end up with a lot of islands that are actually attached to the mainland or to other islands at low tide; if you count at low water, you count hundreds that disappear 10 to 20 feet under at high tide. In most places in this world you might be able to accept Webster's definition of an island as a piece of land smaller than a continent surrounded by water, but not here. Not in Maine. These islands are, like their inhabitants, hard to pin down.

From time to time various earnest landsmen have tried counting Maine's islands. In 1913, for example, a Moses Greenleaf, Esq., was hired to count the islands for the state, but he was only one man (an Esq., at that), and he didn't have a boat, which meant that his transportation—how should we put it—was at the mercy of fishermen. Oh, he got most of the big ones, including the island in Muscongus Bay with a year-round population that had simply been left off previous maps, but either Greenleaf did not consider the little ones important or his island informants considered them too important to let the state know about them.

More recently, someone in Augusta remembered that the state owned all unclaimed islands as a result of the same legislative mandate that had sent Mr. Greenleaf out to count them some 60 years earlier. With Geological Survey maps, they set about counting the number of islands between the Piscataqua and the St. Croix Rivers to the head of tidewater, in order to determine just how many remained in the public domain. The fact that these landsmen counted a few bathymetric circles on the Geological Survey maps, and did not count those islands with more than four houses on them (where the political heat was likely to be intense in the event their titles were not secure), means that you still can't say how many islands are out there. It's one of their essential characteristics.

Out there, apart and between, there are, to be exact, a lot of islands. More than 3,000, anyway; more than on the rest of the east coast combined if you stopped to figure it. The Greeks would simply call them an archipelago, a wonderful word that means "a group of islands in the sea." If the Greeks were writing their myths here in the Maine archipelago, no doubt the stories would resemble those from the Aegean. Zeus would hurl huge stones at the Titans to create new islands from time to time, Bacchus would be having a good time celebrating the power and fertility of nature, and serious Apollo would be much given over to introspection on wave-lapped promontories.

Islandness

In an age when all of us have seen that our entire world can look like a tiny island in and from space, islands have once again become powerful metaphors. Anyone who has set foot on an uninhabited island cannot fail to appreciate the feelings of security, simplicity, and proprietorship that isolated islands are able to convey. To have spent a few days closed in by a thick-o'-fog and missed an appointment on the mainland, or to have waited in the spruce woods and listened to the play of wood warblers, or to have sat on a shore watching the silver moonflecks refracted on the black water makes concerns and cares Back There seem momentarily small and distant.

On quite a separate level, islands present us with a unique opportunity to do something we cannot do on the mainland. Because of their watery isolation from contiguous ecosystems, they become experimental natural laboratories that record the passage of time, *here,* on this exact piece of

Clamdigger.   *Jim Kosinski*

ground. On the mainland, effects of the hands of the past are frustratingly masked by the influences of neighboring pieces of land. It's very hard to sort out. But on islands, each with a unique history, the centuries of human and natural history are carefully indexed in the landscape, and the reading is curious, diverting, and pleasurable.

Another characteristic of islands that scratches at this historical and vaguely scientific itch that most of us feel is that islands are, quite simply, fun to describe and explore. There are very few landscapes in the United States that have been visited so often by such disparate sorts of people who felt compelled to put their impressions in writing. Generations of mariners, naturalists, navigators, explorers, merchants, yachtsmen, and vacationing rusticators have been describing islands since the first sail rose off the southern rim of the Gulf of Maine prior to 1600. Before then, fishermen and Indians described the profits and pitfalls of the islands to each other—though the former left, as is their habit, few records, and the latter left only hints of their lives in archaeological deposits and place names incompletely deciphered.

Finally, because islands are so separate, insular, and entire, ecological differences among them are striking. You don't have to be carefully trained in ecological theory to be struck by the differences between an island that is composed of greenstone and one composed of granite; an island that supports a colony of herons and another that supports a colony of gulls; or an island that once supported a colony of stonecutters and one that supported a colony of woodcutters. Each is presently the domain of a unique combination of plants that limits the appetites and numbers of animals; and of animals that utilize and alter the collection of plants in patterns that depend on their diverse pasts. Plants over animals, animals over plants—the kind of reciprocal, temporal interdependencies in which nature seems to delight.

Islands and the Urge for Wilderness

When it comes to tossing around impressions of the islands out there, it's tempting to think of them as pieces of wilderness. After all, they are largely uninhabited, except by various species of birds and an occasional deer or mink. Perhaps one in 10 has a small summer cabin or fishing camp on it, but mile after mile of uninhabited coastline present themselves for every foot of developed shorefront. Most of the islands are forested by pointed spruces, which obscure dark, mysterious interiors. Protected coves are altogether absent on some islands, so it is impossible to land on their jagged, wave-pounded shores. Perhaps no one has been there much before, at least not often enough to have altered the island's ecology. Perhaps this is the Forest Primeval whispering. Ah, wilderness.

Tending a herring weir, 1920.   *Frank Claes*

Like many other outwardly satisfying ideas, there is a notion that here in Maine, at relatively short distances from the mainland, are inaccessible pieces of New England landscape that have remained untouched, untrammeled, and unchanged since the white man arrived. Unfortunately, this does not hold up to closer scrutiny. The appearance of most of the islands is the result of nearly four centuries of human occupation and alteration. In fact, they are some of the oldest, continuously utilized pieces of landscape in eastern North America. Upwards of 15 generations of European boat-borne people—not to mention the 4,000 to 5,000 years of previous Indian use—have altered island ecologies, in some cases subtly, in other cases dramatically.

The present uninhabited look of the Maine islands is a result of a little more than a half-century of passive neglect following the decline of island populations that was gradual after 1870 and rapid after 1910. The reasons for the exodus are varied and will be traced in the chapters ahead, but all are rooted in the depletion of resources upon which islanders de-

Ferries link a few islands to the mainland.   *Jim Kosinski*

pended or in the disappearance of markets for those resources. For perhaps 50 of the past 400 years, islands have been left in their natural state.

Even if it is deluding to think of Maine's islands as pieces of intact
wilderness, many of them are indisputably special in both the ecological
and the spiritual sense. Islands of all sizes and descriptions lend themselves
to introspective reflections on the relationship between ourselves and the
natural world as we circumspectly survey the way things look from an
island, apart and between. The mainland looks smaller, the soaring spirits
of birds seem larger. A few of these islands are so simple and majestic that
even the most callous of human natures are silenced within their panthe-
istic sanctuaries where experience of the world is direct and elemental.

In ecological terms, these islands support species of plants and animals made rare by too much contact with our own kind on the mainland.
Many of the islands support populations that are at the northern or southern ends of their breeding ranges, and therefore serve as refuges where
genetic diversity is maintained. For many, the concept of genetic diversity
is a bit abstract, but it is easier to grasp the idea that small populations
of puffins or eagles or seals or bird's-eye primrose might have an importance
beyond their small numbers.

Some islands, whether or not they are naturally covered by forests or
grasses, are undoubtedly poorer in species composition after years of waste-

ful, negligent and destructive human uses. But if we use diversity of species on islands as a measure of ecosystem vitality and vigor, many other islands are richer after generations of human alteration. When we succumb to simple strategies of protection, we are often preserving nothing so certainly as the alteration that we have caused to exist in the first place.

If the Maine islands are as various as the pasts to which they remain attached, it makes sense to ask where our human sleight of hand has been just that. On such islands it is important to let things take their course as a way to measure the natural processions and progressions of intact insular ecosystems. But on many more islands, to simply "let nature take her course" begs the question: which, among the thousands of courses available, do we "let" her take?

Aside from the complicated issue of the effects of human hands, there is the matter of the dynamic changes that a tempestuous nature introduces. Islands are subject to the violent moods of their winds, waves, wings, and waters. Everything changes all the time. The infinitely articulated, infinitely modulated biofeedback loops of intact mainland ecosystems are quite capable of going temporarily out of whack on islands without any help from us. Occasionally the oscillation of systems deflects the direction of those systems away from the purposes that benefit us, the beasts who walk upright, to favor species such as mice, snails, or fungi, whose purposes are no more or less grand than our own. When such events take place, there is an urge within most of us to try to deflect those oscillations back to purposes that more nearly benefit us. Whether such activities are reasonable and wholly desirable depends on the unique circumstances at hand. Only one thing is certain: simple and inflexible rules and policies are in no one's best interest.

The tasks at hand on Maine's islands are not to re-create the past, nor to freeze the present, but to consider the future based upon an understanding of the present and past. It is our ability to do so that defines us as a species. Places can be wild without being a wilderness. Places can impress us deeply with their power and mystery, even when generations of our own kind have come and gone before us and left behind unmistakable signs of their occupation—their successes and failures in little pieces of the past cast in stone and wood. In each beat of the sea there is a pulse of a world not human, but there is also wildness enough in a manmade meadow system, as long as we are able to cast aside our ideas about the meadow and to see it as it is.

ISLANDS IN TIME

1

Downwind Histories and Ecologies

The Ecological Setting

Climate as an Ecological Factor

Part of the reason Maine islands do not have more inhabitants frequenting their shores is that the seas around them and the airs over them can be, like a wild animal you have found and made into a pet, very unpredictable: one moment sleek and tame, another wild, ungrateful, even brutal. One reason Maine fishermen talk so much about the weather is that there are so many ways of describing the moods of the wind and water. On islands, the weather determines so much of what you will and will not do; it reduces you to a little part of a much bigger world. From all but the most stupid or arrogant (and out there the two are almost interchangeable) it commands respect.

The climate of the islands is dominated by the influence of the younger sister of the Labrador Current called the Nova Scotia Current, which is a cold Arctic-born tongue of water that curls around the western end of Nova Scotia, slips southwest along the irregular Maine coast until it is deflected east and then east-northeast by the great arm of Cape Cod and its counterpart current, the Atlantic Gulf Stream. Where the offshoot Nova Scotia Current and the Gulf Stream run side by side, miles offshore, the humid, maritime, tropical air condenses over the brisker waters to produce fog—not little-cats'-feet fog, but impenetrable walls of fog. With light southerly or southeasterly flows of air, the fog rolls in, locking up first the outer islands and then the tips of peninsulas. Those who live "down peninsula" can often drive to town and find that the rest of the world is having a warm, sunny day, as the heat of the land dissipates the fog. But on islands there is no escape. The fog often approaches with the stealth of an Indian;

if you are out on the water, your world view changes in a moment from one of passing interest at the interplay of green water, white shores, and blue sky to one of quiet, intense concentration, forcing you to calculate mentally the number of ledges that lie between you and your home harbor.

Maine is in the zone of prevailing westerlies, a simple-enough fact that doesn't distinguish our climate from most of the rest of the East Coast. This simply means that the systems that cause Maine's weather originate to the west of us and move eastward; either they come down the St. Lawrence River Valley, thus creating southeast blows of maritime air drawn into the low-pressure trough, or they head out to sea, often near Cape Cod, to generate northeast gales. Northeasters, though not confined to the spring and fall, are most frequent during these seasons—they are related to the shift in location of the jet stream and are a trial to be endured anywhere, but more so on islands. Northeasters bring in the worst of all weather, so-called maritime polar air, the worst of two worlds—winds both wet and cold are drawn in from the waters surrounding Newfoundland, Labrador, and even Baffin Island. You cannot weather a northeast gale in the spring or the fall on an island without recalling the title of Ruth Moore's collection of poems (the author herself was born and brought up on an island) *Cold as a Dog and the Winds Northeast.*

No matter how tight your house may be, or how many layers of clothing you try to put between yourself and the cold-fingering rain, you feel a northeast gale to your bones.

Because of the way winds clock around the low-pressure cells that produce gales, the trailing edge of a system is composed of a cold front that ushers in clearing air from the northwest—often cold enough to make you wonder if the gale itself isn't the lesser of two evils. Snapping-clear high pressure from the dry polar continental interior cascades in behind a gale; in the summer it drives off the encircling fog within a matter of moments to reveal the long view, the large day; in the winter it whistles day after day, churning up white combing seas that freeze on the hulls and in the rigging of boats.

Most islanders cannot help but have something to do with waterborne occupations for at least part of the year, so gales have a special meaning. Very few island harbors are protected from both the east and the west; you just pay your money and take your chances. But when the winds howl, part of you is listening to the chafe of your mooring pendant or feeling the relentless beating of the sea on wharf pilings and fish-house footings.

If for substantial parts of the year the cold is colder and winds are windier on islands, why do people still persist in hunkering down out there, waiting for the teeth to be removed from the bite of the dog? Part of it is habit, tradition, inheritance, and plain stubborn Yankee independence that is too proud to cry uncle, but the better part of it is participating in the drama, the Titan-like interplay of capricious elements that serve to give all

A sixty foot wave breaks over tops of trees on the south shore of Hurricane Island.
Neil Elam

who stand and watch a primitive belief in the "will of the gods," luck, fate, or call-it-what-you-will. The sea is possessed by its own mood and spirits, and men and women are almost nothing to it.

Then too, there is the matter of the summer, which many of the islands' enthusiastic temporary residents have discovered. Not only are there few landscapes that can match the interplay of colors on "broken islands in the sea" on a high, blue sunny day, but the Gulf of Maine is like a giant thermostat, absorbing the heat of the sun throughout the hot months. Thus summer lasts well into November, when island flowers are still in bloom and gardens still produce long after those on the mainland have turned brown. There may be no other place where the meaning of Indian Summer is so real.

But one day in December it is all over, and the winter is brutally quick about its business: a cold front roars through and sits on towering haunches picking its teeth. The sea is alight with tongues of sea smoke as she gives up the warmth she has harbored for half a year, and we watch and wait. It's called "sitting on a rock" in the North Atlantic.

Natural Catastrophes: Wind, Salt, and Ice

Since the Maine coast and islands are such rough, raw, rocky, cold, and tempestuous places to live, their ecosystems must be adapted to periodic natural catastrophes. Disturbances range in intensity from the spate of yearly gales that batter the coast to an occasional bona-fide hurricane. Over the last three and a half centuries, there have been three storms so ferocious that they make it onto anyone's hurricane scale, Beaufort or otherwise. That's an average of a hurricane a century.

   The storm of August 15, 1635, was the most destructive ever known on the Maine coast. It began early in the morning, when the winds picked up from the northeast and blew "with great fury" for five or six hours, driving up a huge tide 20 feet over normal that flooded islands and coastal croplands. Edward Trelawney of Richmond Island in Saco Bay wrote back to England that the storm "blew down many thousands of trees, turning the stronger up by the roots and breaking the high pine trees in their midst." The hurricanes of 1815 and 1938, though they caused great damage throughout

Thick o' fog. *Gordon Lutz*

New England, did not affect the Maine coast quite so drastically, but the damage nonetheless ran into the millions of wind-thrown trees.

Aside from the obvious damage to trees, storms whose winds exceed 60 knots exact a more subtle toll on island vegetation. They kick up prodigious quantities of salt from the sea and drive it overland in clouds. This kills the leaves and needles on plants, whose tissues dry out as a result of the excess of salt. The composition of the vegetation of low-lying islands may be completely altered after a single storm drives clouds of salt ashore.

Storms that coincide with a high tide can work changes that defy the imagination of our routine-bound minds. The storm of January 12, 1978, not only peaked with the high tide, but it came on a spring high tide at that. The tide, 10 feet higher than normal, caused such havoc that many coastal property owners couldn't recognize their lands or find their homes afterward. As the storm raged for six hours, the rising tide equalized the barometric pressure over land and water. Just as the tide began to ebb, the cold front broke through the trailing edge of the storm and the abnormally high tide began draining out of the bays, driven by a 60-knot northerly flow of high pressure. For those on shore, worrying over their boats, the effect of the passage of the front was frightening. In north-south-trending bays, the water simply disappeared, as though someone had pulled the plug in a tub. Boats that had held on during the morning swung violently around, and a few disappeared with the cascading tide. A dinghy that had been tied to a pier was, 15 minutes later, hanging taut from its painter. It was called a "100-year storm," though it was not a hurricane.

Fish-house in a northeast gale.   *Jim Kosinski*

Wives of fishermen suffer in greater measure from these periodic gales. The histories of islands such as Vinalhaven, Islesboro, Deer Isle, Swans, the Cranberries, and Beals, which contain genealogies of the original settlers, are so full of men lost at sea, it's a wonder that island women continued to participate in the institution of marriage. When a southeast gale struck a fleet at anchor off the Nova Scotia Banks, Cape Sable became a dangerous lee shore for any schooner whose anchor line had parted. A list of the vessels that have been driven up on those shores is quite long enough to have earned the region its name of the "Graveyard of the Atlantic."

To add to these catastrophes to which mariners and other wild creatures must adapt, a long and occasionally brutal winter can dramatically affect island ecosystems. The decade between 1810 and 1820 was the coldest 10-year period on record since data collection began. One year, 1816, Maine had no summer. A late frost hit in July and the first snow fell in August. The only vegetables that grew were a few potatoes. Frozen corn was cut for fodder as islanders prepared for a bleak winter. The winter of 1816 was the first one in 35 years in which Penobscot Bay froze over completely to the Fox Islands and Isle au Haut—the ice was thick enough to allow sleighs to ride to the mainland to buy hay for the famished livestock. In Muscongus Bay, pack ice jammed the waters out to Monhegan, which made the islands completely inaccessible. Twenty years later, all but a few harbors east of Cape Cod were again closed by ice. Although these extraordinary winters worked extreme hardships on everything alive, they also built ice bridges out to the islands that served as colonization routes for fox, rabbit, hare, mice, and other furred animals not accustomed to making the marathon swim out to a new world and a new life.

The Physical and Cultural Setting—
The Bays of Maine

Maine has an immensely long tidal coastline—2,500 miles of shore collapsed accordion-like into a short 250 miles as the crow measures it from Kittery to Eastport. Even this figure of 2,500 miles, which nearly everyone uses to describe the Maine coast, does not include the shores of all the 3,000-odd islands, which, if added together, would increase the estimate by almost half again. The long, sinuous shoreline certainly is good for the fish that depend on the nutrients washed off this coastal acreage and for the fishermen who set off after the fish from the thousand protected coves and bights of the islands and coast—yet it almost defies the generalized description attempted here. Nevertheless, every sort of place should be properly introduced, and it is to that end that this section is devoted.

To see anything at all of the Maine archipelago, you have to see it

The world of small boats. *Jim Kosinski*

from a boat. The Maine islands have always been occupied by the sorts of people who knew how to handle small boats: birch-bark canoes, dories, sloops, coastal schooners, and the many variations of the Maine lobsterboat. Except for a short period of time when steamship companies churned the waters carrying tourists between Boston and various island ports, "you couldn't get there from here" unless you owned a boat or knew someone who did. It's still almost like that. Oh, there are state and private ferries that connect a dozen of the big islands with mainland ports, and mail boats that reach a handful more. But out of 3,000-odd islands . . . well, you do the arithmetic.

No, you simply have to have a small and reliable boat, be able to memorize tricky channels, or better yet, learn to navigate through the rock-strewn waters, and then put up with being wet and cold even in the warmest months of summer. Because these skills and inconveniences require a lot of time and patience, island life is not an attractive proposition to great multitudes of people. For those with ample resources, modern navigation devices can be comforting crutches during the weeks of fog that can descend and obscure even the bow of your boat; and in a yacht that has dry bilges, you don't have to be quite as good a seaman to keep yourself from the long yaw(n) of the sea.

For some of these reasons, many of the people on or about the islands of Maine have spent either a lot of time or a lot of money to get there.

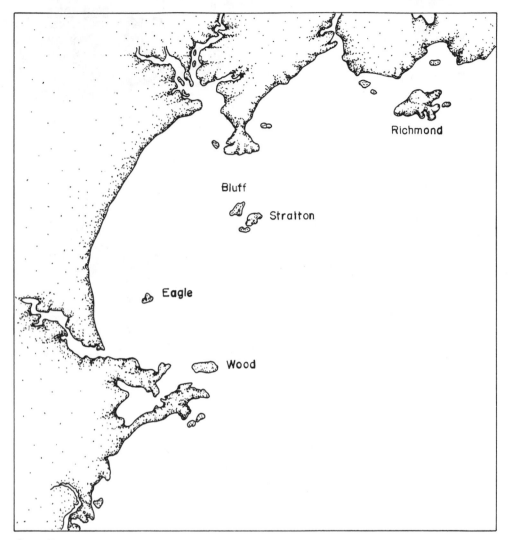

SACO BAY

Maybe it should be different, and maybe someday it will be, but for most of the present century, the islands have been divided among a few fishermen, yachtsmen, and nesting birds. Before that, they were divided among a few Indians, fishermen-farmers, and nesting birds.

Getting to know the Maine islands takes a lot of time—a lifetime—and you cannot be in a hurry. Because most of the people who visit Maine come from more populous places to windward, the most logical water-view proceeds from west to east, downwind; and because the present look of each island is dependent on its past, you'll have to put up with some history along the way. Once we ghost all the way Downeast, however, you'll have to beat back by yourself. In cruising the Maine coast, as in ecological matters, there are no free lunches.

Saco Bay: "Nut Trees and Vineyards"

Unlike all the other Maine bays to the east, Saco Bay has a short and broad topographical configuration, the kind you expect to find when the mainland's massive ridges of rock run parallel to the trend of the shore. Saco Bay is bounded on the main by Biddeford Pool and Cape Elizabeth, and it is really more closely related biogeographically to Massachusetts than to the rest of the Maine coast. Like the rest of the coast southward to Cape Cod, the shoreline is smooth and unencumbered by caves, headlands, or a bewildering array of islands.

Historically, the two most important islands in this broad bay are Stratton and Richmond. Richmond Island was settled a few years before Stratton, around 1627 or 1628, perhaps by men who had accompanied the Englishman Christopher Levett in his exploration of Casco Bay four years earlier. Within a few years of its occupation, Richmond Island officially passed into the hands of an influential Bristol merchant named Robert Trelawney, who established one of Maine's early fishing and trading posts. Some of the most interesting pictures of island life, as well as the larger picture of early colonial Maine, are contained in the *Trelawney Papers,* the correspondence between Trelawney and his agent, Jonathon Winter. Between 1630 and 1645, several vessels were built and launched from Richmond Island. They carried cargoes of fish oil, pine clapboards, and oak staves, all of which were harvested from the islands and nearby waters. At the height of the island's prosperity, 60 men worked in the Richmond Island fisheries.

Two decades before Trelawney's man, Winter, began sending men out to the winter cod-fishing grounds that were handy to the island, Richmond had been visited and described by Samuel de Champlain, the French explorer. Looking for a more suitable location for his country's Acadian headquarters after their disastrous winter on an island in the mouth of the St. Croix River Downeast, Champlain was deeply impressed by what he found on Richmond. The island "has fine oaks and nut trees, the soil cleared up, and many vineyards bearing beautiful grapes in their season." Champlain named it Isle de Bacchus, and he might have been well advised to try to establish a French settlement there. For some reason the French decided on the gloomier climate of the Bay of Fundy shores, and they never were able to establish permanent settlements on the Maine coast.

Stratton Island was settled in 1630 by an obscure Englishman, John Stratton, who cleared the land and established a small farm. He traded a a few goods with the Indians for furs, which were sent back to England to generate a small income.

Whatever else might be said of the early relations between the English and the Indians, trade between the two groups, though desirable from the settlers' point of view, became a vital necessity to the Indians. During unusually severe winters, starvation was a serious threat to the tribes who retreated from the islands and coast in the fall to spend the long winter along the shores of interior river valleys. The introduction of muskets had a dramatic effect on Indian provender: as traditional hunting methods were foresworn, the Indians were at the mercy of the whites for supplies of powder and shot. According to John Josselyn, whose brother owned one of the earliest plantations in Saco, "It was a poor Indian that did not have two guns."

Islands were favorite spots for independent traders to set up business with the Indians, since they could conduct their affairs without adhering to the officially sanctioned rates of the fort truck houses. Trade monopolies in fish and fur were granted to merchants in return for their promise to set up permanent settlements. But until the latter part of the 1600s, trade monopolies were not very effective against the independents, who knew the coast and the local Indians much better. The history of Stratton Island after its first settlement is somewhat hard to follow. It doesn't appear as if Stratton himself stayed very long, but during the remainder of the 17th century, the island intermittently was a trading station.

Today, Champlain's oak and nut trees on Richmond and the small farm and trading station on Stratton have all but disappeared. Richmond is largely covered by spruce growth and Stratton has recently become a multi-specied heronry.

Casco Bay: "All Broken Islands in the Sea"

Casco Bay islands used to be called the Calendar Isles, supposedly because there was one island for every day of a non-leap year—until someone counted them up and found there were 222 (and that is only if you count all the islands that are now connected to the main by bridges, such as Bailey, Orrs, Sebascodegan, Cousins, Littlejohn, and Mackworth). Of all of the Maine bays, Casco has lost more of its islands to bridges—including the ingenious, one-of-a-kind Bailey-to-Orr granite cobwork bridge, which has withstood not only the occasional coastal storm that chews up much of the rest of the Maine coast, but the daily tidal rip that surges through it at a speed of four knots.

Casco Bay is often described in terms of its parallel ranges of islands— an inner, middle, and outer range. It actually has, besides these three, another handful east of Harpswell Neck. Each of these ranges represents the weathered roots of resistant ridges that have relatively recently been isolated from the intervening parallel valleys by the long arms of the sea.

The first European description of Casco Bay comes from Christopher Levett's account of his voyage of 1623. He described the landscape as "all

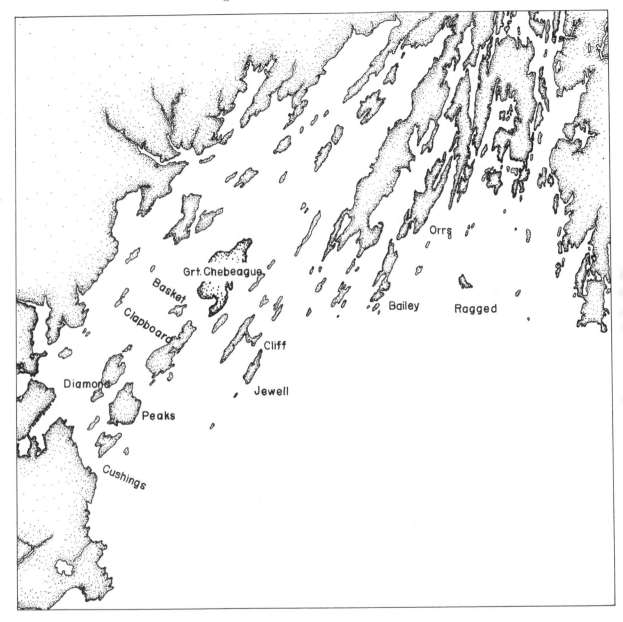

Casco Bay

broken islands in the sea which makes many excellent good harbors where a thousand sail of ship may ride in safety." The word "Casco," however, is apparently derived from an Abnaki term meaning "muddy bay." The different perceptions are due to the fact that the Englishman Levett explored the waters in a small ship looking for deep water and secure anchorages, while the Indians looked for canoe routes closer to the shore and

Bailey-to-Orr cobwork bridge. *Kate Fitzgerald*

handy to mud flats where they could dig clams. Different strokes from different boats.

Though Levett built a fortified house on one of the inner Casco Bay islands in 1624, before he returned to England to raise money for a more ambitious plantation, the first permanent settlement within the present limits of Portland occurred on Mackworth Island in 1632. Like Richmond Island, around the corner of Cape Elizabeth, Mackworth Island was ideally suited to settlement, being an island and therefore easy to defend, as well as being connected by a low tide bar to the mainland and therefore accessible to other settlements along the rivers.

A few of the remaining Casco islands were settled during the next half century: the island of Sebascodegan in 1639, Orrs and Bailey a few years later, Lower Goose in 1658, and Moshier in 1660. Several others were cleared to pasture livestock; the trees were cut up as cordwood and shipped to Boston. The primary settlements of the region, however, were along the Presumpscot, Fore, and Royal Rivers, where deep, rich soils, water, and water power for saw and grist mills were available.

The larger islands, such as Peaks, Great Diamond, Long, and Chebeague, were all important Indian encampments during the summer months. It seems that for the first 150 years of English presence in the Bay, the settlers had neither the numbers nor the nerve to challenge the Indians

Whitehead Cliffs, Casco Bay.   *Rick Perry*

for these valuable island fastnesses to which the tribes repaired every summer to fish, collect berries, and dry shellfish.

Chebeague is an Indian word that translates as "island of many springs,"
and no doubt many settlers were envious of this piece of Indian domain,
since lack of adequate water was one of the factors that limited settlement
of these otherwise highly desirable islands. Until the end of the last French
and Indian War in 1760, the whites settled only the islands that the Indians
did not use. With few exceptions, they used islands at the mercy or suffer-

ance of the Indians, who commanded the islands by virtue of their superior numbers and mobility in canoes. In 1689, for example, 300 to 400 Indians gathered on Peaks Island in preparation for their successful attack on Portland. For most of the 17th century, the Indians simply had a more impressive navy than the settlers.

Around the turn of the present century, long after the Indians had disappeared, several of the larger Casco Bay islands were bought up by associations of Portlanders, who have turned them into other sorts of summer encampments. Within this century, forts and military installations have been constructed on several of these resort islands, ostensibly to protect Portland, one of the East Coast's most important deep-water ports. Most of the state's oil is delivered here in coastal tankers, and several proposals have been made in recent years to establish an oil refinery on one of the islands in the Bay or in Portland itself.

Sheepscot, Boothbay, and Johns Bay: The First Permanent Settlement in Maine

Like Casco Bay to the westward and Muscongus to the eastward, Sheepscot, Boothbay, and Johns Bay are part of the all-but-weathered-away rootstocks of the ancient fold mountains that once were foothills of the Appalachians. Except for Boothbay, these waters are not the well-protected embayments for which Maine is most well known. They have, nevertheless, figured centrally in Maine's maritime history—particularly Damariscove and Fisherman Islands offshore, and Southport Island, which has been connected intermittently to the mainland since 1869.

The Indians were good seamen and regularly visited all of Maine's islands—even those 10 to 20 miles offshore. Their birch-bark canoes were, according to one account, "strengthened with ribs and hoops of wood . . . with such excellent ingenious art as they are able to bear seven or eight persons, far exceeding any in the Indies." Christopher Levett wrote that the canoes "can take an incredible great sea," and Captain John Smith related that the Indians "would row their canoes faster with five paddles than our own men would our boats with eight oars."

The Indians that the Europeans encountered used the islands for summer headquarters for hunting and fishing. From their canoes they hunted for whale oil for heat, seal fur for winter clothing, and porpoise skins to make snowshoes. In the early summer the men collected eggs and young birds from nesting islands, while the women and younger children ashore dried whatever fish the men caught, collected berries, and dug clams, which they shucked out and hung on spruce roots stretched between trees out of reach of the dogs.

So many of the islands show signs of Indian encampments that they must have camped primarily in small family groups or clans spread through-

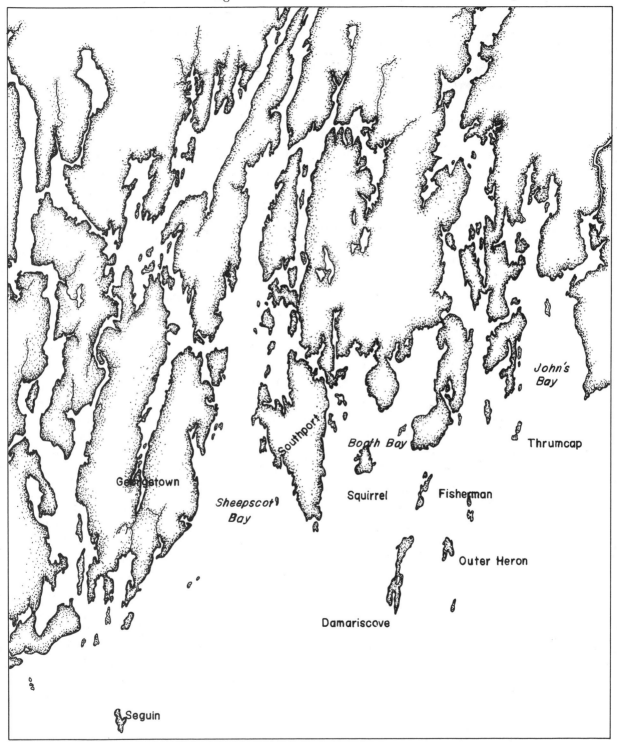

SHEEPSCOT AND JOHNS BAYS

out the bays that the various tribes controlled. There may have been a few
larger encampments on the big islands, but many families must have had
their own island headquarters. At least this was true for the chiefs or sagamores, who returned to the same island year after year: Cocawesco to
Mackworth, Samoset to Louds Island in Muscongus Bay, and Asticou to a
small cove of Somes Sound on Mount Desert Island.

Damariscove Island was probably named after a fisherman, Humphrey
Damarill, an independent trader who set up headquarters on the shore of
the island's southern cove before 1614. Because the hapless Popham Colony
had already failed by this time, Damariscove Island has the distinction of
being the site of the first permanent settlement in Maine. Like Richmond
Island off Cape Elizabeth, Damarill's Cove (or Damariscove) was ideally
situated near an important winter cod spawning ground located a few miles
off the mouth of the Sheepscot River. Along with Monhegan and Matinicus, Damariscove quickly became one of the most important fishing stations
in the mid-coast region. When the District of Maine petitioned the Massachusetts Bay Colony to provide some sort of government for the area in
1687, Damariscove and Monhegan were the two colonies assessed with the
largest tax, a reflection of their greater population.

The Indians who inhabited the region were from a different tribe than
those who confined their summer encampments to the Casco Bay islands.
Though we do not know very much about most of Maine's original Indians,
it appears that each river valley was the home of a separate tribe. While
different authors apply a bewildering variety of names to the various tribes,
it is least confusing to call them by the name of the particular river along
which they lived.

The Sheepscot Indians appear to have been quite friendly with the
English during the early years of European settlement, but whether this
relationship would have lasted very long, we do not know, since the Sheepscots were nearly wiped out in the plague that swept through the coastal
tribes during the winter of 1618–1619. It is estimated that 75 percent of the
Indian population of Maine died during a three- or four-month period.

The Sheepscot, Kennebec, Androscoggin, and Saco Indians were all
closely related to each other and collectively were known as Abnakis, or
"People of the Dawn." The other large group of Indians, whose primary
contact was with French missionaries, was known as the Etchemins. They
consisted of at least three tribes: the Penobscots, the most powerful tribe in
colonial Maine after the plague; the Passamaquoddies; and the Malecites
or Micmacs. John Smith estimated the total population of Abnakis in Maine
at 5,000 and of Etchemins at 6,000. After the plague, the total number of
both groups may not have exceeded 3,000, if we are allowed to make crude
estimates.

The fishermen who were headquartered on islands such as Damariscove appear to have gotten along well enough with the Indians, since their ideas of property rights were similar to those of the Indians. Boundaries were loose and shifting and were enforced by extending control over the utilization of the resource rather than over the ground itself. Relations began breaking down only after farming along the river valleys limited the Indians' access to the tidal flats.

Throughout most of the 19th century, Southport Island was one of the premier fishing harbors on the East Coast. It sheltered a large fleet of schooners that fished the offshore cod grounds. Southport Island was the homeport of several of the most successful mackerel seining vessels, and when the menhaden or pogy fishery boomed, Southport fishermen supplied the oil and fertilizer plants built in Boothbay. At one time, so the story goes, Southport Island fishermen had the highest per capita income of any port in Maine.

In recent years, the Boothbay region has become a necessary stop for autoborne tourists looking for an authentic coastal fishing village. Since the waterfront is now almost entirely taken up by restaurants and other tourist establishments, there are few fishermen left in the harbor. A tour boat runs between Boothbay Harbor and Monhegan. Several of the islands in the Bay have been purchased by associations and developed as private summer colonies in a manner similar to those of Casco Bay. Other islands are private nature preserves, including one that has been a thriving heronry for great blues for at least the past four centuries.

Muscongus Bay: "The Fishing Place"

The substantial rivers, the St. George and the Medomak, and the several smaller rivers that empty into Muscongus Bay, create a lobster heaven. The rivers are warmer than the Gulf of Maine and since the Bay is quite shallow, the water temperature is several degrees higher. The rivers also carry a load of suspended nutrients, which, in combination with the moderate water temperatures, creates ideal lobstering grounds. In fact, "muscongus" is an Abnaki word for "fishing place"—probably referring to smelt rather than lobster, according to Fannie Hardy Eckstorm, whose indefatigable efforts to unravel Indian place names give us one of the best pictures of Indian uses of the coastal islands. Anyone who has tried to navigate Muscongus Bay between June and November can confirm that there are probably more lobster pot buoys per square nautical mile here than any other place in the world. It is not unheard of for the most industrious lobstermen, the so-called crushers, to have 1,200 traps.

Muscongus Bay is steeped in the early history of Maine; depending on whom you believe, it may have supported the first settlement in Maine. At the western edge of Muscongus, Allen Island hosted George Weymouth and his crew for two months in 1605 and was the site of the first religious ser-

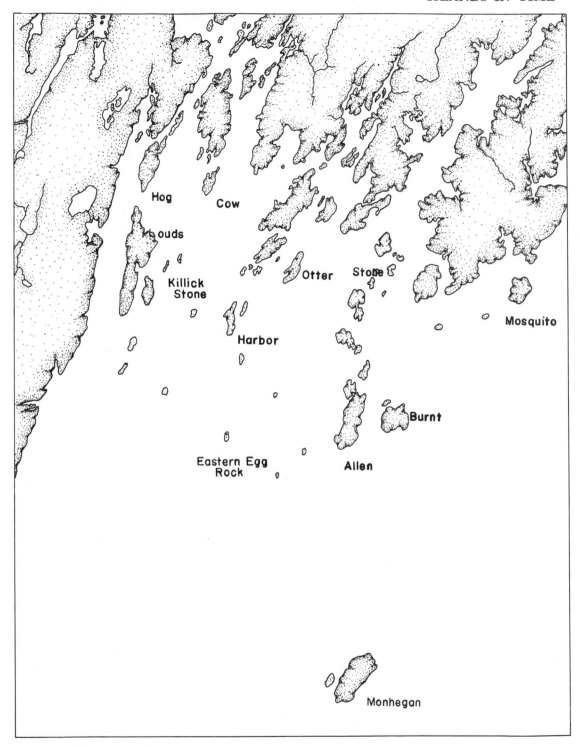

Hog

Cow

Louds

Otter

Stone

Mosquito

Killick
Stone

Harbor

Burnt

Eastern Egg
Rock

Allen

Monhegan

MUSCONGUS BAY

vice held in New England. But after this early flurry of activity, it appears that serious island settlement was slow to develop, no doubt because colonists preferred to huddle close to the mainland fort at Pemaquid during the long, sad Indian Wars.

Warfare between the settlers and the Indians may have been inevitable, given the nearly antithetical conceptions of property rights, but the habit of various Englishmen of kidnapping local Indians to show to the folks back home certainly did nothing to increase the Indians' trust of whites. In 1605 Weymouth and his crew, after being shown around the islands and the mainland by the local Sheepscots for nearly two months, "suddenly laid hands upon [five] Savages, two canoes with all their bows and arrows." According to the early naturalist James Rosier, who accompanied Weymouth aboard the *Archangel*, another Indian, "being too superstitiously fearful of his own good, withdrew himself into the wood" and escaped. Two of these kidnapped Indians later returned to Maine when Sir John Popham attempted to found a settlement on Georgetown Island, but the treachery continued. Captain Edward Harlow kidnapped three more Indians from Monhegan in 1611, and Thomas Hunt, part of John Smith's expedition of 1614, kidnapped 24 more and sold them as slaves in Spain "for a little private gain."

Since the Indian code of law made a whole tribe responsible for the acts of one of its members, the activities of Weymouth, Hunt, and Harlow, among others, set the stage for later terrorist attacks by the Indians on innocent mainland English settlements. In addition, there were indications that some Englishmen intended to make the kidnapping and selling of Indians a regular business. In 1675, after nearly three quarters of a century of increasing hostility between the mainland farmers and the Indians, the first Indian War broke out.

After the first wave of Indian attacks on isolated farms in 1675, the settlers from Arrowsic and Southport Islands evacuated to Damariscove and then to Monhegan. For a short time in 1676, Monhegan sheltered virtually the entire white population of the District of Maine. During the various Indian wars, islands such as Monhegan, as well as Jewell and Cushing in Casco Bay, served as temporary refuges where the settlers retreated to defend themselves.

The end of the first Indian War in 1676 was a distinct victory for the Indians. Every farmhouse between Falmouth and Pemaquid had been burned to the ground; every settler had been killed, captured, or driven away. With peace reestablished, the English settlers could reoccupy their lands, but each planter had to pay the Indians a tribute of a peck of corn. The settlers also promised not to push their land above the tidal waters of the rivers where the Indians were headquartered during the major part of each year. In exchange, the Indians agreed not to go out to "ye fishing islands," presumably Monhegan, Damariscove, and Matinicus.

Island farm. *George Putz*

The first peace soon degenerated into a second war with the Indians, this time with the French actively participating on the Indian side. As the conflict developed, the fighting grew into a war for control of the new continent that had been claimed by both France and England. Pemaquid marked the easternmost stronghold of the English; Mount Desert was the westernmost part of French Acadia. For the next 80 years, everything in between, including the islands, was a war-torn no-man's land. During the second Indian War, which raged from 1688 to 1697, nearly every farmhouse east of Wells was destroyed. Even Monhegan was attacked—by a French frigate carrying a force of several hundred Indians.

During the third war, which lasted from 1703 to 1713, Maine lost between a fourth and a third of all her white settlers, but the Indians suffered more. At the end of the declared hostilities, there were no more than perhaps 300 Indian fighting men remaining east of the Kennebec River, and several of the smaller tribes simply ceased to exist. By 1713 Maine reached the lowest ebb of population. The town of Biddeford in southern Maine was incorporated in 1718, and only two other towns were established in the following 40 years. With the exception of fishermen and fur traders, white men were nowhere to be seen in the greatest part of the territory. In 1720, for example, there was only one house standing between Georgetown and the St. Croix River, and it was located on Damariscove Island.

A fourth war broke out between 1722 and 1725, and about a third of the remaining Indians were killed or died of starvation. At some point during the long and bitter century of wars, the conflict of terror and blood boiled over into what can only be described as genocide. The Indians, their weakened tribes reduced to a few old men, women, and children, were hunted down like animals. Cut off from the coastal clam flats, their last means of avoiding starvation was their cornfields, and these were systematically laid waste. Though the last French and Indian War would not be concluded until Montreal fell to the British in 1760, Maine's Indian tribes had largely been exterminated by 1725.

Today the ecology of Muscongus Bay is dominated by spruce forests, which run down the ridgy spines of most of the long and narrow islands. Many of the islands were used to pasture livestock after the Revolutionary War, when the Bay region began to be settled rapidly, but there are fewer records of island farms here than in Penobscot and Blue Hill Bays to the east. It appears that the settlers of this area preferred to farm in the river valleys, where access to salt-water shipping routes was just as good, and soils were decidedly more productive.

Now every May the Bay's largely uninhabited spruce forests are filled with warblers. Waves upon waves of them wheel in behind a change in the weather pattern, so much so that one day the island woods will be alive with a thousand complicated descants when the day before all was silence enshrouded in fog. The songbirds set up housekeeping in the dense canopies of the trees, stratifying themselves according to their flight skills and their abilities to exploit the different food niches found at a given tree level.

In July, after the woods have been filled with the exacting songs of territorial males for several months, a less skillful choir takes up, as the newly fledged young try to get the words right: "Old-sam pee-dee-b-d, sam-old-bodee-pee, I mean old sam peabody, peabody, peabody"—which is actually the song of the white-throated sparrow (not a warbler at all), but you get the idea.

Penobscot Bay: "Beautiful Ports and Channels"

It is not just an irrational regional preference to suggest that Penobscot Bay is Maine's grandest stretch of water. It is a fact that Penobscot Bay is Maine's largest, measuring 20 miles across from Whitehead to Isle au Haut and trending 30 miles north to the mouth of the equally superlative river of the same name. Giovanni Verrazano, who sailed these waters in 1524, described the Bay as filled with islands "all near the continent; small and pleasant in appearance, but high, following the curve of the land; some

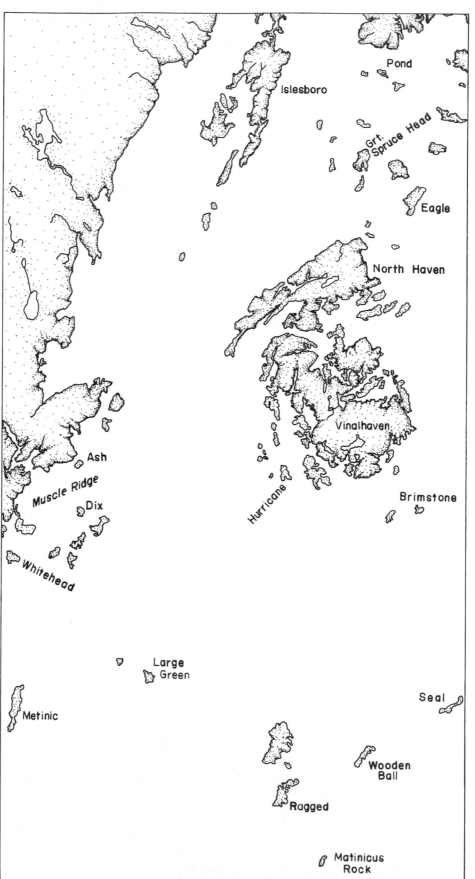

Pond

Islesboro

Grt.
Spruce Head

Eagle

North Haven

Vinalhaven

Ash

Muscle Ridge

Dix

Hurricane

Brimstone

Whitehead

Large
Green

Seal

Metinic

Wooden
Ball

Ragged

Matinicus
Rock

beautiful ports and channels are formed between them, such as those in the Adriatic Gulf in Illyria and Dalmatia" on the coast of Yugoslavia.

Penobscot Bay's topography is diverse. The islands are underlain by a complex of craggy, cliffy volcanics to the northeast; by a greenstone-greenschist association to the northwest; and by an evenly textured, coarse-grained, grey-white granite that stretches from the Muscle (sometimes spelled Mussel) Ridge to Calderwood Neck on Vinalhaven. Such a massive outcrop of granite is called a "pluton," after the Greek god of the deep; in fact, the roots of Maine's coastal granite plutons, according to bedrock geologists, descend near to the fiery depths.

After the Marquis de Vandrieul surrendered to General Jeffrey Amherst in Montreal in 1760 to end a century of warfare, land-hungry men and women from New England towns that had long since cultivated every available acre of land rushed to claim a piece of the eastern frontier. The amount of coming and going on North Haven Island, to take one example, between 1760 and 1775 was phenomenal. Men came singly or with families or with groups of families; some stayed, some went farther east, some gave up and returned to previous homes, and some went home and came back later. For the next several decades, scores of islands in the Bay were settled by squatters who attempted to establish self-sufficient farms and independent fishing enterprises. Few succeeded.

Within 15 years a new war would break out, this one a war for independence from British control of the natural resources—masts, lumber, and

Outer Penobscot Bay—Maine's grandest stretch of water. *Rick Perry*

fish—upon which the livelihoods of Maine's settlers depended. Settlers who moved to the islands for protection during the French and Indian Wars reversed the process during the Revolution, when the British Navy controlled the coastal waters from their stronghold in Castine, which they captured in 1779. Isolated island farms, particularly in Penobscot Bay, were easy plunder for British troops. Raids on salt-water farms by Tory privateers became so commonplace that the term "shaving mill" was coined to describe the boats that cleaned out these farms. Revolutionary patriotism among islanders seemed to be a function of their distance from Castine. The settlers on Islesboro, for example, conducted a thriving trade with the British at Castine, following the old belief that discretion is the greater part of valor, while those on the Fox Islands ambushed the British from the dense woods when patrols came ashore.

After the Revolution, the land rush resumed with the policy of paying off soldiers with land. Trees were cut and islands were burned to create pasture on even the smallest "junk-o-pork" island. By 1820, virtually every island greater than about 25 acres had either people or livestock on it. The census for that year shows 207 hardy souls on the small islands surrounding the Fox Islands, North Haven and Vinalhaven.

After building a cabin, generally the next order of business for islanders was to build a boat, which was indispensable for going to the grist mill or to the mainland to sell produce and obtain supplies. Eventually several families joined together to buy a coasting schooner, which was put in charge of one of the families' sons—20 years of age or so—who would take farm goods to Boston's Haymarket.

Beginning around 1870, island farming and fishing efforts were eclipsed by the granite boom, which swelled island populations to the bursting point. Immigrants from Scandinavia and Eastern Europe were brought to work in the quarries as the nation entered its first period of ambitious public works construction. Because granite could be transported conveniently on coastal schooners, island quarries developed much more rapidly than those on the mainland.

Today these granite-strewn islands are inhabited more often than not by various nesting seabirds and waterfowl. Penobscot Indian legends describe the discovery of islands by following birds, and even the most remote islands have huge colonies of fish-eating avians. Matinicus Rock, at the outer rim of Penobscot Bay, is the principal Maine residence of puffins and razor-billed auks. In 1979, a pair of eagles still maintained an aerie in Penobscot Bay, having been pushed out of all other bays to the west, where they used to nest as recently as 1970.

Merchant Row to Jericho Bay: The Heart of the Mid-Coast

Though the islands in this stretch of water have not arranged themselves neatly into well-defined bays, when taken together they constitute the heart

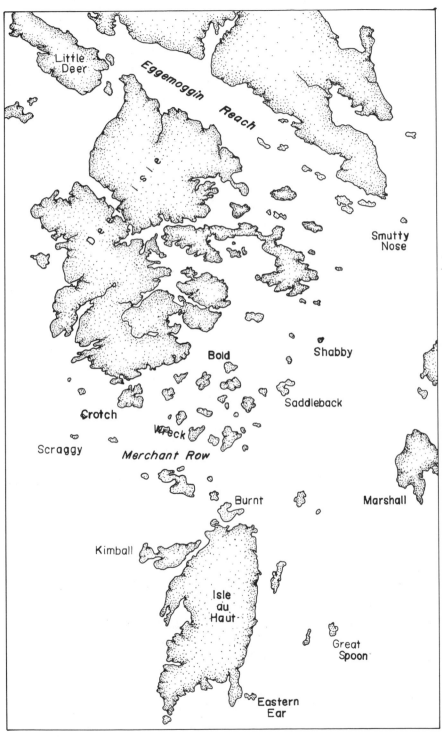

MERCHANT ROW TO JERICHO BAY

of the mid-coast world of islands. Year-round communities persist on Swans, Frenchboro (Long Island), Isle au Haut, Deer Isle, and Little Deer Isle (the inhabitants of which still refer to themselves as islanders, even though they have either the best of both worlds or the worst of two worlds since the suspension bridge was completed to Sedgwick in 1937). With the many summer cottages that have been built on islands in Merchant Row, this area continues to be one of the more densely populated parts of the Maine archipelago.

One of the interesting historical patterns of settlement after 1760 on Deer Isle—a pattern that was repeated on other islands—was that many north-facing shores were settled earlier and more densely than southern shores. The determining feature for island farmers probably was the chilling effect of damp fogs, which roll in off the Gulf of Maine and set back crops on seaward-facing shores. The northern shores of Northwest Harbor and Smalls Cove on Deer Isle were settled before most of the rest of the island's southern shores, suggesting the initial island settlers placed a higher priority on growing crops rather than on catching fish. Even on Vinalhaven, a traditional fishing community from earliest times, the northern Thorofare side was settled before Carvers Harbor on the island's south side.

The islands in this region were settled earlier than most of the mainland because the sea provided convenient access to neighboring farms and to distant eastern seaboard markets. Before there were good roads on the mainland, long voyages via sea were easier and less costly than even short expeditions overland. The settlers of Swans Island, for instance—most of whom were sailors who served in the Revolution or the War of 1812 before becoming fishermen—used boats to visit each other's homes rather than go to the effort and expense of building a road across the island's rocky and rugged interior.

Between 1820 and 1845, many Swans Islanders were entirely engrossed in building ships, brigs, and schooners used either for fishing or to transport cordwood and lumber to market. James Swan, one of the early speculators in island real estate, offered to give 10 acres of land to any fisherman who owned his own boat. The fact that Swan owned the island's tidal sawmill meant that he certainly intended to recoup his investment when islanders brought ship timber to be sawn.

As in Penobscot Bay, the islands of Merchant Row and Jericho Bay are underlain by granite. Because granite is resistant to the agents of erosion, which are also the agents of soil formation, the soils of these islands are among the most shallow and sterile on the coast. Some of the diversity of field and forest landscapes in Merchant Row is a result of the 18th- and 19th-century practice of burning islands to create pasturelands. Though pretty to look at, the cycles of burning and overgrazing have run the shallow soils downhill, and the bleached bare bones of the granite outcrops still poke though their thin grass skins.

In 1880 Merchant Row (like Penobscot Bay) became a world of boats carrying granite. Individual quarries, called motions, were pounded out of hardrock on half a dozen islands in Merchant Row and Casco Passage, and major quarries were established on Swans, Deer Isle, and Crotch, one of the last Maine island quarries to furnish granite to the cities of the Atlantic seaboard.

To yachtsmen today, the waters of Jericho Bay are a rock-strewn treachery, particularly in a fog, when the exact location of any vessel is vague at best. To all but the herring fishermen of the area, the silver lining is that these half-tide ledges are whelping and haulout grounds for something like one out of every five seals that inhabit Gulf of Maine waters. Until recently, it was a rare fisherman who passed up an opportunity to practice his marksmanship on these pinnipeds, which allegedly dine on a strict and steady diet of fishermen's profits.

Blue Hill and Frenchman Bays: The Arms of Mount Desert

No other stretch of Maine's coastal waters is defined so completely, so gigantically by the land that rises up out of the sea as are the desert-mountains above Southwest, Northeast, Seal, and Bar Harbors. So much has been written about Mount Desert among all other islands that further attempts can only retrace old ground. Here it is enough to concentrate on some of the islands that ring the fractured granite shores of the Big Island. The bedrock of the islands surrounding Mount Desert is of different composition than the granitic pluton that defines the rounded contours of Pemetic, Norumbega, Cadillac, and Champlain Mountains. To the west, Long and Bartlett Islands are primarily underlain by an ancient covering of the country rock into which an ancient volcanic vent intruded. To the south, the Gotts, the Ducks, and the Cranberry Isles are composed of the hardened deposits that issued forth from millions of years of extrusive activity. To the east, the steep, austere topography of the Porcupines and Ironbound are defined by a massive inclined sheet of diorite, which, like a slab of inerodible cement, gives them a ramp-like shape.

With the exception of Little Placentia Island, now called Great Gott, the islands of these bays were not settled until the conclusion of the French and Indian Wars. However, in 1688, when Sir John Andors, Governor of the Massachusetts Bay Colony, sent a whaleboat along the Maine coast east of Pemaquid to survey French occupation, the expedition found "Petit Plaisants" (the Little Beautiful Island) occupied. We don't know anything about these two families, but they must have been inconspicuous or politic enough to have avoided the enmity of both France and England, who spared no efforts to destroy each other's unprotected settlements along the coast of Maine.

After Montreal fell to the British, the islands south of Mount Desert

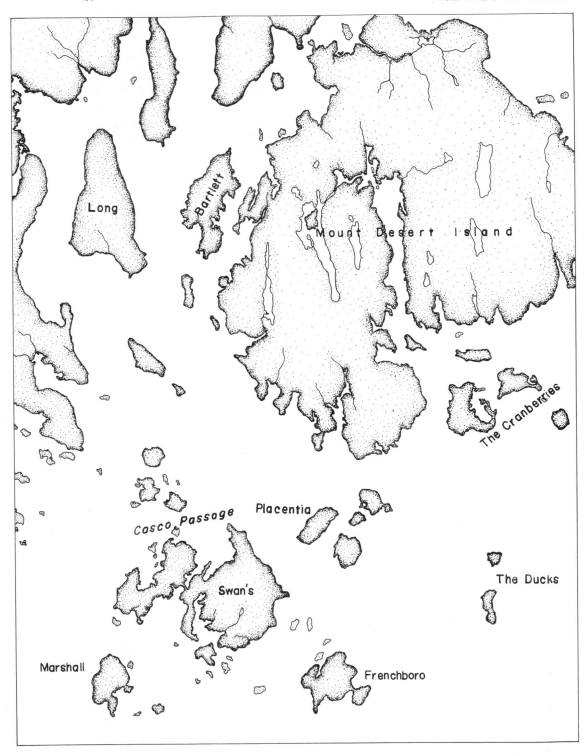

Long

Bartlett

Mount Desert Island

The Cranberries

Casco Passage

Placentia

The Ducks

Swan's

Marshall

Frenchboro

BLUE HILL BAY

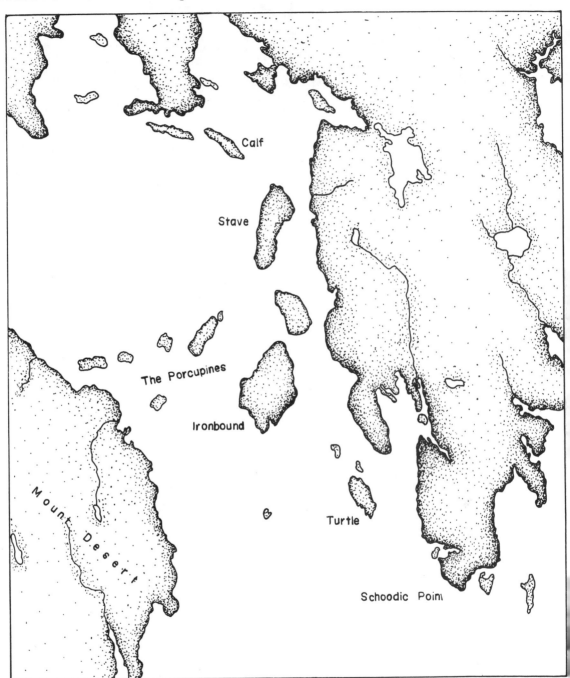

FRENCHMAN BAY

Island were settled rapidly. The Cranberry Islands, named for the extensive swamps where bog cranberries could be collected for winter preserves, became important fishing and shipping stations because of their many small,

Glacial sculpturing of Mount Desert hills.   *Jim Kosinski*

protected harbors. A county atlas published in 1886 shows eight herring smokehouses on Little Cranberry Island; herring became a specialty export from these islands during the latter part of the 19th century. To supplement their incomes during the winter when fishing was slow, islanders shot birds for feathers or cut wood on the uninhabited islands for the Boston cordwood market. By 1860, virtually all the islands around Mount Desert had been cut over at least once, with the possible exception of the nearly vertical-sided Bald Porcupine, which, to this day, supports a forest association different from the others in the Bay.

In 1830 the Cranberry Isles, together with Sutton and Baker, petitioned the State Legislature for separation from Mount Desert Island. The islanders cited the inconvenience of attending public meetings across the water on the main island, since they had "nearly all their trade business and common connections among themselves," and not with those other people across the way. One of the inescapable facts of island living is that the more time you spend "islanded," the less you feel compelled to go anywhere else for any reason.

In 1926 much of the undeveloped acreage on Mount Desert was given over to the federal government to create a national park. Since then, a few of the outlying islands have been purchased or donated to what has become Acadia National Park, but recent efforts to acquire more islands for public recreation have been condemned so roundly in coastal and island towns that the Park has been forced to withdraw its plans for expansion.

As in the past, the islands will continue to be the haunts of those who have spent either the time or the money to get there on their own. It's a system that might be called unfair and unequal, but at least it has worked to the advantage of the variety of nesting bird populations. Despite the invasion of millions of summer tourists to Acadia, the big island and several of the smaller islands support nesting pairs of eagles that are no doubt attracted to the great many craggy niches on these cliffy islands. Two of the islands at the outermost edge of this group even house fragile underground cities of burrow-nesting seabirds—the secretive Leach's storm petrel, whose colonies persist only on a few inhospitable Maine coast islands.

Narraguagus and Pleasant Bays: Getting Sparse

These two bays whose waters spill back and forth into one another are bounded on the main by Cape Split and Petit Manan Point. Petit Manan was named by Champlain, whose charts of the Gulf of Maine have given us more permanent place names than those of any other explorer: Grand Manan, Mount Desert, Isle au Haut, and Burnt Coat. Champlain had a knack for coining good descriptions of the natural features that mariners encountered for centuries afterward. Having said this, one must concede that Champlain's name of Petit Manan for the peninsula's resemblance to Grand Manan is a little far-fetched—since it looks nothing like the high, rugged shores of the Canadian island—but it must be a reflection of the relief felt by sailors after making a landfall on an uncharted and treacherous coast.

As you go farther east, even today, the settlements on the islands and along the coast get fewer and farther between. The same situation was true in 1760 when the British Admiralty began the painstaking process of charting the waters of their newly expanded empire. The *Atlantic Neptune* was the first great marine atlas of the eastern coast of North America; it covered the waters of the Florida coast to the Gulf of St. Lawrence. The New England charts were produced by an engineer named Samuel Holland from on-the-spot surveys conducted between 1764 and 1773. In addition to showing water depths and the locations of all serious hazards to navigation, the *Atlantic Neptune* showed settlements and even ownership boundaries on the islands and along the coast of Maine. Obviously no expense was spared. It was virtually the only comprehensive view of Maine that existed for the next 50 years, and it gave the British an enormous advantage over the colonists in naval matters during the two wars that the two countries fought.

But east of Schoodic Point, even the information from the *Atlantic Neptune* becomes rather sparse. In all of Narraguagus and Pleasant Bays, the only islands correctly named in the *Neptune* are Little Manan (Champlain's landfall), Bois Bubert (literally "the woods of Bubert," an unknown Frenchman), and Shipstern. Flint and Norton Islands are misplaced, and the mariner's most important landmark, Pigeon Hill, is located on Dyer Neck, one peninsula to the west. Most of this confusion reflected the fact

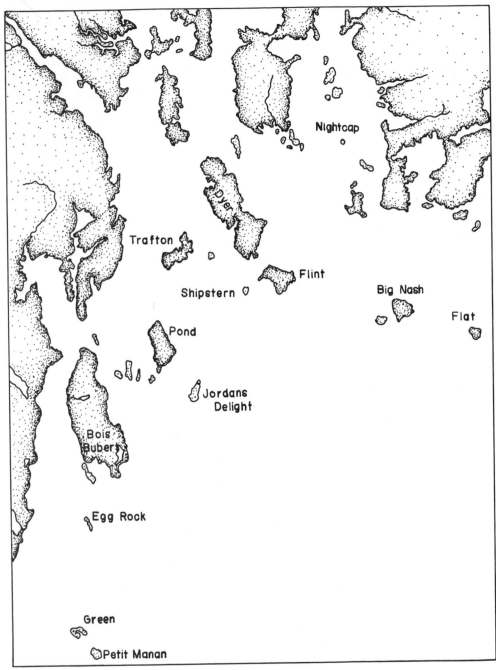

NARRAGUAGUS AND PLEASANT BAYS

that the area was so sparsely settled that reliable information for local place names was hard to come by.

All three of the rivers that empty into these waters are still important runs for anadromous (Greek, meaning "up-running") fish—alewives, smelt,

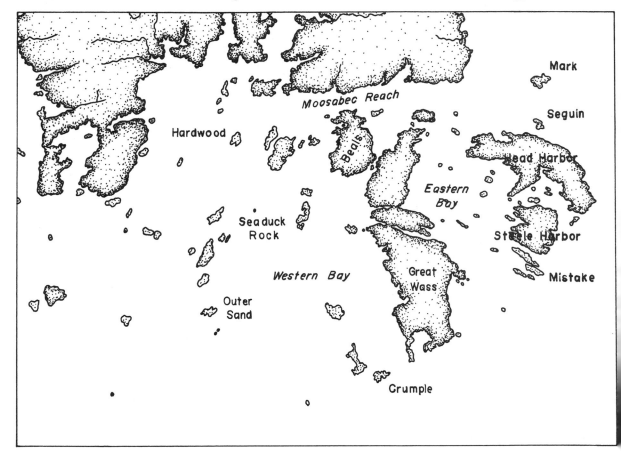

EASTERN AND WESTERN BAYS

and striped bass—and the Narraguagus River is still one of the most famous Atlantic salmon rivers on the East Coast. These fish runs explain not only the variety of homemade fish weirs or traps—which have in their day provided small fortunes for the fishermen who correctly guessed where to place them—but also the diversity of fish-eating birds that nest here. One small island halfway up the Bay hosts no fewer than six nests of the normally territorial osprey. The two grassy islands off Petit Manan Point are the site of Maine's largest nesting colony of terns, a mixed-species colony of Arctics, commons, and roseates.

Eastern and Western Bays: Subarctic Ecosystems

The farther east you go, the more subarctic the coastal ecosystems look. Blueberry barrens are interspersed with larch or tamarack swamps and peat bogs. Rare arctic flowers occupy the extreme tips of islands and peninsulas, where the climate is raw, cool, and damp for all but one or two months of the year. Probably because of the incredibly long winters, the area was never rich or prosperous. Instead of lovely old mansions built by clipper-ship captains there are the small one-and-a-half-story Cape Cod houses of fishermen, woodcutters, and "outlaws," the men who administer their own conceptions of justice according to private codes, feuds, and traditions. In the old days they were called pirates.

Champlain, who was so successful with his place names, stopped in these waters on his second coastal voyage. Samuel Eliot Morison believed Champlain dropped anchor in the Cow's Yard between Head Harbor and Steele Harbor Islands, which is still one of the few protected deep-water anchorages east of Schoodic Point. Champlain named the islands Cape Corneille, or Cape Crow, for the black birds that made their presence known to him in raucous fashion. It is perhaps a little unkind to take issue with Champlain's faulty naming of these birds, especially since Cape Corneille is now known by the less attractive name of Black Head, but for the sake of argument, the birds he saw were probably ravens, a shy species that has been replaced by the smaller, gregarious crows that have made a habit of following humans around the globe.

The waters of Eastern and Western Bays surround four large islands—Beals, Great Wass, Steele, and Head Harbor—which, together, form the easternmost granite pluton of the Maine coast. Beals Island, a well-known lobstering community, was the last coastal island to be ceded to the main-land when a suspension bridge was arched over the swift tidal waters of Moosabec Reach in 1957. The smaller islands around Beals, like those in

Cool, damp spruce woods.   *Rick Perry*

Merchant Row, have been burned and grazed for upwards of a century and today look quite bony.

The ledgy waters of Eastern Bay have remained important haulout grounds for a large number of harbor seals that have made a scientific study of the distance between themselves and approaching boats. Most of the largest haulouts are at low water, just beyond the accurate range of a rifle shot.

Englishman Bay: Puffins or Rogues

No one knows the names of the first Europeans to settle on the islands in this bay, English or otherwise, but by 1769 there were two log cabins on Roque Island, the largest island in the Bay. Island place names often reveal something of their history or ecology, but in the case of most of those in the Roque Island group, the derivations are conflicting and obscure. Great

ENGLISHMAN BAY

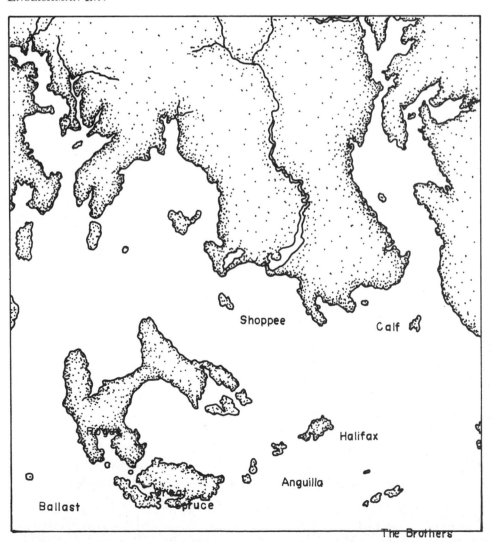

Shoppee

Calf

Rogue

Halifax

Anguilla

Ballast

Great Spruce

The Brothers

and Little Spruce present no problems, except that they were called Parson's and Rough's Islands in two different editions of the *Atlantic Neptune*. Double Shot is a topographic reference, and Halifax would have been named by an Englishman, but Anguilla sounds more Spanish or Portuguese, like "aguila," the word for eagle in Spanish. In fact, eagles still nest in good numbers in the area.

In the case of Roque itself, Samuel Morison has suggested it may be an abbreviation of Isle des Perroques, a name that French explorers gave to places frequented by the "sea parrots," or puffins, they found on the islands of the North Atlantic. While there is no doubt that puffins were once found on several other Maine islands than the few to which they are now confined, it is a bit unlikely that they would have nested on Roque itself, since they are burrow dwellers and prefer exposed sea cliffs. The Brothers Island at the outer edge of Englishman Bay or Libby Island at the entrance to Machias Bay would have served better. Another problem on Roque is the record of its mainland connection by a low-tide gravel bar until 1805, and this would have served as an avenue of entry for all manner of predators, chiefly raccoons, that are deadly to puffins.

A more plausible explanation for the derivation of the name Roque is that it is a corruption of Rogue Island, referring to its use by pirates, known then as privateers, who raided passing merchant ships. In fact, there is a record of one John Rhoades, who headquartered his pirate fleet at Machias in the early 1700s and conceivably used the high headlands of Roque to post lookouts—on a clear day, Mount Desert is visible from the summit of one of the promontories.

Among the yachting fraternity, Roque Island is most well known today for its magnificent Great South Beach. There is also a belief among yachtsmen that upon completion of a successful passage east of Schoodic, where secure anchorages are difficult to find, fogs more prevalent, and coastal towns full of skeptical inhabitants, one has earned entry into an exclusive club. It is more a rite of passage than a sailing passage. The reward for success is to anchor off the long, arcing, white sandy beach, which stretches for nearly two miles between the shoulders of two immense headlands, and congratulate yourself for a fine bit of navigating. Of course, in these days of fancy navigation gear, the challenge is not quite as real as it was 20 or 30 years ago, when the mystique of "Roque or broke" was prevalent, but the reward hasn't changed much: the Great South Beach is as surprising and pleasing a landform as one could hope to find on this rocky, fogbound coast.

No one has adequately explained why there is such a long, perfect white sandy beach here and not another one like it until you hit Small Point at the mouth of the Kennebec 150 miles farther south. A good guess, though, is that the two headlands of Roque trapped a massive tongue of ice as the glacier retreated across the landscape 13,000 years ago. The melting ice dropped its load of sand and gravel, which has been held in place and protected from the onslaught of storm seas by the unique arrangement of the

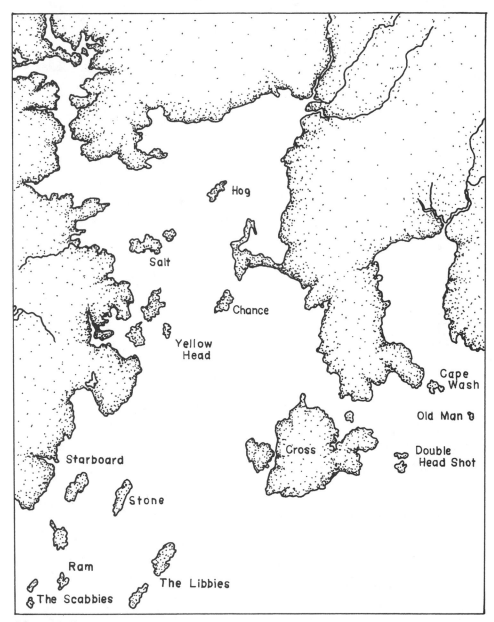

MACHIAS BAY

fringing islands. The sand moves up and down the beach over the years, transported by harbor currents, but it is, if we can speak of shifting sands in such terms, quite stable. The passage from Schoodic to Roque may not be material for myth and legend, but the Great South Beach certainly is.

Machias Bay: Volcanic Arches and Caves

Machias is an Indian word that describes the "bad little falls" of the Machias River, where the present town is located. Machias was settled earlier than

Cross Island sea cave.   *Lolly Cochran*

many other parts of the coast because of the commercial possibilities afforded by the easily harnessed water power tumbling over the rocky cascades.
Enormous quantities of timber were sawn into boards, shingles, clapboards,
shooks, and deals for the export market by the early settlers of Machias.

The names of the islands at the entrance to the Bay derive from some of the town's earliest inhabitants—Stone, Libby, and Foster. It's hard to say how Scabby Island at the western edge of Machias Bay got its name, though it may have been named in the same spirit as Ragged Arse Island at the entrance to Penobscot Bay.

The Machias Bay islands, like those of Englishman Bay, have a more rugged and forbidding topography than islands farther to the west, reflecting the change in bedrock that underlies the coast east of Jonesport. The southern shores of most of these islands are formed of brittle, fractured, needle-shaped volcanic rocks that have been cut by intrusions of other igneous rocks known as dikes. Many of the dikes have eroded away, leaving narrow, vertical-walled crevices and a world of arches and caves that discourages most foot traffic. In fact, the access to foot traffic along the shore of Cross Island, the largest of the Machias Bay islands, was an important consideration for the life-saving station that was built there in 1879. Crews patrolled the shore night and day, rain and gale, to watch for foundering vessels off its rugged perimeter. Telephone stations were located at various shoreline points on this 1,500-acre island, not only to connect the far reaches of the island with the life-boat station, but, one suspects, to ensure that on dark and stormy nights the patrol did not lose heart and only pretend to make the circuit of the island.

Cobscook Bay: Oil and Eagles

Cobscook Bay is distinct from other sections of the Maine coast. Here the old river valleys run northwest-southeast, or perpendicular to the trend of bedrock in Casco, Sheepscot, Muscongus, and West Penobscot Bays. Cobscook is a system of concentrically curving bays, peninsulas, and islands formed from the partial submergence of these arc-shaped valleys and ridges carved in folded shales, slates, and sandstones. When sea level rose following glaciation, it flooded a cross valley that connected the inner and outer longitudinal valleys to create the topography we see today.

Cobscook Bay is connected to and is an integral part of Passamaquoddy Bay—known to most Americans since Franklin Roosevelt's time for the power potential of its enormous tides, up to 24 feet when moon and sun line up twice a month. More recently, Cobscook Bay has figured in the public discussion of whether or not the Pittston Company will build an oil refinery in Eastport. Of the many points of discussion in the heated public debate, none is more central to the outcome than the effect the refinery might have on Cobscook Bay's population of northern bald eagles. Recently the eagle has been declared a rare and endangered species—the only bird species in Maine to receive this form of federal protection.

Depending on the year, about eight or 10 pairs of eagles maintain nests along the shores and on the islands of Cobscook, away from the disturbances of civilization and near the productive fisheries that the waters of the Bay support. It is the only area of Maine where the eagles are reproducing fast

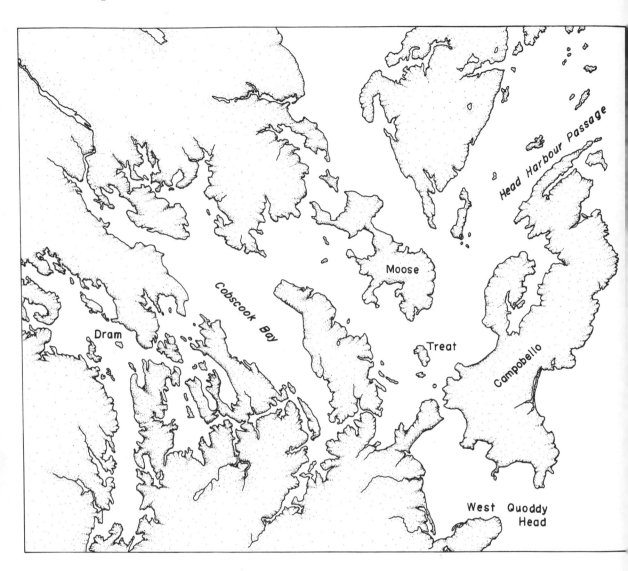

Head Harbour Passage

Moose

Cobscook Bay

Dram

Treat

Campobello

West Quoddy
Head

COBSCOOK BAY

enough to offset their annual losses. The fear, of course, is that a refinery
—either by its daily presence or as a result of an oil spill—would harass this
last flourishing population. For its part, Pittston has presented a disin-
genuous plan to protect the eagles in the case of a spill. They would not
allow any of them to eat fish contaminated by the spill, but, like some kind
of corporate Pied Piper, would lead the eagles off into supposedly uncon-
taminated areas and feed them there! It's easy to hear them now: "Here
eagle, eagle, eagle."

2

The Gulf of Maine: Cod, Haddock, Herring, and Hake

THE MATTER OF LEIF ERIKSON and the Vikings aside, it seems likely that the original discoverers and occupiers of the Maine archipelago were expeditions of unnamed fishermen who pursued schools of herring and cod successively farther and farther across the North Atlantic in search of more productive fishing grounds. So, a description of the marine features that combine to make the Gulf of Maine one of the most productive bodies of water in the world is a good point of departure for describing the islands themselves. Not only do these waters define the outline of the rocky shores, but the fishermen who came to the islands early and stayed late have subsequently and indisputably been a major influence on their ecologies.

Geomorphology of the Gulf of Maine

Geomorphology is another word for shape of the land and the shape of the bottom of the Gulf of Maine is its most distinctive feature. The Gulf is an enormous, 36,000-square-mile backwater of the North Atlantic Ocean—a partially enclosed sea. It is a young sea, as seas go, having been dry land until 15,000 years ago, when glacial meltwaters inundated what had once been rolling hills and valleys. If you remember the tale of the Chinese man who could swallow up the sea, you get an idea of the effect of Pleistocene glaciation. Nine million cubic miles of the sea were swallowed up in ice and then spit back into the ocean where the ice melted.

The bottom of the Gulf of Maine is irregular and shallow, averaging only about 35 fathoms over its great breadth. The underwater topography

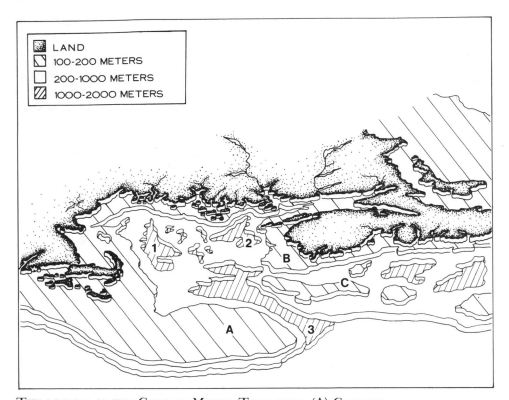

THE BOTTOM OF THE GULF OF MAINE. THE BANKS: (A) GEORGES;
(B) GERMAN; (C) BROWN'S. THE BASINS: (1) WILKINSON; (2) JORDAN
(3) NORTHEAST CHANNEL.

of the rest of the eastern coast is much simpler than that of the Gulf of
Maine. Along the rest of the eastern seaboard, a coastal plain of varying width
slopes gradually away from the land's edge to the continental shelf, where
the sea floor drops off sharply into the depths of the ocean.

The outer perimeter of the Gulf is formed by Brown's Bank on the
east, Georges Bank on the south, and Nantucket Shoals on the southwest.
These remarkably productive banks serve as a barrier and protect the Gulf
from the intrusion of warm, sapphire-blue waters of the Atlantic Gulf
Stream. Without them the long tropical fingers of the Gulf Stream would
invade the basin of the Gulf of Maine, which acts as a nursery for the 500
million tons of seafood harvested there annually. The intrusion of the
Gulf Stream might make swimming less of a feat, but it would also make
fishing less productive, since its warmer, saltier waters have, on the rare
occasions they find their way up and over the banks, disastrous effects on
fish populations adapted to the strict temperature regimens of Maine's waters.

Scattered inshore of these major banks are innumerable smaller banks
and ledges—Platt's, Stellwagen, Fippinnies, Jeffrey's, and the wryly named
Hue and Cry Bottom, Minerva Hub, Mistaken Ground, and Kettle Bottom,

to name a few of the hidden pieces of underwater topography of the Gulf of Maine.

In part these underwater banks and ledges are the result of glacial scouring, and in part they are the topographic remnants of the rolling coastal plain, which has been flooded by rising seas. The composition of the shelves and basins varies from hard rock to sand, gravel, clay, ooze, and shell fragments. Together they represent an incredible variety of habitats for the diverse marine assemblages that spend portions of their lives feeding over or around them.

On the landward side of the Gulf of Maine, five enormous river systems—Merrimack, Piscataqua, Kennebec, Penobscot, and St. John, not to mention scores of smaller rivers—empty fresh water and suspended nutrients into the Gulf's basin. Collectively these rivers supply something on the order of 100 billion gallons of fresh water annually to Maine's partially enclosed sea, and this has a direct and measurable effect on salinity, and therefore on fish egg survival. Fish egg survival and larval growth of most saltwater fish are enhanced by slightly reduced salinity. Some of the Gulf's most productive spawning grounds lie at the mouths of these rivers, where both the reduced salinity and the increased availability of dissolved nutrients combine to create fish-development factories. Since an estuary is a body of seawater into which fresh water mixes, technically the entire Gulf of Maine is an estuary, one of the most biologically productive ecosystems in the world.

Although the Gulf of Maine stretches along the shore of two other states, it is named for Maine, since by far the greatest portion of the Gulf lies off Maine's shores, and until 1910 Maine boats and fishermen were the most numerous in these waters. It is no exaggeration to say that the Gulf of Maine is the most distinctive body of water on the eastern side of the North Atlantic.

The Biochemistry of Cold Water

Most of us grew up believing that the oceans of the world represent an enormous biological potential that would feed us for the rest of eternity if we could just learn to exploit it a little more cleverly. But this is a myth: biologically the oceans of the world are deserts. Except for a very few places in the world—the Gulf of Maine is one—there is not enough plant life to feed a handful of fish, never mind the civilizations of the world.

Almost the opposite relationship between latitude and productivity exists on land as in water. By and large, on land as you move south toward the equator, terrestrial ecosystems become more productive; that is, the biomass or weight of all living things within a given ecosystem (a forest,

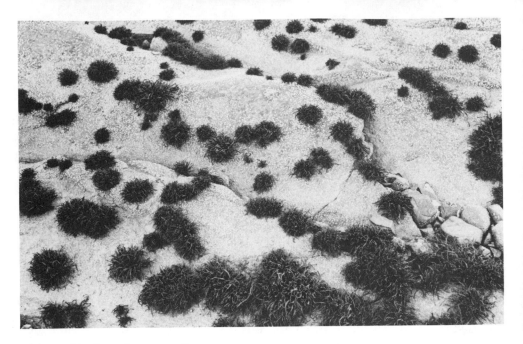

Urchins and rockweed.   *George Putz*

for example) will increase. No one should be surprised to learn that an acre of tropical rainforest has more biomass than an acre of the northern spruce-fir forest. In marine ecosystems, however, as you move away from the equator and toward the poles, productivity increases primarily as a result of the increased concentrations of life-supporting dissolved gases—carbon dioxide and oxygen—that cold water is able to carry. In warm water these gases evaporate more quickly, which is why they are less capable of supporting large concentrations of marine life.

Aside from limited supplies of oxygen and carbon dioxide, most of the world's oceans have preciously small quantities of nitrogen and phosphorus, critical ingredients for all animal metabolic processes—even those of tiny animals that float on the surface of the sea. Whatever the supply of these nutrients in a marine ecosystem, they tend to grow scarce over time, since they are at the mercy of the force of gravity. Floating plants and animals feed on them as they slowly filter down through the water column to bring a portion of the scarce resources back to the surface, but it is a losing battle. More and more of it eventually finds its way to the bottom, where it is either incorporated into sediments or into the food chains of bottom-dwelling creatures. Either way, the nutrients are largely lost to the floating planktonic life that supports the great schools of oceanic fish.

The lost nutrients are replenished at the ocean surface in one of two ways. Nutrients are either dissolved in the runoff from a nearby landmass or carried up from the depths by a bottom current that rises to the surface. This latter process—called vertical mixing or upwelling—occurs where two currents collide or where a current hits a shoal or shelf and, like an air current, accelerates up its slope.

In the Gulf of Maine there are a few significant zones of vertical mixing where two bottom currents collide and one rises to enrich surface waters. The most notable zone of upwelling is a thin band offshore of Matinicus Island that stretches northeasterly toward Grand Manan Island. But the greater portion of nutrients is supplied to the marine food chains of the Gulf of Maine through the conduits of the rivers that empty into the sea. Fresh water is less dense than seawater, and the rivers' discharge literally flows downhill over the heavier salt water to fertilize the sea. The gentle counterclockwise rotation of the currents in the Gulf of Maine—pushed by the flow of the rivers and driven by oscillation of the tides—distributes the dissolved nutrients over a large portion of this partially enclosed sea. It's a dynamic system whose mysterious ways we are just beginning to appreciate.

Food Chains; Water vs. Land

For any species that can breathe dissolved oxygen in water, the Gulf of Maine is a great place to live, since it is a more stable environment than land. The seasonal temperature variations in the Gulf of Maine are on the order of 20° F., while those on land fluctuate five times as much. This causes all kinds of hardships for terrestrial life; deciduous trees must drop their leaves, birds go south for the winter, and many warm-blooded animals burrow underground to sleep it off. But marine life in the Gulf of Maine just shifts slightly, horizontally or vertically, in the water column to find a more comfortable temperature and a supply of food. Marine animals are less affected by the precession of the equinoxes.

In the Gulf of Maine there is also the matter of the endless conveyor belt of tides and currents that brings food to the animals; the great majority of the creatures just float in the right places and eat what comes along. Imagine land animals adapted to feeding on airborne particles of food strained out by some sort of terrestrial equivalent of gill rakers, so that they can just move about the landscape looking for wind currents, for floating pastures of plenty. The gaps between mountains or near the tops of high hills, where the wind accelerates up and over the landscape, would be places where current feeders could congregate and filter out the food that swept by endlessly. At sea, storms increase the food supply by tearing it loose from undersea footholds and carrying it around by tidal currents past the palates of scavengers. Alongshore, rocks are tossed about endlessly and crush a great many other animals. Even the scavengers become meals for other scavengers when they are caught off guard by a big wave.

Many animals weigh about the same as the water in which they live, and they expend less energy moving about, not having so much gravity to

Food chain: dinoflagellates—copepods—herring.   *Kate Fitzgerald*

offend. Because water is more dense, however, the creatures have a harder
time overcoming its inertia. No animal in the ocean can even begin to
approach the speed at which many birds fly or fleet ungulates (antelope,
gazelle, and the American quarter horse, for example) gallop. Possible exceptions to this generalization are the marine mammals that propel themselves by whiplike up-and-down movements of their flukes (or tails), which
sets an oscillating wave over their skin, thus increasing laminar flow and
reducing friction. This means that some species of whales are among the
sleekest creatures in the world, if the combined qualities of speed and grace
are the qualifying characteristics.

Ocean animals have more food available to them than those on land
and less need of it, since their stable environment requires less energy to
move about. Because they are cold-blooded, they have no internal temperature controls that require the burning of energy to generate heat or the
evaporation of water to reduce it. A shrew, on the other hand, must literally
eat every waking minute if it is to survive, due to its small size and conse-
quent high rate of heat loss.

When land animals reproduce, they must not only provide eggs with
food, but enclose them in a package that won't dry out. Leaving aside marine
mammals, most animals in the ocean produce small—even tiny—eggs that
need no accompanying food factory, nor protection against drying out.
As a result, they can afford the biological luxury of laying an extraordinary

number of eggs. The tiny animals feed and grow on what is all around them; they do not have to hunt for water or conserve it. Where food is found, it is abundant, so food storage is not an important evolutionary consideration. For all of these reasons, marine animals are, in terms of behavior, less specialized than terrestrial animals, which are often channeled ecologically into cooperative modes of behavior to find food. In the sea there are few social animals comparable to ants or bees, unless you count the coelenterates—jellyfish and sponges—which are loose collections of cells that congregate to form a single animal but can live on their own.

Green Light and Green Water

The play of light on surface waters also helps define the special productivity of carbon dioxide-enriched cold waters of the Gulf of Maine. Because light rays are more slanted when they strike the earth's surface at the higher latitudes, they do not penetrate the water as deeply; and because light is restricted to the surface layers, the great concentrations of plant life that fix the sun's energy into green life are also confined to the same regions. Where there are dense blooms of surface plant life—diatoms and dinoflagel-

The play of light and water.   *Jim Kosinski*

lates that collectively make up the floating phytoplankton—more of the light is absorbed nearer the surface. This is known as a positive-feedback loop: more light confined to the surface means more plants, and more plants at the surface absorb more of the light. This interplay between sunlight and plant life in the Gulf of Maine creates living green water. Over most of the surface of the globe, the sea is blue—a reflection of the color of the sky. But in the rich waters of the Gulf of Maine it is a lively and murky green—the sign that the water is full of food. Rarely in the Gulf of Maine is underwater visibility anything like in the clear water of the tropics, where planktonic life is much less concentrated.

Long days at high latitudes can be too much of a good thing for surface-living planktonic animals—copepods, little shrimp called krill, and the whole world of odd-looking larval forms of crabs, lobsters, squid, and emaciated shapes with bug eyes and big mouths that you wouldn't believe will turn into fish. It is during the day that this collection of not-yet-fish, crabs, lobsters, and what-not is most vulnerable to other species of marine animals with a temporary size advantage. During the free-floating stage that most marine animals must go through, great numbers fall prey to some distant marine relative. But the delight of the marine world is that the tables soon are turned and animals that were prey weeks ago become the predators of smaller members of the same species that had just pruned their ranks. It's as if half-grown rabbits, with a slight size advantage over baby foxes, could turn the tables and have fox for dinner.

Because of this eat-and-be-eaten arrangement of life in the water, most of the planktonic animals that feed on diatoms spend the daytime near the lower limits of light penetration and migrate upward to feed after the sun sets. Plankton-eating fish such as herring follow their prey up and down in the water column from night to day, but they are most easily caught at the surface when the sun goes down. Schooling herring or sardines at night disturb multitudes of luminescent animals and thus often reveal their presence to fishermen, who look for the play of eerie green lights on the night-time water.

Competition and Predation

If life in the ocean is so good, why have the last several hundred million years of evolution been a process of marine forms struggling out of their watery pastures and onto the surface of land, which is hotter and colder and drier and in almost all ways less habitable? Survival in the sea is tenuous until a creature gets big enough so that it does not make a convenient mouthful for something bigger. The intensity of predation and competition for inevitably scarce resources must be twin driving forces for land coloniza-

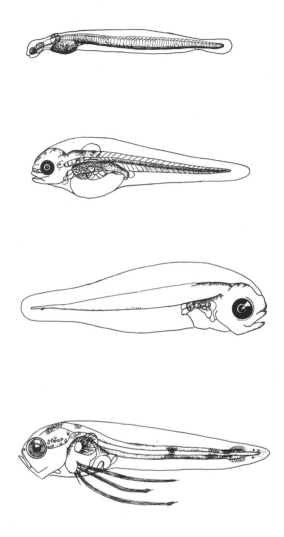

Larval forms of herring, haddock (middle two) and cusk.   *Kate Fitzgerald*

tion. This dynamic is most visible in the intertidal region, where the common marine plants and animals stratify themselves into the neat zones that the naturalist Rachel Carson described: the barnacle zone, the periwinkle zone, the rockweed zone, and so on. Recent studies of the way these creatures maintain such a rigid stratification indicate that the upper boundary of each zone is primarily determined by a creature's physical tolerance to drying out. The lower limits of the zone, however, are determined by competition

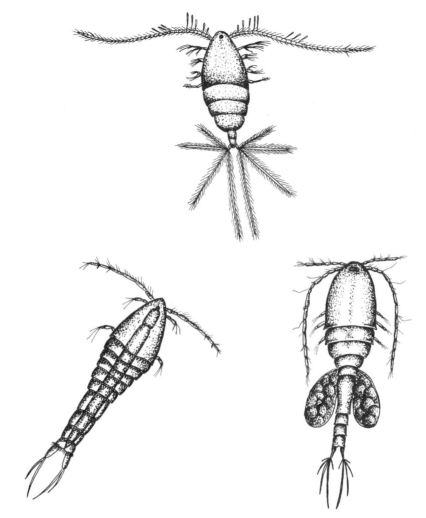

Copepods: *Calanus, Canthocamptus* and *Cyclops.*   *Kate Fitzgerald*

and predation. When you look at a diverse marine intertidal zone you can almost hear the struggle for a foothold slightly above and beyond the reach of the snapping mandibles of their competitors and predators below.

For most of us, who are used to thinking in terms of terrestrial systems, the cyclical nature of marine food supplies is hard to understand. In a few places like the Gulf of Maine, where all the ingredients are present for an incredibly rich assemblage of marine life, the total supply of food is vast, but it disappears temporarily as cycles come in and out of synch with each other. Consider the tiny floating crustaceans called copepods, which make up a great portion of the Gulf of Maine's zooplankton. Copepods feed on blooms of phytoplankton and are in turn fed on by small fish. Some copepods can go through an entire life cycle—birth, reproduction, and death—

in 10 days. An individual female copepod lays 50 eggs, which can produce 1,250 individuals 10 days later, which produce 31,250 in the next fortnight, 781,250 in the following, and so on. At the beginning of the cycle, there is perhaps one copepod for every decimeter (a four-inch cube), but by the fourth generation, there will be 500 copepods per cubic inch. Soon they exceed the numbers of the phytoplankton upon which they feed, and a die-off results. If a school of fish find them first, however, there is a great finned feast, which fattens fish until the next randomly created meal presents itself —that is, until the copepod cycle synchs with a planktonic bloom and the whole cycle begins again.

Cycles of abundance of fish happen at unlikely times in lucky and likely places. If they are to be successful, fishermen, like fish, must be adapted to taking advantage of temporary concentrations of marine life. There is enough shrewdness in the business to sustain the good fishermen who prosper year in and year out. But make no mistake, the best fishermen are those who combine the likely with the luck.

Fisheries' Histories

> Never could the Spaniard with all his mines of gold and silver pay his debts, his friends and army half so truly as the Hollanders still have done by this contemptible trade of fish . . . But this is their mine and the sea the source of those silvered streams of all their virtue.
>
> Captain John Smith

The search for productive fishing grounds, especially those frequented by cod, lured European fishermen into the far corners of the North Atlantic; lured them, indeed, to discover and explore the shores of New England. Most of the history books write it somewhat differently, since these fishermen were not inclined to keep journals, chart voyages, or record exploits— the stuff from which history is made. In fact, these European fishermen who certainly sailed to Newfoundland for private profit before Cabot's voyage of 1497 were in a sense antihistorical, since they were preternaturally jealous of new and uncrowded fishing grounds and were (as they still are today) secretive about their movements. Casual pieces of information from the official port records of English towns such as Bristol, and indirect information from Breton and Basque ports, are all that modern historians have to go on, but the records are still there for those who like their history to be neat and tidy.

The commercial advantages of the cod fishery made it hugely appealing to merchants in towns whose ports faced the Atlantic. Where cod were found, they were both abundant and easy to catch. They were taken on handlines from the earliest times, and later on longlines or trawls—a series of hooks attached to a long line held down at each end by anchors, and buoyed by floats. They are large fish, averaging 20 to 30 pounds in the early days of the European cod fishery, easy to split and clean, and, because their flesh is not oily like that of mackerel and herring, they could be salted and air-dried without turning rancid.

Throughout the Middle Ages, cod were taken in greater and greater numbers farther and farther out to sea, a livelihood that required the training of capable seamen, the emergence of a seafaring culture, and the building of larger and more seaworthy vessels. The cod is a cold-water fish, widely distributed on rocky bottoms of both sides of the North Atlantic. It was pursued out to the Faroe Islands and then to the waters surrounding Iceland. It was inevitable that sooner or later some fishing vessel would press farther west to find the immense cod grounds—the Grand Banks—off the southern shores of Newfoundland.

In the early 16th century the Grand Banks of Newfoundland were considered to be the greatest fishing grounds in the world by those who caught cod offshore and who went ashore to salt and dry their catch at the innumerable coves and headlands of the new land, the Newfoundland. By the second decade of the 1500s, there were the English fishermen, plus 50 other French, Basque, and Portuguese vessels fishing in Newfoundland waters. By the end of the century, the number of vessels had increased to 350 or 400. Eventually, whether driven south by a gale during a transatlantic crossing or driven to pursue cod on new grounds, one of these vessels sailed into the Gulf of Maine. Perhaps in this case the fishermen did not precede the true explorers—at least they didn't precede Verrazano, who explored the inner waters of the Gulf of Maine during his epic coastwise voyage of 1524 and gave the European world its first written description of the shores and islands of Maine. But the fishermen came to Maine's fishing grounds early, to set up drying yards or flakes on the outer islands and trade with the Indians long before Champlain, Weymouth, and Smith explored the islands for the crowns of France and England.

The Winter Fishery

Sometime after 1600, another undocumented discovery by other unknown fishermen changed the course of Maine's history. The inshore winter spawning grounds of cod were discovered. Like other groundfish such as hake, pollack, and haddock that have moved into cooler, deeper waters to feed during the summer months in the Gulf of Maine, cod move into shallow waters in the winter. Unlike the other species, however, cod go inshore to lay eggs during the winter months. Cod mass in enormous numbers in well-defined locations in accessible waters slightly south of Isles of Shoals, off Cape Eliza-

Flake yard on Vinalhaven—1890.   *Frank Claes*

beth, off the mouth of the Sheepscot River, and off Boothbay. Rather suddenly it became possible for fishermen to catch another full fare of cod,
thus doubling the profits of the merchants who underwrote the costs of the
voyage. Within a short period of time, the owners of fishing vessels realized
that if they set up year-round settlements in Maine to supply the needs of
this lucrative new fishery, they could make a great deal of money.

Even before privately financed year-round fishing outposts were established, the winter fishery became the most lucrative Gulf of Maine fishery.
John Smith—who not only explored the coast of Maine in a small boat in
1614 but caught enough fish during his stay to turn a handsome profit at
the conclusion of his voyage—was one of the early popularizers of the idea
of a Maine winter fishery. He did not exaggerate when he wrote that the
cod that had fattened themselves all summer long were more valuable when
caught during the spawning season: "Each hundred is as good as two or
three hundred in the New-found-land . . . and you can have your fish to
market before they have any." The practice was to leave England in January,
reach Monhegan or Damariscove Island in March, set up stages, and begin
fishing. By June a full fare could be caught; by September it was dried and
on its way to Spain or to some other Mediterranean port, all this long before
the Newfoundland boats could deliver their fish.

Islands such as Isles of Shoals, Richmond, Stratton, Damariscove, Monhegan, and Matinicus—all of which were handy to the winter cod grounds—became important outposts for this new fishery. Jonathon Winter of Richmond Island, the agent for the influential Bristol merchant Robert Trelawney, wrote to his employer that the best catches were landed in January and February: "If you propose to follow fishing here, you must expect to have your ship here by Christmas."

Richmond Island's winter fishing was done in small boats called shallops, with a crew of four. A fifth crew member stayed ashore to wash the salt out of the boat and dry the fish when the shallop returned from a two- or three-day trip to the cod grounds. The fish were "kenched" on board, which involved stacking them so that they would drain. Drying the cod, called "making fish," involved placing the fish on flakes inclined at an angle to keep the sun from parching them. During storms they were mounded up; at night they were covered with wooden boxes. Making fish became a community enterprise during the heyday of the cod fishery.

The full-grown and fat cod that weighed between 40 and 60 pounds were sold on the continent; the smaller cod that were not good enough for the Spanish or Portuguese markets were sold to the Virginia colony. Dried fish of inferior quality—they may have been salt-burned and spotted or simply not as full-fleshed, but still were wholesome and sweet—were packed in casks and sent to the West Indies to be fed to plantation slaves. Other products from this fishing station included "core fish," or corned fish, which were salted in brine without being dried, and "traine," or cod liver oil. "Dun" was a product peculiar to the Isles of Shoals. Pollack caught in the summer and cured in the sun without much salt were piled together and covered with marsh hay until they "ripened." Dun fish became a high-priced specialty product in the Mediterranean.

The success of the cod fishery depended on an abundant supply of bait fish, usually herring, for both handlines and longlines or trawls. According to John Smith, "the savages compare their store [of herring] in the sea to the hairs of their heads." Herring were caught throughout the year, but most prolifically in the fall. By Janathon Winter's account, the bait herring used by Richmond Island fishermen were caught under light sail at night with open drift nets. After several profitable years of fishing from Richmond Island, the herring failed to appear, and Winter was forced to send to England for salted North Sea herring to make his annual fare of cod. Even in the pre-industrial days, the herring fishery was notoriously unpredictable.

"Such Stubborn Fellows"

A good number of the larger fishing enterprises headquartered on various islands off the coast of Maine were financed by a group of wealthy and influential noblemen known as the Plymouth Council. The Council was headed by Sir Ferdinando Gorges, who had underwritten the cost of the ill-fated Popham Colony at the mouth of the Kennebec River. The new Plymouth Charter of 1620 gave Gorges and his Council a monopoly over fishing in Maine's waters, where previously the right to fish had been granted to all Englishmen.

Gorges proposed to sell licenses to fishermen at a rate of 83 cents per ton, which would have amounted to approximately $100 per vessel—a lot of money in colonial America—for the right to harvest the fish that stood between them and starvation. A regent of the King was sent to Maine to demand the fees, but he returned without collecting a farthing, complaining that the fishermen "are such stubborn fellows."

As the importance of Maine's fishery increased for domestic food and trade, so did the clout of her stubborn fishermen. In 1729 a colonial ordinance was passed to protect the rights of access of fishermen to the shoreside for drying fish. The ordinance specified that the first 40 feet above the high-water mark was reserved for use by any fisherman to erect stages or flake yards to dry his catch, regardless of who owned the property. It was a significant development in the history of Anglo-Saxon property rights that has filtered down in diluted form today. Regardless of what the fine print of the law reads today, fishermen still behave, to the utter consternation of landsmen, as if they have a natural right to the shoreline. But the near shores of the sea have been an essential resource since colonial times, and the protected shorelines are one of Maine's most significant natural resources as far as her fisheries are concerned, so it is easy to understand why and how conflicts between landsmen and fishermen develop, and why the two often regard each other with mutual suspicion.

Groundfish and Fishing Grounds

In the years between 1770 and 1800, the population of Maine quintupled. A land rush was on; the eastern frontier opened up at the conclusion of the long and terrifying French and Indian Wars. Suddenly there were more people pouring into the state and many more mouths to feed. Before the Revolution there were about 60 vessels employed in the fisheries from the District of Maine. Only a few of these went to the offshore banks such as Georges or Brown's. The greatest number fished the smaller banks closer to shore—Spot of Rocks, Saturday Night Ledge, Old Man's Pasture, Sousouwest, Kettle Bottom, Schoodic Ridges, and Clay Bank from berths at Isles of Shoals, Damariscove, Monhegan, North and South Fox Islands, Swans, and Deer Isle. They could fish from smaller, less seaworthy boats on the inshore banks, and therefore they did not need a large initial invest-

Wreck—Monhegan Island.   *George Putz*

ment to go into business. The Isles of Shoals had probably the largest Gulf
of Maine fishing station before the Revolution. Appledore, the biggest island
in the Isles of Shoals group, had a population that fluctuated between 300
and 600 and annually cured 300,000 quintals (pronounced "kentals"; a
quintal equaled 112 pounds), mostly for the Spanish and West Indian
markets.

The early fishing was done in chebacco boats, double-ended sprit-rigged
ketches that averaged 15 tons. They made day trips to the fishing grounds.
By 1810 the chebaccos had increasingly been replaced by the jigger or
pinky—a larger double-ender with a small cabin where there were two
berths for the crew and a fireplace with a wooden chimney. The 20-ton
pinkies, which were the most popular boats until around 1840, sailed with
a foresail and large mainsail only. The pinky was an ideal boat from which
to work the inshore banks. Full forward and sharp aft, deep and heavy,
she could work to windward, ride a sea equally well under sail or at anchor,
and then scud quickly home. Virtually no other type of working fishing boat
was built for 20 years. Pinkies took a wide variety of groundfish: cod,
pollack, haddock, and later halibut. In the seemingly endless matter of
changing tastes, halibut was considered a "trash fish" until the 1820s. Haddock and pollack were not as large as cod and were more difficult to cure.
In fact, the haddock was despised by cod fishermen until the 1870s, when
they began icing the fish at sea for the fresh fish trade.

Haking inshore.

Gradually, however, the inshore groundfish stocks began to be depleted. The year 1832, for example, was the highline year for the inshore cod fishery. In years following, fishermen were forced to go farther out into the Gulf of Maine to make a full fare. The pinkies were eventually succeeded by larger and larger schooners, which were capable of making trips to the outer banks—not just Georges and Brown's but the Nova Scotia banks as well.

The "bankers," averaging 40 tons, would make two trips, called fares, to the outer banks in the summer months. Each fare lasted five or six weeks. Once at the banks, the schooners anchored, and the crews of perhaps six men fished with handlines from stations around the deck called checks; planks were made and fitted for that purpose. They usually fished for six days at a time; on Sunday most of them observed the tradition of visiting each other's boats, called "coving."

Though we usually associate the bank fishing with men longlining from dories, this innovation did not hit the bankers until 1858 when the *American Eagle* from Southport Island loaded eight 13-foot dories on deck and returned with a full fare in half the normal time. Within a year or two, handlining from deck became a thing of the past. On a good voyage to the banks, the crew could wet the salt in less than a month and then haul up anchor to run downwind "cross-legged and split open" back to homeport.

Once back home, the fish that had been lightly salted and kenched during the voyage were salted again and laid out to dry on the flakes, at which point the shares of the voyage were figured up. A good fisherman could earn a living of $800 to $1,000 per year. However, the best-paid member of the crew always was the cook, who never fished. Instead, he spent most of his waking hours below, providing the men with such dishes as "joefloggers," "smother," and "duff," which roughly translate as pancakes, pot pie, and pudding. The real staple of these voyages, however, was dundefunk, a rich combination of fried pork, molasses, and bread, which could take the chill off anyone standing all day on deck with a handline.

On Vinalhaven, to mention but one island fishing community, the fishing industry grew each year until 1860, when the Civil War disrupted markets. At that time 75 to 100 vessels, most of them schooners, were part of the fishing industry. Four steam freighters were used to haul the cured fish to Boston. Several hundred more were employed ashore building boats, outfitting the vessels, supplying bait, and pursuing the time-consuming process of curing the fish. In all, something like 700 islanders on Vinalhaven, out of a population of 1,200, made their living from the sea.

"Gummint" Policies

One of the first acts of the newly formed First Congress in 1789 was to enact a measure to encourage and protect the country's cod fishery, which had suffered heavily from the loss of its most profitable market—the British West Indies—following the Revolution. Congress voted to pay a bounty to all vessels in the codfish trade; this amounted to $2.50 per ton for the largest vessels in 1792, and it increased to $4.00 per ton by the end of the War of 1812 to offset the effect of the establishment of a Canadian three-mile fishing limit. Provided a vessel fished four months out of the year, these bounties remained in effect until after the Civil War. No one became rich from the federal support, which amounted to perhaps $360 per year for the largest schooners—three-eighths of which went to the owner and the rest was split up among the crew. But it unquestionably had the effect of stimulating the rapid expansion of Maine's fisheries. Between 1797 and 1807, the tonnage of the Maine fishing fleet doubled. By 1820 the Penobscot District, which included most of the island fishing communities, surpassed the Portland District for the first time. By the end of the decade, 2,600 men were employed in Maine's fishery, and countless others ashore depended upon its productivity. In 1830 Maine harbored one-fifth of the nation's commercial fishing tonnage. By 1850 the tonnage had more than doubled, and by 1860 it had doubled again, so that the value of Maine's fisheries was second in the nation. Even more important, Maine had twice as many fishing establishments as any other state. For hundreds of communities, fishing had become a way of life.

Then, suddenly, at the close of the Civil War, Congress abolished the bounty system. Five years after the bounties ended, the number of boats in the salt-cod fishery was cut in half. Thirty years later, fewer than a dozen Maine fishing vessels remained in the trade. It would be interesting to go

Metinic Island pier.   *Susan St. John*

back through the Congressional Record of the debate over the abolition
of federal bounties for cod fishermen and compare it with the kind of

rhetoric that landsmen use today in discussing the American fishery. It seems likely that by the votes of men representing agricultural districts, an entire way of life was voted out of existence. It literally dissolved overnight. Towns that had once been profitable sank into disrepair and desuetude.

It is difficult to understand now—and was doubtless more difficult for the fishermen to whom it happened at the time—what the legislators thought they would accomplish by ending the bounties. It was not as if the fishermen made great fortunes from their trade; the bounties did mean, however, as subsequent events proved, the difference between profit and loss; between a small return and economic collapse; between gainful employment and idleness. For with the decline of the offshore fishery, something else much more valuable disappeared: a way of life that might have kept alive skills, attitudes, and a kind of hardiness—in short, a culture—based upon harvesting the productivity of the sea, which, once gone, takes generations to recover. Now that Maine, along with other East Coast fishing regions, has begun the long process of gearing up technologically and psychologically to take advantage of the 200-mile limit, it is worth considering for a moment the pervasive effects of a distant and seemingly isolated historical event.

The Silver (Sided) Age of Maine Fishing

Schooling fish are smaller in general than groundfish, and fin for fin, they are more numerous than the species that only stray from their deeper shadowy redoubts to rise to the occasion of an unusually sumptuous school of surface swimmers. Though D. H. Lawrence was referring to love rather than fish when he wrote that, "There are many fish in the sea, but most of them are mackerel," the picture is accurate enough, since mackerel is probably the most abundant species of fish along the Atlantic coast, though in any given year in the Gulf of Maine, they may be outnumbered by both herring and menhaden (pogies).

School fish such as mackerel, pogy, and herring feed on floating masses of small animal and vegetable sea life, which are so abundant in the Gulf of Maine, but it is likely that for the most part they utilize different species of food. It has been established that the oily menhaden has a diet so unlike that of mackerel and herring that the adults do not compete with these other species for food. Pogies strain diatoms through a series of intricately layered gill rakers, which act as a kind of fine-mesh tow net as they swim through the water, processing microscopic sea vegetables into oil and protein. Both mackerel and herring feed chiefly on copepods (from the Latin, meaning "oar-legged," referring to the way these oceangoing crustaceans "row" through the water). Fishermen will often find mackerel packed with "red feed," or cayenne, a species of copepod known technically as *Calanus*. Her-

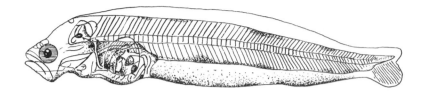

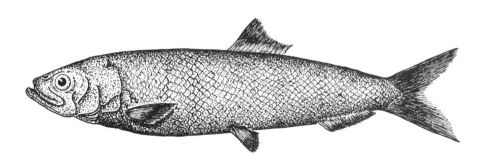

Herring, larva and adult. *Kate Fitzgerald*

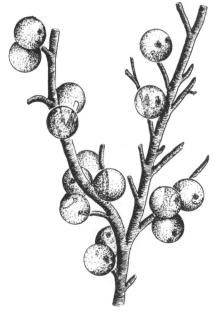

Herring eggs on rockweed stipe. *Kate Fitzgerald*

ring more commonly eat a smaller copepod known as the *Pseudocalanus,* but neither mackerel nor herring confine their diets exclusively to these two copepods. At the right time, and in the appropriate locale, they will consume prodigious quantities of most of the other species of floating crustaceans and their larvae. Since most mackerel are caught in the southwest corner of the Gulf of Maine, and herring predominate in the northeast corner at the mouth of the Bay of Fundy and in Passamaquoddy Bay, they seem, for the most part, to have divided up the spoils geographically, except where their schooling frequently overlaps.

To some extent the matter of division of the food among adults of different species misses the point. It seems likely that the abundance of both the mackerel and the herring, and for that matter, almost all other commercially important species of finfish, depends less on the food that is available to them when they are adults than when they are small fry. It's all very mysterious, since the smallest and newborn fish are the most difficult to find in the expanse of the sea, and the outlines of their movements from the time the eggs hatch to when they reach commercial size are only dimly perceived. The facts are few but suggestive. The annual production of eggs is usually sufficient to create a new age class, but there seems to be an inverse relationship between the number of adult mackerel present in any given year and their breeding success; that is, the fewer the adults, the more fry that survive.

Henry Bigelow, the oceanographer who, more than any other single person, has contributed to our knowledge of the physical and biological dynamics of the Gulf of Maine, supposes that the number of both mackerel and herring in any given year may be most directly related to the kind of winter the fish experienced. If they emerge from their deep winter hideouts in good physiological shape (which seems to be related to the number of adults that have been competing for the copepod food supply), then a high proportion of the eggs will hatch and provide strong young fry that are better able to elude the snapping jaws of other hungry marine creatures with the temporary advantage of size. Of course, even in a good hatch, the young fish can be decimated by killing temperatures or salinities, or they can perish from a simple lack of food. In the telling, it's sometimes surprising that we ever get a chance to eat a fish stick or a sardine sandwich.

Mackerel

In 1816 Abraham Lurvey of Mount Desert Island invented the mackerel jig—a small hook with a shiny pewter sinker for its shaft—and initiated the era of jigging for mackerel, which would last until 1865, when Southport Island fishermen figured out how to catch them in a seine. For 50 years the jiggers and elegant mackerel schooners, with their two gaff-rigged topsails, would whiten the bays of Maine in a Silver Age of fishing.

The year 1831 was the highline year for mackerel jiggers, whose boats had to be faster and more trim than the pinkies, since schools of mackerel arrived unpredictably and disappeared as quickly. In years that the mackerel were abundant, a masthead lookout could spot upwards of 50 separate schools at one time. The wake of mackerel is less compact than that of either pogy or herring, so from his high position a lookout could recognize their shadowy movements, even at depths of eight or 10 fathoms. Mackerel jiggers chummed the school to the surface by grinding up oily herring and pogies thrown in the water. When the mackerel started feeding, the jigs were dropped over and the voracious mackerel were pulled out of the water as quickly as lines went in the water.

But the competition among boats was occasionally as fierce as the feeding. There are gripping accounts of an elegant, well-handled mackerel schooner jigging fish, only to have another one round up on her stern and heave-to to leeward and steal the school. In one day in 1850, 300 mackerel vessels were counted off Portland alone: 300 boats jigging for mackerel to pickle in brine and ship in casks to Boston, New York, and a hundred other world ports. That was back in the days when Roman Catholic holydays were celebrated by eating fish; back in the days, indeed, when Catholics were impiously called mackerel snappers.

When purse seines were introduced by the Southport Islanders, the mackerel fishery changed overnight. Suddenly, the catches were so huge that it began to be impossible to clean and salt the fish before they spoiled. The Penobscot Bay islands were the center of the seining business. Hansen Joyce from Swans Island was the highliner for the entire New England mackerel fleet for seven years running, between 1875 and 1881; that's something like winning the American League batting crown for seven years in a row—which no one has ever done. In 1831 the mackerel catch from the Gulf of Maine had been 76 million pounds; in 1880, at the height of the most prolific concentration of mackerel the Gulf of Maine has ever seen, 294 million pounds were landed from United States and Nova Scotia waters. The glut ended in 1885. One hundred million pounds of mackerel were landed, but the fishery then fell into a calamitous decline that lasted for 25 years. In 1898 there was not a single mackerel boat left in the Swans Island fleet, where there had been 34 boats 15 years earlier.

The mackerel fishery rose and fell before there was much regulation of management of fish stocks in the Gulf of Maine. If and when Maine fishermen begin to report the kinds of catches that were common between 1880 and 1885, certainly the scientists will step in and, through the application of biological principles backed by the force of law, will try to preserve the resource from overfishing. The fishermen who are antihistorical will see it as a bunch of pointy-headed intellectuals trying to ruin a hopelessly temporary but undeniably good thing. Those of us on the sidelines can count the highline years and add up the catches to see whether the scientists will be able to make a good thing last longer for the fishermen, or whether the fish will simply appear and disappear according to cycles that might be better left to magic and superstition.

Herring

From the earliest syllables of recorded time, herring have been the most important food fish in Western Europe. They school in northern waters of both sides of the Atlantic and spawn in shallow waters, where they have been caught by almost every conceivable way of taking fish.

Torching for herring was one of the earliest methods employed by Maine islanders to take this fish. When the herring move into coves at night to feed at high water, they are attracted to light, which in the early days was provided by burning pitch-pine boughs but later by rags soaked in kerosene. When the herring rose to the surface, they could be scooped out of the water with buckets. Fish traps or weirs were also used to snare herring inshore. The earliest weir was simply a brush fence strung across the mouth of a cove—it was low enough that the fish could swim over it at high tide but they would be trapped when the water ebbed. Herring weirs became increasingly sophisticated over the years, not only in their placement to capture the maximum number of fish, but also in their construction. Today most stationary weirs consist of a long leader of net hung on stakes that leads the school of herring to the "bib pound," which has a hook-shaped opening; this leads into another smaller pound and then finally into a "pocket." When a school has been trapped, the weir tender simply closes the doors to the pound as he rows in, driving the herring into the pocket, where they can be taken out of the water. Building a stationary weir of this sort is a time-consuming process, occupying a crew of men for several months each spring. Today stop seining, where a cove is shut off, is a more popular way of catching the herring, but the greatest number are taken in purse seines— a net that is pulled around a school and then "pursed up" from underneath to trap the fish. The school usually has been located from the air by a spotter plane.

Ever since the beginning of serious fishing for herring, Eastport has been the center of the industry, because the particular combination of environmental conditions around the mouth of Passamaquoddy Bay attracts these fish in greater concentrations than any other section of the coast. In 1808 the first herring were smoked in Eastport—primarily for an export market. By 1900 this industry had grown to a six-million-pound-a-year business. That same year, 72 million pounds were canned as sardines and another 2.5 million pounds were salted down for bait. Just before the turn of the century, there were 68 sardine factories in Eastport.

It is the unhappy fate of the herring to be a prey species for almost every other fish in the sea: cod, pollack, hake, mackerel, bass, salmon, tuna, shark, and whales. The voracious silver hake is often so relentless in its pursuit of the herring that an entire school of thousands of fish is occa-

Stop seining: a shut-off in Gaston's Cove.   *Rick Perry*

sionally driven up onto shore. Not only do herring feed many of the fish of the sea, but they also supply seabirds with a major portion of their diet: gannets, razorbills, puffins, and gulls of all sorts pick them off the surface of the water, often at the very moment when they are being pursued from below by some fish bigger than they. Hit them high and low; it's an old trick, but it hardly seems fair.

Herring spawn in the late summer in three to 30 fathoms of water over many different types of bottom—rock, pebble, gravel, but never over soft mud. A single gravid female lays something like 30,000 eggs, which sink to the bottom and cling in clumps to everything from seaweed to pebbles to pot warp and anchor rode. They will grow to be four to seven inches long during their first two years, when they are called sardines. By the end of their third year they are larger than 10 inches and frequent deeper waters. The largest catch ever recorded from the Gulf of Maine occurred in 1946, when 219 million pounds were taken. The greatest number of these weighed about ½ ounce, which meant that something like six billion fish were caught. That's six thousand million—or, if you like, 6,000,000,000 individual creatures produced in two years of growth out of this rich green sea.

Like other Gulf of Maine fish, the number of herring caught each year fluctuates greatly. It appears that a single age class that has a poor spawning

Tending the pocket of a herring purse in East Penobscot Bay.   *George Putz*

year can affect population levels for many years to come. An 1881 case study of a particular group of Bay of Fundy herring showed that these fish received no recruitment of young fish for about 10 years and finally seem to have disappeared from the area after the last ones died of old age. Likewise, during exceptionally good spawning years, when environmental conditions are optimal, billions of new young fish are added to the population and will continue to produce some young until the next big spawning year occurs. The reason that herring catches are so unpredictable from year to year appears to be largely a result of the great fluctuation of the survival of the spawn. The survival of the spawn is in turn determined by the interaction of such factors as water temperature, salinity, the effects of tides and currents, and the physiological condition of the adult females when the eggs are laid. All of this makes it understandable why marine biologists can quickly get into trouble when they try to predict the levels of fish populations.

Lobstering

Lobstering, Maine's most lucrative fishery in terms of the value it brings fishermen, began as a pastime for those too old, too young, or too feeble to make the trips to the offshore waters for groundfish. Some say that catching lobsters for a commercial market began in Cundys Harbor in Upper Casco Bay in the 1840s. Perhaps, but it's likely that a lot of other fishing villages would make a similar claim.

On Swans Island in outer Blue Hill Bay, lobsters were not sold until after 1850. Occasionally a fisherman might collect some small lobsters from along the shore—the larger ones were thrown back as unfit for family use—but no one thought of lobsters as a commercial species until relatively recently. For instance, 1857 was the first year that a smack operated between Swans Island and Boston to haul the lobsters to market. The first of these vessels were "dry smacks," which carried lobsters packed in seaweed and ice. But the lobster mortality was high, and the boats were soon replaced by "wet smacks," which had watertight bulkheads with one-inch holes drilled through the planking to provide the live cargo with a continuous supply of fresh seawater.

The difficulty of hauling live lobsters to market led to investments in lobster canneries, which soon increased the price. Vinalhaven was one of the first towns to have a cannery. One opened in 1847, and by the 1870s there were enough canneries in operation around the mid-coast region that the price of lobsters had increased from a nickel each to 10 cents per pound. "Shorts" brought a penny each. By the end of the 1870s prices were high enough to begin attracting fishermen into the business from other fisheries.

During the old-men-and-young-boy days, lobstering was done from dories or wherries of the Gloucester and Swampscott types. With the decline of the cod fishery after the Civil War, and the disappearance of the mack-

The incredibly various Maine lobster boat.   *George Putz*

Foggy day off Bantam Ledges.   *George Putz*

erel after 1885, more and more fishermen invested in their own boats and
went to work for themselves. Friendship sloops soon became the most popular lobstering boats, since they were weatherly and would keep pointed up
into the wind when the lobsterman left the helm to haul and rebait his
traps. By 1897, according to estimate of the new Maine Sea and Shore Fisheries Department, there were 142 lobstermen fishing in Maine waters.

By 1900, the Vinalhaven pound, located in a little embayment on the
island's western shore, was handling 200,000 pounds of lobsters annually,
and steam smacks were hauling the catch to Boston fish markets. With the
introduction of the first make-or-break gas engines around 1903, lobstering
came of age. Although the early engines were considered dangerous—a
sternman who wanted to smoke, for instance, was encouraged to get in a
dory that was towed behind—auxiliary sloops soon dominated the business.
The two-cycle 4–10 horsepower engines were meant to be used when the
wind failed, but "it was only a short time before we saw all sail set and
the engine running wide open," according to one of Vinalhaven's historians.

In 1885 an energetic lobsterman would fish between 100 and 150 traps
—which looked much like the wooden ones still used today. The early
traps were made of spruce boughs and laths, but after the destructive marine
teredo worm invaded Maine waters, traps had to be constructed of oak. In
1885 lobstermen already were complaining about the bitter competition in

the fishery—how a man used to be able to make $4 or $5 a day hauling traps but was reduced to $1 a day as more men set to lobstering.

While the fresh lobster market could realistically sell only those lobsters big enough to make a meal (10½ inches and up), the canneries bought lobsters of all sizes and sold them primarily to a foreign market. By 1886 there was enough concern over the decreasing size and numbers of lobsters caught in Maine waters to induce the legislature to pass the "short lobster law." But most lobstermen took a dim view of the effort to regulate their fishery, and bitter howls of protest went up. The coastal town of St. George went so far as to pass a local ordinance that any fines levied by the state for taking short lobsters were deductible from the fisherman's next property tax bill.

After a decade of argument, the evidence of declining catches simply could not be denied. In 1906, after 10 years of occasionally violent controversy, the lobstermen recognized that the taking of "shorts" had to stop, and they formed the Lobstermen's National Protective Association.

Though lobsters are crustaceans, and it would be foolish to draw exact parallels with finfish, it seems significant that the most carefully regulated fishery in the state of Maine is also one of her most stable. Since 1960, the annual catch of lobsters for the state of Maine has consistently remained between 18 and 20 million pounds. What began as a way to employ old fishermen and young boys became, by the 1970s, a very lucrative way to earn a living, replete with deductible 40-channel CB radios, four-wheel-drive pickup trucks, and mid-winter Florida vacations. No one in his right mind would want to take this away from those who work hard for the living they earn; sometimes, however, it's just a little hard to swallow all of their emphatic excoriations of fisheries biologists.

On a Clear Day You Can See for 200 Miles

Well, not quite, but ever since Congress passed the Fisheries Conservation and Management Act in 1976, known as the 200-Mile Limit (over the bitter protests of West Coast fishing interests and the strenuous opposition of Secretary of State Henry Kissinger), the outlook for Maine fishermen has been a lot brighter. For the first time in 15 or 20 years, there are new fishing vessels in many Maine harbors that are not just bigger lobsterboats designed to fish farther and harder for the limited supply of a luxury shellfish resource.

In 1962 Canadian boats entered the Gulf of Maine fishery in significant numbers for the first time. Within the next few years they were joined by the subsidized fleets of Russia, Poland, and East and West Germany. These European countries had undertaken aggressive national efforts to replace their fishing fleets, which had been destroyed during World War II. These foreign fleets outnumbered and outfished the declining American fleet, whose customers' tastes turned away from fish and toward a seven-day-a-week diet of beef, pork, and chicken.

While Americans fell in love with meat fattened off the bounty of the American grain enterprise—an enterprise supported in part by the availability of cheap fossil fuels, which are used in everything from fertilizers to pesticides—Europeans continued to depend on less expensive sources of protein. In the heady days of America's meat-and-potato diet, probably no one much noticed or cared that the American fleet was falling into disrepair and that traditional fishing grounds were relinquished to foreign fleets. But with a suddenness that surprised many of those who follow national political events, Congress began to listen to the warnings about her moribund New England fishing fleet.

The valuable offshore banks were being drastically overfished by large, efficient, subsidized, and, most important, unregulated foreign fishing vessels. The Gulf of Maine haddock catch had averaged 48 million pounds annually between 1917 and 1961. By 1965, landings had reached 150 million pounds, the highest on record. With the appearance of the foreign effort, the catches began to decline. Cod, which peaked at more than 50 million pounds, declined to a paltry 13 million pounds by 1973. And the herring industry, already suffering from declining domestic demand, suffered year after year of poor catches. The 1970 catch of 36 million pounds was the lowest since 1938, and it was tempting to believe that the voracious

Sunset over West Penobscot Bay. *Jim Kosinski*

appetites of the offshore fleets, which could seine up whole age classes, were responsible.

After four years of living under the 200-mile limit, Maine fishermen were told by federal fisheries biologists that they, too, were capable of overfishing the resource. The traditional enmity between domestic fishermen and biologists, which had been buried while the biologists made their case against the foreign fleets, quickly resurfaced when cod quotas were set in 1978. The honeymoon was brief. At a time when many fishermen had made substantial investments in new gear and boats, and the New England fishery had experienced its first good years in decades, the cod quotas could hardly have been timed to be more unpopular. The problem is that no one really knows how many fish there are in the murky depths of the Gulf of Maine. Fisheries biologists unquestionably know a lot more than they did even a few years ago, but until they are able to make reasonably accurate predictions of future population levels, on the basis of an understanding of the ecological relationships among all the major species of fish and the unique environment of the Gulf of Maine, their theories will remain just that. And they will play to an exceedingly skeptical audience of hard-nosed and raw-boned independent businessmen. On a clear day you can see a long way out into the Gulf of Maine, but some days it gets a little thick.

3

Island Landforms: Cliffs, Caves, Cobbles, and Domes

"It is perhaps a little indelicate to ask of our Mother Earth her age. . . ."
Geologist Arthur Holmes, 1913

Long Island—Round Island

IF YOU IGNORE THE BORDERLINE CASES that ruin any generalization, Maine's islands come in one of two shapes: they are either long and narrow like the islands of Casco and Muscongus Bays, or they are rounded and domed like Mount Desert, Deer Isle, Swans, Isle au Haut, Vinalhaven, and Beals off Jonesport. The bedrock underlying these islands controls their topography: the region from Casco to Camden is primarily underlaid by the rootstocks of ancient fold mountains, while the remainder of the coast is dominated by the remnants of volcanic activity.

To understand how these shapes come about, you must understand that over the immensely long periods of time by which geologists measure these things, the earth's surface has been quite plastic. Mountains rise and disappear; rivers flow off the highlands and carve intersecting networks of valleys; even oceans fill, flood the land, and drain away. The study of the rise and fall of land forms is called geomorphology, and there are few places in the East where geologists have such a field day in studying the restless movements of the earth's surface as in the frozen rocks of Maine's shores.

As a science, geology is not very old, certainly not as old as the rocks that geologists study. One of the reasons that geology and geomorphology are not more venerable professions is that over most of the surface of the earth, rocks are covered by a thick blanket of soil, so the Big Picture is obscure. Certainly geology has been greatly aided in this country by an unexpected

72

The bedrock controls the topography. *Jim Kosinski*

source: the interstate highway system. If you see a small group of people standing on the shoulder of a freeway staring intently at the side of a road-cut, it's easy to understand that geologists are greatly indebted to the construction crews for laying out these dramatic rock tableaux. The same kinds of tableaux are presented on the wave-scoured shores of Maine's rocky islands and are a geologist's heaven. A prime example of this occurred during an afternoon I spent with a geologist, who bent over a small outcrop on a Casco Bay island for a half hour or more. When he stood up, he pointed to a series of sinuous crenellations in the outcrop and said, "This is a third-order fold of an ancient mountain chain and is good evidence of a continental collision."

The story of Maine is written on her rocky shores. Before trying to trace the path of drifting continents, a story whose patterns are only dimly understood, or trying to find mountains that have disappeared, we should try to appreciate the origin of Maine's rocky coast. Originally, most were layers of sediment washed off some proto-North American landmass and deposited in a shallow sea, where the pressure of layer after layer of additional sand, silt, and gravel cemented them into sedimentary rocks.

Then, over incomparably long geological epochs, these sedimentary rock layers were pushed up out of their horizontal beds, ultimately to become part of the long mountain chain we now call the Appalachians. Easterners will be happy to hear that, through careful analysis, geologists have calculated that the Appalachians must have once stood higher than the present-day Himalayan range. Thirty thousand vertical feet of sediments have been worn away from this great mountain range.

Mountains are formed in a variety of different ways, through processes collectively known as orogenesis (from the Greek words, *oros,* meaning mountain; and *genesis,* birth). The Appalachians are called fold mountains, and to understand how they were formed, you have to imagine what happens if you stand at the edge of a heavy rug, the far end of which is against a wall, and begin pushing with your foot. First there are little bulges in the rug, and as you continue to scoot the rug toward the other end of the room, the bulges expand into undulating ripples and finally develop into a series of folds. Never mind what force your foot represents; it's enough for a moment to understand that the parallel ridges that characterize the Maine coast, interior lowlands, and coastal islands from Cape Elizabeth to Cape Jellison at the head of West Penobscot Bay were formed when rock strata were pushed into broad folds. In the process, one might add, the sedimentary rocks were subject to deformation from the heat and pressure that inevitably accompany crustal movements. Today these are called metamorphic rocks—mostly quartzites and micaceous schists. But that's probably more than most people need or want to know.

Beginning at the western edge of Penobscot Bay, in a group of islands called the Muscle Ridge, the bedrock changes from the metamorphic remnants of fold mountains to a world dominated by granite. Granites of all textures, shades, varieties, and colors (reds, pinks, greys, blues, whites, and everything in between) form the basis of a chain of islands that continues Downeast for some 75 miles.

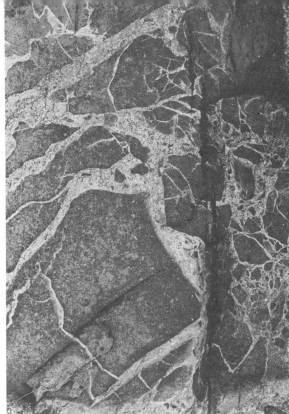

LEFT Magma is melted rock. *George Putz*
RIGHT Granite is frozen magma. *George Putz*

Granite is really nothing more than frozen magma, and magma is rock that has melted beneath the earth's crust. All this melted rock is the result of collisions of continental plates, but the more easily visualized results were volcanoes—immense, violent, eruptive volcanoes pushed up onto the earth's surface by the force of increasing quantities of molten rock. Two-thirds of the Maine coast is composted of the remnants of a long period of volcanic activity, when it was literally a ring of fire—so much so that technically the coast is described, in the terms of one of her best-known geologists, as "The Bays of Maine Igneous Complex."

Most of the effusions of ash and lava that were coughed up from the fiery depths, and the above-ground portions of the volcanoes themselves—the vents and cones—have long since weathered away. In fact, these extrusive portions of the volcanic episode are only preserved to any significant extent in northern Penobscot Bay, in the so-called "Castine Volcanics," and south of Mount Desert Island in the "Cranberry Isles Series." What has remained is the less erodible molten rock that collected in the volcanic necks and subterranean reservoirs of magma; in other words, the granite itself. It is only after epoch upon epoch of geologic time that the reservoirs of frozen granite have been exposed.

The islands at the western end of the coast are long and narrow, a result of the creation of fold mountains, but granite islands are rounded and domelike, for the same reasons that drops of liquid mercury collect into rounded bubbles when dropped on a reasonably flat surface.

The crustal events that pushed the western Maine coast into fold mountains and the eastern Maine rocks into volcanic eruptions resulted from the collision of two ancient tectonic plates. The theory known as "plate Tectonics" has taken a long time for geologists to embrace whole-heartedly, since even to them it appeared implausible when first suggested by the German geographer Alfred Wegener at the turn of the century. The idea first occurred to Wegener after simply remarking upon the hand-in-glove fit of the east coast of South America and the west coast of Africa. But too many convergent lines of evidence lead to the conclusion that continents indeed drift around from place to place in the course of geologic time.

Geologists now figure that the surface of the earth is divided into 12 major plates that "float" on a viscous mantle, somewhat the way the shell of a hard-boiled egg rests on the egg's innards. Because of the convection currents within the super-heated core of the earth, these plates are driven into each other by the turbine-like force of the swirling molten rock.

In our part of the world, some 500 million years ago, an ancestral North American continent was separated from a single Eurasian plate by a shallow ocean called "Iapetus." As the Eurasian plate drifted westward, the heavier oceanic plate on which Iapetus had formed collided with ancestral North America, folding the continental crust into what became the Appalachian mountain range. As the story continues, the Iapetus plate between the converging continents was forced to plunge under the North American plate, forming an arc of volcanic islands where a portion of the oceanic plate broke. Very much the same kind of process is apparently now occurring where the Pacific plate is drifting into the Asian continent, creating an arc of volcanic islands that we know better as the Japanese islands.

"The problem I have with geology," a friend recently said, "is that it's so abstract." Maybe so, but the next time you drive down Merepoint or look at the frozen plutonic shores of Vinalhaven or Mount Desert, perhaps "fold mountains" and "volcanic arcs" will now make more sense.

Mountains in the Sea

To the professional geologist, the landforms of the Maine coast must present a slight irony. Geologists are always trying to explain to a disinterested public that the study of rock shapes and landforms is determined by events that occur so gradually, over such incomparably long time spans that they must be measured not in thousands or even millions but in hundreds of millions of years, at rates nearly imperceptible to our febrile minds. Even though the rocks of the Maine coast are easily as old as all that, the present shape of the coast has been determined more decisively by the events of the very recent past than by all the millennia that passed before.

But there's a good analogy to make it all understandable. Take the six "days" of *Genesis* (God rested on the seventh) as a figure of speech for what has actually been something like four billion years. On this scale, one day equals something like 667 million years, so all day Monday and Tuesday creation was busy getting the world going. Life didn't begin until Tuesday noon, and the intricate living web of species took the remaining four days to develop. The dinosaurs appeared, but five hours later they were gone. Christ was born and walked through Judaea at three minutes before midnight on Saturday; the Industrial Revolution happened a fortieth of a second before midnight, and so on.

On this scale, for most of Wednesday the Eurasian continent drifted into the North American plate, pushing up the enormous chain of the Appalachians and circling the edge of what would become the Maine coast with an arc of volcanic fire. And yet Maine's islands were not separated from the mainland until perhaps 10 minutes before Saturday midnight.

The reason that there are so many islands off the Maine coast, and so few to the south, has to do with the phenomenon of ice. A wall of ice flowed downhill like white molasses from the frozen wastes of the Arctic and covered Maine as far as its outer banks with a kingdom of ice a mile high over the highest point of land. Before the creaking, shuddering glacier of mobile ice and snow ground over the landscape, Maine's coast had been much like that of the remainder of the Atlantic coast: gently sloping coastal plain with sandy beaches and salt marshes. What is now the Gulf of Maine was a rolling topography of coastal lowlands with an occasional granitic dome breaking the horizon.

The effect of the ice was drastic. Someone has taken the time to calculate that an acre of ice one mile high weighs on the order of seven million tons. The burden of the ice warped the land down along a weak zone in the crust that trends approximately northeast-southwest, tilting this entire crustal block toward the sea. Then within a very short period of time the ice melted. It melted into floods—Noah's flood? Rivers of incomparable magnitude surged into the sea and began to fill it up as the sea itself began filling the coastal lowlands. At glacial maximum, about one-third of the world's total fresh water was frozen in ice, compared with the present three or four percent, which is tied up in polar ice caps. Nine million cubic miles of ocean were pulled up onto the land and held as ice. When this water was released, the worldwide level of the sea rose, but it was especially dramatic along the Maine coast, where the crust had been warped down. Some of the effects of the melting ice must have been cata-

Beach of glacially transported cobbles. *Jim Kosinski*

strophic. When you stop to consider that the world's rivers today empty unendingly into the sea without affecting sea level—the Amazon River alone pours a billion gallons a second into the Atlantic, yet the sea is, to use a Biblical phrase, "never full"—the glacial meltwaters must have been incredible torrents of sediment-laden water.

On the Maine coast the sea sent long fingers onto the land, it flowed up the old river valleys, all the way to Millinocket on the Penobscot and near Greenville on the Kennebec; it flowed over the outer banks, which had been dry land, and completely submerged the coastal lowlands to form the Gulf of Maine. After several thousand years of flooding, the uneasy land, relieved of the weight of the ice, rebounded somewhat and most of Maine's islands were born from around the receding waters. True enough, some of the highest islands had remained dry even during the worst flooding, but the majority of them must have been submerged, since there is evidence that Mount Desert's high hills, now 200 feet above sea level, had sand beaches that were once lapped by wind-driven waves off the Gulf of Maine.

It is because of the epoch of Pleistocene glaciation that Maine's is called a drowned coast, not, as my nephew recently thought, because so many sailors had been washed overboard into her seas.

As to the question of whether sea level off Maine's shores is rising or falling, there is, among the fraternity of geologists, no unanimous agreement. The sea, like the land, is restless and fickle. She may appear to be rising along one section of the coast and falling elsewhere. But a few records from the 19th century are illuminating. In the 1804 edition of the *American Coast Pilot,* which provided mariners with one of the few reliable sets of directions for navigating Maine's rock-strewn waters in the era before charts were widely available, there is the following note for sailing east of Schoodic:

> In standing in [from "Skutock Hills"] for this island, you will see a small place called Titmanan's Island [Petit Manan]. There is a bar that runs from the shore to this little island which is about one league from the land and has a few bushes on it. The bar is covered at high water but bare at low water.

Anyone who has crossed the Petit Manan bar when a falling tide is kicking up short, steep seas against a smoky sou'wester will agree that it would almost be better if the bar were uncovered at low water today so that everyone would have to go around it, rather than smash through those violent waters.

The speed with which the level of the sea is rising relative to the land might be determined from an examination of the shore of Gott Island. From a late 19th century description by Dr. H. M. Small, Swans Island's historian, we have a rare glimpse into the changing relations of land and sea. He wrote that the roots of a "thorn tree" (hawthorn or locust) planted next to the first house built near the shore of the island in the 1680s were, at his time (1898), hanging loosely over the bank, and that only a portion

Columnar jointing in basalt outcrop, Saddle Island.   *Jim Kosinski*

of the cellar hole remained. Is there nothing sacred left—not even houses built on stone foundations?

The Little Picture: The Geomorphology of Place Names

The study of the origins of place names can be a riveting form of entertainment. The Maine coastal islands present an unlimited challenge to someone who will one day provide the definitive explanations for how 3,019 discrete pieces of island real estate (not to mention innumerable pieces of the bottom of the Gulf of Maine) were named by generations of Maine sailors and islanders. If none of the islands that are currently inhabited had names, no doubt they would come to be called by some of the same names they were first given. An island with a bold granite southern shore that shimmers in summer sunlight should rightly be called White Island. There would be a number of Long and High Islands, a few Sand Islands, a scattering of Washerwoman Ledges where the surf foamed up over a half-tide ledge, perhaps one or two Crotch Islands if this didn't cause too much blushing—although around the turn of the century this was reason enough to rename more than one Crotch Island.

But many of the islands and ledges that were named for their geophysical features would have different names now. Who has even heard, in these days of imported textiles and polyesters, of a thrumcap, which was a round hat made of four leftover pieces of homespun called thrums. Would we still call the myriad of smooth-rounded ledges by these whimsical names: Sugar Loaves, Junk o' Pork, Ladle, Colby Pup, or Virgin's Breasts? Probably not.

Popplestones, Cobblestones, and Killick Stones

Long before Maine's rocks were quarried for lime and granite, the shores of her rocky coast provided more humble products. One of the first of these was ballast for vessels serving the early coastwise trade. One island off Jonesport is still known as Ballast Island. Another, Great Spoon Island off Isle au Haut, was no doubt named for its high inverted spoon-shaped hill and long trailing handle, which makes up the cobble beach. On the early British Admiralty charts, however, it was called Fill Boat Island. Both islands have exposed beaches where smooth round rocks were easily collected to ballast the holds of homemade sailing vessels.

Somewhere along the line, someone realized that large wave-smoothed stones, free for the taking off Maine's shores, could be sold to city merchants intent upon cleaning up their streets. Dirt, in a matrix of horse manure, hardly made city streets pleasant to negotiate. These "popplestones," as they came to be called, were the first (but not the last) Maine rocks used

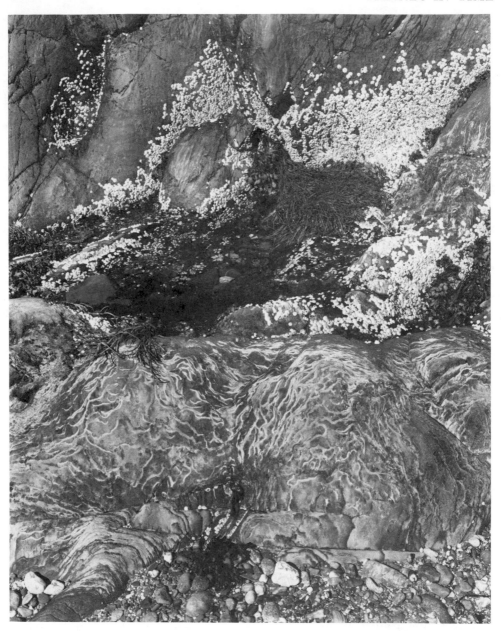

Greenstone outcrop and intertidal.   *Rick Perry*

to pave the streets of East Coast cities. Popplestones were probably also the first ballast ever sold for profit, and they provided employment in the early 1780s to Maine islanders.

The ingenious use of the materials at hand was simply another case of making a virtue out of necessity. Illustrations of this could be multiplied indefinitely, especially on the islands where specialized occupations were

Killick stone anchor.   *Kate Fitzgerald*

slow to catch on; men and women were expected to be good at everything
or at least be able to cope with what they had.

Maine's rocky coast not only had an abundance of cobblestone coves
for popplestone streets but also provided here and there just the right-
shaped rocks that could be fashioned into small anchors known as killicks.
(Iron for anchors was almost unheard of, and in any case it was too expensive for the self-sufficient island economies.) Rather long and thin
stones were necessary for this handmade anchor; these were found chiefly
in the western bays from Casco to Muscongus, where the trend of the
bedrock nicely fit the desired shapes. One island in Muscongus whose shores
are covered with just the right-shaped rocks is still called Killick Stone. A
neighboring island is called Stone Island, though whether this was for its
economic importance or for an unknown Mr. Stone is anyone's guess.

Pocket Beaches and Rocky Headlands

Out of 2,500 miles of shoreline, Maine has perhaps 60 miles of sandy beach,
mostly in the southern part of the state, which seems biogeographically
more a part of Massachusetts than of Maine. There are more sandy beaches
on Casco Bay islands than elsewhere, owing to the fact that the Androscoggin River used to empty into the Bay before its course was altered
hard left into Merrymeeting Bay. But these beaches are unfortunately sited
on the north sides of islands, so that sunbathing has never been as diverting here as other places.

In place, then, of sandy beach fantasies, the littoralists in Maine have
had to make do with the hard, cold facts of life. The shores of Maine islands are made for solitary pursuits, such as taking yourself quite seriously

on an exposed promontory during a gale after being spurned in love. Or dancing at midnight just out of reach of the breakers that surge in and out after a front has passed and the moon lets your life come shining.

A lot of printer's ink has been spilled over the varieties of marine life that attach themselves to the seemingly uninhabitable rocky coasts of Maine. But the point is well taken; it is the ever-shifting sandy substrate that makes an intolerable habitat for living creatures. On a rocky shore, all that is required of you is rootedness or a little glue on the soles of your feet or your backside to be witness to the endless crescendos and ensembles of life.

The coast's rocks are also made for children, or those who can think like children, who can remember what it was like to be small and overwhelmed by the enormity of the world around them. It is true that Maine's sea cliffs are in places awesome, even to the most jaded eye—Monhegan's White Head and Mount Desert's Otter Cliffs, each calling itself the highest sea cliff on the east coast of the United States come to mind—but almost every other mile of shore has precipices for a childlike eye. Not long ago, returning from the West Coast with a friend, we found ourselves driving down Vermont's Champlain Valley, where my friend had spent a few summers in his childhood. He told me of the magnificent cliffs over the lake, where he used to stand and survey all of creation. We decided to try to find them. We studied the woefully inadequate road map for clues, tried to recall the name of the town, crossed and recrossed several roads (which turned to dirt down near the lake), asked at a gas station, a country store, and at last stumbled on it. Certain that we were near the spot, we got out of the truck and wandered down to the shore, where my friend fell into an embarrassed silence. The cliffs seemed to have shrunk over the last

Pocket sandy beach. *George Putz*

two and a half decades; they stood just six or eight feet over the lapping waves of the lake. No matter, it *had* been a breathtaking kingdom: it is our imagination that has been reduced.

The outthrust jawbone of a rocky headland or peninsula, like a street fighter, dares something to hit it, and a storm sea is only too willing to comply. A point of land focuses wave energy at its outer edge, while coves are treated more gently. Waves bend around promontories and headlands. As they bend, they lengthen, become less steep, and spill some of their energy, so that they can be quite tame as they curl into a cove. If the cove is fronted with a deposit of glacial till—the mixed bag of sand, silt, gravel, and cobbles scraped up off of Canada and transported into New England— these waves will rework the deposit. They will transport the silt offshore, leaving the larger rocks nearly in place and distributing the sand along the horseshoe arc of the cove to form one of the innumerable pocket sand beaches on the islands. A beach is really a kind of natural seismograph recording the climate of wave energy: slight currents transport silt; a 2½-knot current transports inch-round stones; a storm wave packs three tons of power to a linear foot of shore; and so forth up the Beaufort Scale. A granite boulder on Matinicus Rock, calculated by a stonecutter to weigh 100 tons, was moved 12 feet during the lifetime of one of the island's lightkeepers.

Rock outcrops succumb to the pressure of both air and water. As waves curl in on a shore, they trap air under their rolling crests. When a wave breaks on a headland, large amounts of trapped air are driven into the rock crevices, where it is compressed all the more. It acts on the same

This unique wave built beach is reshaped by every major storm. *George Putz*

Vertical joints produce vertical cliffs.
Jim Kosinski

principle as compressed air driving a jackhammer, and the results are the same. Given enough air, the compression can burst rocks apart at the seams. Once a seam appears, water flows in, freezes, expands, and works further havoc on the rocky shore. In the telling, it's surprising there are any cliffs and headlands left at all.

The rock forms of the Maine coast are so irregular and diverse not only because wave energy and bedrock units vary from place to place but also because these forces of moving air, ice, and sea work differently in various bedrock types and on different patterns of naturally occurring jointing systems. Jointing in bedrock refers to the series of fractures and fissures in rocks that result from the crystalline microstructure of the mineral constituents. Along most of Maine's shores, the jointing planes of the bedrock dip gently toward the sea. But occasionally, as a result of the cooling history of granite or volcanic rocks, vertical stresses develop. And vertical joints produce vertical cliffs. Otter Cliffs on Mount Desert are exceptional not only because of their uninterrupted system of vertical jointing but also because the erosional forces attacking the cliff are creating a sea stack—a chimney of rock separated from the parent cliff. This has recently become a popular site for rock climbers to practice human fly routines over the white combers.

Sea caves, rock arches, and other architectonic rock renderings exist in a number of well-visited places at Acadia National Park, including Anemone Cave and the Ovens. But these most delicate and ephemeral of all rock formations exist in dozens of other places in the islands or along the rocky shores. Even as the forces of time waste at the wall of caves and arches, the masterful hands of the sea are busy carving more.

There is a story among the fishermen near where I live of a cave on an island from whose entrance you can see clear through to the other side at low tide. It's enough to make anyone skeptical, or at least to make me skeptical, since I am somewhat unnaturally tuned against fish stories. And yet there is a relative, if not absolute, truth to the story. Low tide is the only time when the entrance of the cave is exposed. When the surge is not too strong and you have calculated your timing right, you can enter the eerie sea vault, which opens up above like some Jules Verne proscenium, and head for the heart of this mysterious island. It might be compared to falling Alice-in-Wonderland-like into a hole in the sea. The farther back you go, the more you wonder what you are doing there. It must be like being inside a chambered nautilus; you can feel the sound of the sea before you hear it. Farther ahead is a pinpoint of light. If you have enough nerve to make your way along the cool, wet walls of this tortured fault chasm bisecting the island, it suddenly becomes clear that without measuring or arguing about it, it *is* the other side of the island. And then you want to get out, because you cannot help but reflect that when the winds and seas begin to build, this might be just the place to pass an eternity.

The Hard Facts of Life About Quarrying on a Hard Rock Island

And there in ragged greyness lay the quarry
"This pavin' motion," my companion said,
"Was goin' to make me rich and made me poor.
'Twas in the eighties I began to work here,
When the great cities paved their streets with blocks
A nickel a piece they were, and I could reel
Two hundred blocks or more each blessed day."
Wilbert Snow

There is some urge within most of us to dignify the hardships of work by speaking of it in terms of its past glory. Enormous stone vaults were pounded and blasted from the unflinching granite on some 33 Maine islands from Friendship to Jonesport, but there are precious few histories of the Maine island quarry years that included what these men of hard rock thought of the work. More often historians have written about the large towns of 2,000 or more that sprang up almost overnight (and in many cases disappeared as quickly) on islands such as Clark, Dix, High,

Stonecutters' cabins on Hurricane Island around the turn of the century.

and Hurricane. Other histories have listed the impressive number of buildings that were constructed of the rocks of this-and-so island quarry. Indeed, it is some kind of testament to the era that such lovely and elegant structures as the Cathedral of St. John the Divine and the Metropolitan Museum of Art and the capacious New York City Public Library and the Philadelphia Post Office and the Naval Academy buildings in Annapolis were once silent, solid hefts of rock on the shores of Maine's far-distant islands. The Scots, Italians, Finns, and Swedes who came to American shores of opportunity were happy enough to be here and have paying jobs, but the cost in labor and lives was high, just as in previous eras of constructing monuments to a forgetful future.

Although small island quarrying operations had begun as early as 1792, the first granite commercially quarried in Maine was cut in 1826 in Vinalhaven to build the walls of a prison in Massachusetts—it's almost as if the men themselves were aware of an historical irony in the making. With access to inexpensive water transportation, island quarries had a natural advantage. In the Vinalhaven area, which would become the center of this trade, a second quarry opened in 1846 on Leadbetter's Island, just across the Narrows on the west side; a third, the so-called East Boston Quarry, opened in 1849. There were three more by 1860 and seven others between 1860 and 1880.

The early quarries primarily provided rough granite for breakwaters, forts, and lighthouses—many of the latter to mark the unforgiving Maine coast itself. With the end of the Civil War and the beginning of the first massive government works program, contracts were let for federal buildings of all sorts, sizes, and descriptions: post offices, customs houses, libraries, train stations, and the like. By 1890 Maine led the nation in the production of granite.

Until they were declared illegal, these public building projects were financed by "fifteen percent contracts," which specified that the companies supplying the granite could tack an additional 15 percent on the costs of delivery for their profit margin. It didn't take long for some government watchdog to figure that this way of doing business was not necessarily in the public interest. The financial belt-tightening that followed made conditions worse for those who worked in the quarries. By the time the 15 percent contracts were a remnant of the past, competition among the granite quarries, which had mushroomed along the coast, had become intense. Bids that determined wage levels were often so low that men could not keep their board bills clear at the company stores that became regular features on company islands like Hurricane, Dix, and Clark Islands.

A frieze carved on Vinalhaven for New York City Customs House.

The Technology of Quarrying: The Rift, the Lift, and the Hardway

Granite lies in sheets of varying thickness over the surface of the land. Because of the internal structure of the granite's mineral constituents (translucent quartz, white or pink feldspar or dark flecks of mica and hornblende), granite fractures along right-angle planes. And there is something within us that likes a right angle.

Mineralogy aside, an experienced stonecutter is able to tell how the grain runs in an unbroken piece of granite. Quarrymen used to speak of the plane of granite in terms of its "rift," which runs perpendicular to the horizon and in most Maine granite was oriented along an east-west axis. The "lift" of the granite (what geologists call the "sheeting" of granite) runs parallel to the horizon, and the "hardway" runs at right angles to the rift.

The earliest attempts to cut granite in homemade quarries, called "motions," involved locating a "toe" where the lift thinned to an edge. There a man could trace out straight lines of the surface, chisel along it, and drill a series of quarter-inch holes, which he would fill with dry pine plugs and pack with mud. If he had calculated the rift correctly, he would return the next day and the swollen pine plugs would have split the stone. Of course, using soft "pumpkin pine" to cut hard white granite was not the most

The rift, the lift and the hardway at
City Point Quarry, Vinalhaven.   *George Putz*

efficient method of quarrying the stone, and more modern means of using feather and half-round wedges quickly replaced the older system.

When the demand for rough blocks for the busy city harbors of the eastern seaboard created what might be called a Maine granite industry in the 1850s, quantities of rock began to be shaken loose with charges of black powder. "Lewis holes" were two 4-to-6-inch holes drilled side by side and filled with blasting powder, packing, and a fuse. Blasting in the early days was notoriously unreliable, and when a charge failed to go off, someone had to find out why, and, in finding out, frequently earned an obituary in a local newspaper. Had a generation of quarrymen been canvassed, no doubt they would have awarded their own Peace Prize to Alfred Nobel, the Swedish chemist who invented the more reliable dynamite in 1867.

The division of labor in a quarry usually involved a blasthole team and a drilling team. The top drill holder was one of the quarry elite—his steady hand and nerve held the finely tempered star bit in place while two others whaled away with sledges, taking turns and counting out a cadence. One slip of a sledge and the top drill holder joined the company of the three-fingered people. A correctly tempered drill did not bounce when struck by a sledge; it rotated perhaps a quarter-turn in place and slowly bit into the granite.

The sheets of granite widened toward the center of a main quarry face due to the natural jointing patterns in the rock. This trend of the lift, as quarrymen spoke of it, allowed them to cut single pieces of enormous dimensions. The four rough columns for the interior of the Cathedral of

The flywheel for the steam driven air compressor at Hurricane Island.   *Rick Perry*

A galamander was used to haul large stones.   *Kate Fitzgerald*

St. John the Divine were 64 feet long and 8 feet in diameter and weighed 300 tons. An earlier piece of granite cut for the monument to Major General John Ellis Wool weighed half again as much as the cathedral pillars and was at the time the largest single piece of granite ever cut from solid rock. Since granite quarrying everywhere has fallen on hard times, the best guess is that this record still stands.

Though all the early cutting was done by hand, the stones were hauled by wagons, called galamanders, driven by yokes of oxen. By 1900, steam-driven air compressors were used to replace some of the more grueling hand work, and with the introduction of machinery, fewer men were needed to run a quarry.

One of the interesting historical sidelights of the island quarry era is the complementary role played by another island community to the west. Chebeague Island in Casco Bay built boats to carry granite; and for the initial period, they supplied *all* the boats that worked the coast of Maine. At first, Chebeague Island sloops carried rock ballast from the shores of Casco Bay islands to the expanding Portland shipyards. So it was only natural that they should have gotten into the business of hauling granite to build coastal forts and breakwaters. By 1870, about 50 Chebeague Island craft coasted along the islands carrying granite. The vessels, originally rigged as sloops but later rerigged as schooners, were beamy, full-bellied craft manned by crews who knew how to handle rock, and most important, how to stow cargoes. In the early days, paving stones—the bread-and-butter product from island quarries—were sluiced aboard the sloops, but later they were loaded by derricks. A load of 60,000 paving stones headed for Boston, New York, or New Orleans was not uncommon, and there is a record that in one 12-day period, 320,465 paving stones cut on Hurricane Island were shipped from its stone wharves.

At the height of the era, there were quarries on 33 islands along the

Bald Island near Vinalhaven, quarried to construct
Rockland's breakwater. *Rick Perry*

coast of Maine, and not even the industrious crews from Chebeague Island
could handle the daily quarry production. George Wasson, one of Maine's
maritime historians, has written, perhaps with more poetry than truth,
that when a vessel became too creaky to carry lumber from Bangor or
cordwood to the Rockland lime kilns, she was considered "none too ripe
for the stone business," and was often loaded to the scuppers with huge
blocks of granite. For many granite schooners, and the crews who slept on
deck, their destination lay only a matter of fathoms away.

The End of an Era

The first concrete house in the United States was built in Port Chester,
New York, in 1874. Although there is no record as to whether it was a
tasteful piece of architecture, the handwriting was quickly visible on the

walls of this new building material. Cement-making was apparently a skill that had been familiar to the Romans, though one lost in what westerners are fond of calling the Dark Ages. It was rediscovered in 1824 by an engineer in Portland, England, and it is still known to many as Portland cement.

The introduction of the cheaper and easier-to-handle building material was probably the ultimate cause of the decline of granite quarrying on Maine islands, but it was not the only cause. The end of lucrative government contracts, the construction of railroads on the mainland, and labor unrest all laid blows on an increasingly moribund industry.

Nowhere was the end of the era more dramatic than on Hurricane Island. The island had been bought in 1870 for the preposterous sum of $50.00 by a retired Civil War general who had fought at Bull Run. Davis Tillson had a reputation of being a petty tyrant, probably all the worse for owning his own island, which he ran as he pleased. When Hurricane Island separated from the town of Vinalhaven in 1878, it had its own post office, bank, pool hall, bowling green, bandstand, ice pond, ballfield, boarding houses, and 40 cottages. Hurricane was justly famed along the coast for its cutting and polishing shed. It was said that no granite took polish as well as Hurricane's fine-grained grey-white granite.

For 45 years the Superintendents of Works on Hurricane had been named Landers. First John Landers and then his son, Tom, had run the day-to-day activities on the island, whose population at one point reached 1,500. But when Landers died on Hurricane in 1915, it was excuse enough for the Hurricane Island Granite Company, in financial difficulties anyway, to announce they were closing the company store and ceasing regular runs to the mainland. A kind of panic ensued as quarrymen, stonecutters, blacksmiths, paving cutters, tool sharpeners, tool boys, lumpers, stone boxers, teamsters, and their families rushed to catch the last boat. Most of them left half of their worldly possessions behind and many never returned.

For years Vinalhaven people who visited Hurricane described the eerie pall that hung over the island. Tools were literally set down in place; huge, half-carved stones stood where they had been hauled into sheds or set down on their way to the wharf. Everything was as if hundreds of people had disappeared overnight, which is not a bad description, since that is precisely what happened.

Of all the human purposes that islands have served, none has left such permanent marks as the brief granite era. No island along the Maine coast has been so thoroughly reshaped as the 10-acre dome of granite off Vinalhaven lately and accurately called Bald Island. Near the turn of the century it was literally blasted out of the water and hauled across Penobscot Bay to create the Rockland breakwater. Bald Island now looms up, particularly out of an early-morning fog, like a piece of lunar landscape that has fallen out of orbit and landed in West Penobscot Bay.

Among other unanticipated benefits, abandoned quarries provide pre-

Skating on Vinalhaven. *George Putz*

mier swimming holes and skating ponds for a good number of island communities. For the greatest part of the summer the Nova Scotia Current
makes ocean swimming something of an ordeal, although it can be chal-
lenging to acclimate your body like the rest of the marine biota to the
bracing Arctic-born water. Hurricane Island Outward Bound School has
proven as much to a generation of disbelieving students, but for teaching
young children how to swim or for lying around in the water like a fat
frog or manatee, nothing quite matches a quarry swim in August and September. The best island quarries are deep, full of dark and still water, and
have little hidden niches along their sides—perfect for sitting motionless
as stone and watching the birds make trips back and forth along the cliff
face, or the comings and goings of island sylphs playing along the shore
with little children.

   The irony of the quarrying era is not only that this irreversible use of
islands has produced such diverting and useful landscapes, but that we
have come to see the granite period and the monumental architecture that
it produced in such a romantic afterglow. If someone today proposed to
supply stones from Maine islands for city development, it would be roundly
and righteously condemned. Since the quarrying was conducted in the far-
distant past, it has achieved a respectability it would be denied today.

4

Island Vegetation: Yew, Aspe, Hazel, and Spruce

THE LONG FINGERS of the sea comb through the unseen island networks of air and soil to create special worlds not found at mainland sites. Fantastic forests, from an Alice in Wonderland dream, are shaped by airborne particles of salt kicked up by a storm sea and implanted in the young bark of spruces. The bark swells in physiological tumult from the salt stress and produces burls—rounded globes that are suspended from the trunks and limbs of trees like Rip Van Winkle's bowling balls.

The composition of island vegetation is dominated by the influence of the cold Arctic-born water currents described in Chapter 1. The Nova Scotia Current cascades southwesterly along the Maine coast from the tip of Nova Scotia. Where warm southerly air piles over the cold water, fog is generated. Day in and day out, somewhere in the Gulf of Maine there is fog, which rolls in to hide the islands when the winds are light and southerly.

In ecological terms, the fog provides an additional ambient source of water and is utilized by a variety of ancient orders of lichens, mosses, and ferns that are capable of extracting moisture directly from the air. Lichens, mosses, and ferns form lambent emerald carpets atop rocky isles and constitute a much more important part of island flora than of mainland forests. Old man's beard *(usnea* spp.), locally called spanish moss, is a long, wispy, grey-green lichen that hangs from the limbs of fog-exposed spruce and gives them an ancient, battered look even when the trees are young and thriving. The forest floors of islands are miniature cities of these odd plants that are part algae, part fungi. Various shield lichens *(Parmelia)* are set in among gracile sprigs and rounded thalli (shoots) of reindeer, ladder, spoon, goblet, and scarlet-crusted lichen (all species of *Cladonia—C. degenerans, C. rangei-*

96

Burls suspended from the trunks and limbs of island spruce.   *Rick Perry*

ferana, C. verticillata, C. gracilis, and *C. conista).* One of these rock-encrusting lichens is the beautiful, vibrant yellow and orange *Xanathoria* lichen, which encoats rocks like spilled paint from the tideline to the height of the land. Hairy cap, broom, pincushion, and sphagnum mosses are interspersed throughout the lichen growth and, when viewed on hands and knees, it all looks like a Lilliputian landscape. . . . slightly dreamy.

Island forests are covered with lambent carpets of lichens, mosses and ferns.   *Sharon Kosinski*

Lichens perform a rather more important ecological function than merely making one wonder what it must be like to be little. They are the first growth of any sort to colonize bare rock and secrete a mild organic acid that begins to dissolve their hard-rock holds and initiate the processes of soil formation. Little bits of mineral soil collect in crevices and crannies, facilitating settlement by a variety of other plants with more demanding requirements. Without lichens, many of the Gulf of Maine islands that support luxuriant forests would have remained as bare as the days when the glacier scraped them clean.

The cold winds blowing in off the Gulf of Maine create a more boreal climate in May and June. Because Arctic species flower earlier than others and can set seed more quickly under adverse conditions, they have leap-frogged down the chain of outer islands much farther south than on the mainland. In ecological terms, they have filled a vacant temporal niche. An ecological niche is just a concept, part of the accepted ecological doctrine these days, but it is useful for explaining certain phenomena. It's easiest to explain with reference to animals. Take the passenger pigeon, which was a colonial-nesting forest bird feeding on forest insects until its habitat was

Hairy cap moss. *Rick Perry*

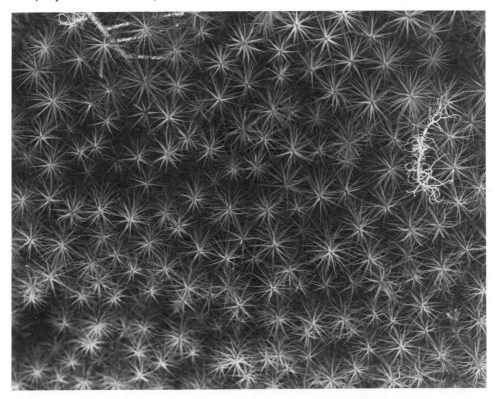

Bunchberry or ground dogwood.   *Jim Kosinski*

greatly reduced and its numbers decimated by market hunters. When it became extinct, seeds and insects that supported the original population were
still alive and well. The concept suggests that sooner or later, something will
utilize those resources—something, in other words, will fill the passenger
pigeons' niche (it is probably the starling that has most completely filled
the niche).

Arctic wildflower species are rare in Maine, since they are at the extreme southern end of their range; they are also among the most beautiful
of island flowers—pale oyster leaf (*Mertensia maritima*), delicate bird's-eye
primrose *(Primula laurentiana)*, a small gentian *(Lomatagonia rotatum)*,
Greenland sandwort (*Arenaria groenlandica*), mats of astringent crowberry
(*Empetrum nigrum*), and the loveliest, most delicate of all the arctics, roseroot stonecrop) (*Sedum rosea*). Even their names are lovely. There is an
island east of Schoodic Point whose sheer, 60-foot roseroot-covered cliffs
subtly change color as the flowers bloom and set seed. Roseroot is dioe-
cious—that is, the male and female flowers are borne on separate plants.
The yellow-tipped male flowers of roseroot appear shortly before the red-
tinged female flowers, which ripen into orange seed capsules. The walls of
the island pulse in shades and combinations of yellows, reds, and oranges
as the season progresses; it is unspeakably beautiful.

The forests of the islands are primarily composed of spruce. White
spruce or "cat spruce" (because of the odor of the sap when it is cut) is the

ABOVE LEFT Crowberry (*Empetrum nigrum*).   *Kate Fitzgerald*

ABOVE RIGHT Roseroot stonecrop (*Sedum rosea*).   *Kate Fitzgerald*

most salt-tolerant of the spruces and is found along the edges of the islands; red spruce crowds island interiors. Balsam fir, an important component of mainland conifer forests, does not do well on islands, probably as a result of the cool, damp, foggy climate, which presents ideal growing conditions for various wood-eating fungi that have an appetite for fir. Island forests often take on the appearance of a multistoried layer cake, with spruce on top and fir underneath. Because fir is a more aggressive seed producer, and fir seedlings outgrow spruce seedlings, the understory of an island is usually dominated by balsam fir. Within this sea of fir saplings, you can find an occasional spruce if you look carefully, but they are outnumbered, often a hundred to one, by fir. Yet if you came back 50 years later to the same spot, you would find a grove of pure spruce. In the interim the hardier spruce outlive the temporarily more numerous fir. The fir dominate the site for 10 or 20 years, but they soon begin to drop out of the race for the sky, one by one, victims of both fungi and suppression. As the fir trees die, spruce spread their branches and root network to occupy more and more growing space, and they will eventually form a pure stand, which in exceptional circumstances will persist for 150 to 200 years: spruce on top, fir underneath.

Mature spruce forests now cover perhaps 90 percent of the islands east of Cape Small, although if we are to believe the accounts of the mariners who sailed along the island shores and occasionally landed to cut firewood and replenish their water, there is reason to believe island forests used to be significantly more diverse.

The Original Island Forests

Which explorers to believe and how to decipher their tantalizingly brief written descriptions presents a world of problems, but two things become quickly apparent. First, the vegetation of the islands' forests, then as now, was the realm of the rugged, slow-growing, shallow-rooted, indomitable spruce. That said, let the second point be made that island forests were originally collectively a good deal more complex; they were made up of many more species than at present, and the disappearance of many of the more commercially desirable species has had effects that today impinge directly on the lives of islanders, and to a lesser degree on their occasional visitors.

The credibility of the early explorers is weakened by the fact that many of them were tempted to gild the lily of their exploits. Glowing accounts of new lands made their voyages seem more significant, and if these voyages were to be remembered down through the crowded centuries, the returning heroes needed to awaken interest in further exploration and investment— investment, more often than not, by merchants probably no less skeptical then than now over the prospect of spending money, even to make more money.

John Cabot, who laid the foundation for England's claim to the entire northern half of North America, was one of the best at stretching the truth. He described the rocky Newfoundland coast as a land with fertile soil and mild climate, suitable for the production of silk, and forests full of the valuable Brazilian greenheart tree. Others who followed were not so inaccurate, yet most of them described the new land only in terms of its "profits." Very few of them described its disadvantages.

The one notable exception among those explorers was Christopher Levett, who wrote in the 17th century with refreshing sense of humor:

> I will not tell you that you may smell the cornfields before you see the land, neither must men think that corn doth grow naturally or on trees, nor will deer come and look on a man until he shoot him, nor the fish leap into the kettle, nor on the dry land, neither are they so plentiful that you may dip them up in baskets, [or] which is no truer, that fowls will present themselves to you with spits through them.
>
> But certainly there is fowl, deer and fish enough for the taking if men be diligent. . . .

On first reading, Mr. Levett seems appealingly reliable, and he turns out to be even better than he sounds. In England Levett served as the "King's Woodward of Somertshire," in charge of the harvest of timber from the large, intensively utilized King's woods. Many of the early 18th century descriptions came from the pens of gentlemen of good estate or of men of the sea (such as John Smith) who turned out to be skillful fishermen, or of adventurers who were bound for glory, but through Levett's eyes we have an unsentimental and insightful description of the vegetation of the islands and the coast of Maine. Levett was the first forester to cast an appraising eye on the value of the islands' timber.

Levett sailed for New England in 1623, making a landfall at Isles of Shoals, upon which he saw "neither one good timber tree nor so much good

ABOVE LEFT Jewelweed (*Impatiens capensis*).   *Kate Fitzgerald*

ABOVE RIGHT Seaside rose and rosehip (*Rosa rugosa*).   *Kate Fitzgerald*

ground as to make a garden." One of these treeless rocks of granite is still known as Cedar Island, and Celia Thaxter, the daughter of the innkeeper who turned this tiny archipelago into Maine's first island resort, has described finding a cedar root imprisoned in a cleft of granite. It is possible that these all-but-barren islands once supported a ragged growth of salt-tolerant spruce that was cleared off by the nameless 16th century fishermen who certainly made this island a headquarters to set up their flake yards or fish stages, but the presence of cedar trees seems unlikely.

From the Isles of Shoals Levett made his way to the Piscataqua River, where he gathered his men and set off in the late fall in an open boat to explore the coast eastward. Through the next several months Levett half walked, half sailed or rowed his craft between "Pannaway" and "Capeman-wagen," or what would become Portsmouth and Southport Island. He was caught in gales and snowstorms; he rowed up the rivers that poured out of the forested interior, met with the Indians, cheered his often cold and hungry men, landed on many of the islands between the two ends of his journey, and built a fortified house on one of them.

Along the way he carefully described the condition and value of the timber growing on the islands and the main, suggesting industries that might be developed from the harvest of the woods. It is notable that Levett

ABOVE LEFT Beach grass (*Ammophila brevigulata*).   *Kate Fitzgerald*

ABOVE RIGHT Sea celery (*Ligusticum scothicum*).   *Kate Fitzgerald*

described poor timber at several places he visited. One such was the place
he called Capemanwagen, at the eastern tip of Casco Bay—a region of "little
good timber and less good ground," most likely referring to the absence of
pine and oak, the two most commercially necessary timber trees for all sorts
of colonial enterprises.

Undoubtedly the long rocky peninsulas and the exposed portions of
outer islands supported forests dominated by spruce. Even today the distribution of spruce along the coast is strongly correlated with the degree of
exposure to maritime climatic influences.

As early as 1524, when Verrazano cruised nearly the entire eastern seaboard, he described the coast of Maine as "full of very thick woods of fir
trees, cypresses and the like, indicative of a cold climate." Not a bad description for the few words he devoted to 2,500 miles of tidal coastline, but
it points up the problem of determining when is a rose not a rose, or a fir
not a fir. Common names for forest trees changed from place to place and
from era to era. The British, who exhausted their supply of mast pines very
early in their history and began to import Scotch pine from the Baltic, more

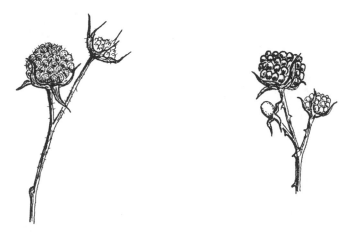

Red and black raspberries (*Rubus spp.*).   *Kate Fitzgerald*

often than not referred to pine as Baltic Firre. In fact, the word "pine" was almost never used to describe the various species of this family that were so important to shiphaulers, millwrights, and carpenters. Pine was called firre by Rosier, who listed it along with hazel and aspe among "the profits we saw." (Hazel probably meant hazelnut and aspe referred to the aspen or "popple.") Maine's balsam fir appears to have been called a yew, since it resembles this common English tree species (the native American yew is not a tree at all, but a pretty shrub that is commonly used as a decorative planting around northern homesteads). To make matters worse, it is equally possible that the yew, which is not a yew, might have been hemlock, which also resembles the English yew. Although white pine is almost unknown on the coastal islands of Maine today (although it still grows on the islands in the brackish estuarine rivers that flow into the sea), it was evidently an important component of the original island forests. Clapboard Island in inner Casco Bay was one of the first-named islands in the area, and as early as 1630, Jonathon Winter was writing enthusiastic reports to England of the supplemental income derived from men who made clapboards out of Richmond Island's soft pumpkin pine for the export trade.

Rosier, the gentleman who accompanied Weymouth to Muscongus Bay, described the mast stock of enormous pines he called "firres" growing on Allen and Burnt Islands from which "issueth turpentine in so marvelous plenty. This would be a great benefit for making tar and pitch." The history of Swans Island mentions that an early settler moved to the eastern side of Swans and cut an immense growth of pines. It seems fairly evident that white pine once had an important place within the sheltered forests of many islands west of Mount Desert.

Hemlock was probably never an important island forest constituent, although the town histories of both Islesboro and North Haven mention

ABOVE LEFT Goose greens (*Plantago oliganthos*).   *Kate Fitzgerald*

ABOVE RIGHT Beach lettuce (*Sonchus oleraceae*).   *Kate Fitzgerald*

tanneries, which presumably relied on local sources of hemlock bark for the curing of farm hides. These industries seem to have died out quickly on both islands, suggesting that the local supply of hemlock was rapidly exhausted.

Island Hardwoods—Fragile Forests

The situation with regard to hardwood growth in island forests is less difficult to sort out, primarily because European forests were composed of many of the same kinds of trees. Levett, Rosier, Smith, and Gilbert all mentioned the oaks found on both the islands and the mainland. "Oaks of excellent grain, straight and great timber," are the words Rosier used. Besides the important oaks, many of the explorers noted the presence of other hardwoods. As mentioned earlier, when Champlain landed on the shore of Richmond Island in 1605, he was impressed by the luxuriant groves of oak and nut trees as well as vines of wild grape, which is why the Frenchman gave the name Bacchus to the island. It is not entirely clear just what the trees were, but five years later when Raleigh Gilbert and Sir John Popham were exploring the islands and nearby shore of Casco Bay for a plantation site, they described immense oaks and walnuts "growing a great space asunder, one from the other as our parks in England, and no thicket growing under them." Both Levett and Smith mentioned the presence of chestnut in Maine's forests; Levett found chestnut trees on the islands of Casco Bay, and Smith described them inland east to the Penobscot River. An account published in 1865 of a visit to the White Islands off Boothbay described the islands' forests as composed of spruce, oak, and hickory. It seems likely that chestnut, walnut, and hickory all were occasional components of the forests of at least a few of Maine's islands.

The 1805 *American Coast Pilot* gave instructions for coasting east toward Mount Desert as follows: "Steer east by south which will carry you between the Ship and Barge and 3 islands which you leave on your larboard which are covered with large rock maple trees." These three islands could only be Pond, Opechee, and Black Islands of the Casco Passage at the western edge of Blue Hill Bay. All of these islands are notable today not for hardwoods, which have disappeared, but for their dense spruce growth. Incidentally, this particular Black Island is not named for its "black growth" of spruce as are several Black Islands, but apparently for an eccentric hermit named Black who rowed to Somesville twice a year to buy supplies with golden guineas he is supposed to have salvaged from the wreck of a British warship.

On a British Admiralty Chart of the Maine coast published in 1760, the island now known as Hardwood Island in Blue Hill Bay was charted as Beech Island, and many of the early island descriptions note the presence, and in some cases the preponderance, of beech groves. Beech is a close relative of the copper beech, which is widely distributed throughout Europe and would therefore have been easily identifiable. Swans Island, according to the town history written in 1898 and the verbal recollections of its earliest inhabitants, was covered with a hardwood forest. Many of the town ancients could remember discovering enormous stumps where even in 1898 only spruce was found. The early records of both Baker Island off Mount Desert and Roque Island mention magnificent stands of the smooth grey-barked beech.

Ash and yellow and white birches were forest species also found by the Europeans and early settlers on the islands. It is a reasonable guess that the Indians headquartered on Diamond and Chebeague Islands collected ash saplings for basket stock on islands in Casco Bay. There is even a Basket Island. Even distant Monhegan, lying three leagues out to sea and exposed to the severest of maritime climatic influences, supported oak, birch, and beech along with its "firres" or white pine, according to Rosier.

No doubt the original forest cover increased in complexity as the explorers penetrated up into the bays from the exposed outer islands. The original survey lots of Islesboro, laid out when the island was settled shortly after the Revolutionary War, provide a rare glimpse into the composition of the presettlement forest: "About 20 acres swampy spruce and hemlock. 80 acres beech, birch, maple middling; good land but rocky hard land. 5 miles to mill by water." And certainly as the explorers proceeded eastward, where the climate became cooler and fogs more prevalent, the forests were seldom much to write home about—at least this was the conclusion reached by Champlain, who described the cover of the Isle des Ranges (islands in a range—a good geographical description of the Downeast islands: Cross, Libby, Brothers, and Head Harbor) as "covered with pines [probably he meant spruce], and other trees of an inferior sort." The name Ragged Island for two of Maine's outer islands—one at the edge of Penobscot Bay (originally known as Ragged Arse) and one on the outer rim of Casco Bay— suggests an irregular forest cover, and as anyone who has looked at a wind-stunted spruce clinging to an exposed headland will tell you, they do look desperately ragged and poverty-stricken.

Although many more of the islands were at one time forested, not all of them supported groves of trees, ragged or otherwise. A colonists' petition for settling Fisherman Island off Boothbay in 1687 asked that Squirrel Island be included in the grant, since Fisherman was "void of wood either for fire or other use." Seal Island, at the entrance to Penobscot Bay, was described by Samuel Argall in 1610 as "nothing but a rock, which seemed to be a very rich marble stone." Large Green Island, lying just to the west of Seal, was similarly bereft of tree growth.

It is worth stopping for a moment to consider the name Green Island, which is shared by no fewer than 19 Maine islands and could conceivably have described the look of an evergreen forest. Checking back again with the wonderfully informative 1760 edition of British Admiralty Charts of the coast of Maine, several still-named Green Islands appear. One of them is the low, sprawling nubble lying between Isle au Haut and Marshall Island; it is chiefly distinguished as a colony of mixed-species seabirds whose rich and copious excretions give a well-fertilized, luxuriant look to the island. Without a doubt, many of the treeless islands of the Maine coast remained so by virtue of the nesting gulls, cormorants, and "shitpokes" (great blue herons) that inhabited them.

From this rather exacting dissertation of the changing fates of forested islands, it is evident that many species that were earlier present and notable are now gone. Walnut, oaks, beech, hard maple, chestnuts, hickory, ash, yellow birch, hemlock, and white pine are conspicuously absent from all but a few island forests. No doubt the most significant reason that walnut, hickory, oak, and beech have almost disappeared from the islands is that their heavy seeds float out and become established on islands rather irregularly. Once the last individual of a heavy-seeded species is harvested from an island, it may be an eon before time and tides interact favorably to reestablish the hardwoods there.

While there are good reasons that many island hardwoods have passed into the realm of historical footnote, it is also true that many were put to great and good uses. Still, there is something here that should give us pause.

Though the effects are somewhat masked on the Big Island America, where seed sources are not so vulnerable, the cutting of trees can dramatically alter the composition of future forests. Perhaps the chief lesson to be drawn from the disappearance of so many island tree species is that although trees themselves might be rugged, forests are fragile affairs.

Shipbuilding, "Better Cheap"

It is unlikely that any industry or occupation has had such a significant and lasting effect on island forests as a century of shipbuilding. It is simply incredible to think of the numbers of vessels that were hewn out of Maine's forests from the period after the Indian Wars until the steel-hulled, steam-powered ships ended the Age of Sail. To try to count the numbers of trees that went into even the most humble of craft makes one realize that much of the original forest growth of Maine's islands could at one time be found whitening one of the world's seven seas. There are few coves, inlets, or tidal streams, however small, that did not at one time have a vessel of some description cut and launched from its shores. In fact, since the cutting and sawing of lumber was the chief motive for settling Maine's forested shores, it was no exaggeration to say, as did one of Islesboro's shipbuilders, that a man could lay a keel and build his vessel on a timbered shore from which he cut both ship and cargo.

Though several of the British explorers recognized the military significance of Maine's supply of mast timbers, it was again Levett, the King's Woodward from Somertshire, who saw the value of the diversity and abundance of tree species that could make Maine the shipbuilding capital of the world, as she indeed became:

> I dare be bold to say also, there may be ships as conveniently built there as in any place of the world where I have been and better cheap. As for plank, crooked timber and all other sorts whatsoever can be desired for such purpose, the world cannot afford better.

Although the islands' shipyards never came close to matching the commercial tonnage of ports such as Bath, Wiscasset, and Thomaston, the numbers of small vessels built and launched from islands is a good deal larger than the official records suggest. For one thing, building and launching a boat for an islander was strictly a personal affair, unlike the launching of a large coasting schooner, which was always a great town event. But a few men or fishermen launching a sloop or a pinky schooner from the shores of an island was not a great deal more remarkable than someone buying a new truck today. Probably your neighbors were aware of it, but the rest of the world took no great notice. In many island communities, almost every male inhabitant of the town at some point in his life built a vessel of some sort.

Boat wood.   *Jim Kosinski*

Fishermen built vessels for their own use out of any material they could get their hands on for the right price, which usually meant next to nothing. Enterprising islanders were part farmer, part fisherman, logger, what-have-you, so that boatbuilding simply became another skill that had to be learned with the tools and materials at hand. Reuben Carver, the premier boat-builder of Vinalhaven between 1820 and 1880, built a vessel almost entirely out of spruce—from a spruce keel and stem and stern pieces to spruce timbers and planks. As the joke went on the island, when she was launched, her crew hoisted a jib made of spruce and she sailed to Boston with a deck cargo of spruce cordwood. It's probably not far from the truth.

Island shipyards on North Haven, Vinalhaven, Islesboro, Isle au Haut, Deer Isle, Swans Island, and Cranberry Isles produced an astonishing number of schooners (185) averaging 90 to 110 tons, as well as a scattering of brigs, barks, and even full-rigged ships, such as the 200-ton *Lucy* and *Nancy*.

As William Fairburn's monumental six-volume history, *Merchant Sail*, pointed out, very few of the Penobscot Bay shipyards could be considered permanent; the builders moved as soon as the timber of an area was cut out, only to relocate in some new area in which the necessary stock of planking, knees and ribs, masts and keels was still found rooted upright along the rocky island shores. Some idea of the great weight of these trees comes from the fact that shipbuilders often chose to move a shipyard to a new

A prodigious amount of wood went into this
three-masted schooner. *Frank Claes*

location in the midst of a good growth of uncut timber rather than leave
the yard where it was and move the timber to it.

As most histories of Maine are quick to point out, the first vessel built
in the New World was the pinnace *Virginia*, which was constructed during
the winter of 1609 by the ill-fated Popham Colony and launched from the
shores of the Kennebec River. Shipbuilding moved slowly eastward throughout the 1700s, but it did not really reach a critical mass until after the
Revolution. By 1790 there was a shipyard on Hooper Island in Muscongus
Bay. By 1796, four schooners and a sloop had been launched from the shores
of North and South Fox Islands. In 1800 David Thurlow settled on the
island across the Thorofare from Deer Isle (which bore his name until it

was changed to Crotch Island 60 years later), built a sawmill, and launched 17 vessels, including a 150-ton brig, before 1840. Similar efforts were underway at Vinalhaven's "Privilege," Deer Isle's "Privilege," Swans Island, Isle au Haut, Islesboro, and the Cranberry Isles. In Casco Bay, it appears that the major yards were located on the rivers, whose waters were more protected, but the islands were used as sources of local raw materials.

While the supply lasted, keels were cut from white oak, as were stem and stern posts. Keelstock was always in critically short supply, since suitably shaped large, clear white oak, free of defects, was not found everywhere, even in the so-called "virgin forest." White oak is desirable as a ship timber chiefly because the integral arrangement of its water-conducting cells (xylem) inhibits the free flow of water through them once the tree has been cut—unlike similar cells of its relative the red oak. As a result, white oak is much more resistant to rot than almost all other ship timbers. Fairburn suggests that northern colonial white oak was so abundant in the early days of shipbuilding that often nothing but the heartwood of these trees was put into American-built vessels. White oak was never as common in Maine as

Cordwood schooners in Rockland Harbor, 1873. *Frank Claes*

red oak, but an 1816 report on the economic condition of the District of Maine, commissioned by the Commonwealth of Massachusetts, put the northern limit of white oak somewhere east of the Penobscot River Valley. Today white oak is rare north of Portland, and almost unheard of on islands.

For the rest of a vessel, the materials were not so critical. Floors were of red oak or beech, their topping planks of almost any species that was handy: spruce, hemlock, white pine, or cedar. Ash was used for oars, rock maple for cabins and finish, hackmatack (larch) for knees, hornbeam or ironwood for hand spikes, and locust or spruce limbs saturated with pitch for treenails. Masts and spars were of white pine when it was handy, but spruce spars became more common as pine supplies dwindled.

It is difficult to estimate accurately how quickly ship timber supplies dwindled, since the original island timber supply differed greatly from area to area, depending on bedrock, soils, topography, and the degree of maritime influences. But if you consider that for one ship of the line the British Admiralty required at least 2,000 oaks (not counting other trees), it is easy to understand how whole forests could disappear. Half the vessels that Deer Isle, Vinalhaven, and North Haven would build had already been launched prior to 1830. Most of the shipyards continued to operate until close to the turn of the century, but their heyday had passed. On the mainland, however, the boom lasted at least through 1855, when fully one-third of the nation's entire tonnage of vessels for the year consisted of vessels built in Maine shipyards.

Lumbering for Cordwood, Kilnwood, and Pulpwood

Why are staves and clapboards and firewood and kilnwood less noble products of island forests than the high-bowed, round-bellied, faired and true wooden hull of a ship, whether brig, bark, or schooner? Something in the asking hints at the answer. It may not be rational to conclude that wooden ships were a better use of island forests than the very products they were often built to carry, but it is hard to escape the impression that these products might better have been cut from mainland forests, where the effects of the cutting are repaired more quickly.

From the earliest times, red oak and beech trees were felled on islands to be riven into staves. There are islands today in Casco, Penobscot, and Frenchman Bays whose name Stave dates from this use, although their hardwood forests have long since been replaced by dark spruces. Levett, the practical forester, wrote that Maine's supply of beech and oak was "excellent timber for joiners and coopers. No place in England can afford better timber for pipe staves." (In Europe, staves were used to make great casks called pipes for the storing of wine.)

Later, when a brisk trade developed between the American colonies and the West Indies, cargoes of staves were sent south to be assembled and were returned full of molasses. As early as 1784, a Captain Parker of Yarmouth (as we are informed by William Rowe) complained:

> I have this day seen the choicest timber cut down and sawn into staves. Transient men come down in gangs and cut from the islands, of which there are now 19 on Chebeague, and several vessels cutting their load.

While Captain Parker may have known ships better than forests, you can hear him wincing through his description of the girth of trees felled for the stave trade that he probably would have preferred to go into his boat. One oak was so broad at its stump that a yoke of oxen could be turned around on it.

William Jones, a native of Maine, was sent to Cuba as a young man by a merchant to assemble the shooks of staves that had been jointed and crozed and were ready to be fitted in place. The record indicates that this Mr. Jones returned to Peaks Island in Casco Bay to open up his own cooper's shop in 1840, but he had to close down 15 years later because the supply of raw material was exhausted.

The cordwood trade was carried on from the time of the earliest settlements to supply Boston with winter fuel. Islands with good anchorages were visited routinely and 20 or 30 cords were cut for a deckload to carry upwind to Boston. It was good winter work when fishing and farming were slack. One of Pemaquid's settlers shortly after the conclusion of the long Indian Wars related that most settlers' "whole living depended on cutting firewood and carrying it to Boston and other towns more than 150 miles from them."

One of the institutions that determined the speed with which islands were settled was the proximity of the tidal-powered saw and grist mill. At Roque Island the dam operated on both ebb and flood tides; the tide turned a grist mill on one bank of the small embayment known as Paradise Cove and a sawmill on the other. The first settler of whom there is a record on Vinalhaven was one Francis Cogswell, whose name seems to have fit his occupation. He set up a tidal sawmill, no doubt attracted to the heavily forested shores, the steady surge of water in and out of the harbor, and the ease of shipping his product to a ready market. The name "Privilege," which was given to the small protected coves and inlets along the coast and islands of Maine where sawmills were built, gives an idea of the importance attached to such places by the original settlers.

We don't know when the timber supply of various portions of the coast was exhausted, but George Hosmer mentioned the abandonment of the Deer Isle sawmill in the early 1800s, "as the best of the lumber had been cut off in the vicinity." Morison reported that most of the first forest growth around Mount Desert Island had been cut off by 1870.

It is certain that in Penobscot Bay most of the forested islands had been cut over at least once prior to 1870, since the voracious kilns of the lime industry were headquartered in the Rockland area. Ever since limestone was first slaked into lime mortar in 1733, the expanding lime industry depended on an enormous and uninterrupted supply of wood to fire the kilns. By 1835 some 150 kilns were producing three quarters of a million casks annually. Several hundred vessels were ranging the coast for fuel for the kilns, which burned 30 cords at a crack. These ragged-looking "kiln-wooders" often had their decks stacked so high with cordwood that it is said the helmsman steered by directions shouted from the bow.

Incidentally, it might be added that next to carrying granite, a cargo of lime was the next most dangerous coasting assignment, since lime burns when it gets wet, and as any sailor knows, seawater has a habit of filling the bilges of even the tightest vessel. In such an eventuality, the only course was to head the craft to the nearest shore while trying to seal all the hatches and air passages into the hold with lime plaster, hoping that the cargo would not become hot enough to burst into flames. Once at anchor, the vigil began. If every crack into the hold had been sealed successfully, the fire went out. But as often as not, the fire could not be smothered, and the vessel had to be scuttled, which would swell the cargo in the hold to the bursting point, warping ship timbers and deck beams into unseemly and unseamanly shapes.

The last serious wave of island forest cutting began around 1920 and lasted until the early 1960s. The St. Regis Paper Company plant at Bucksport on the Penobscot River was set up to offload four-foot pulpwood from tug-driven barges. "Pulping" an island was a means of generating additional income for islands whose populations and economic fortunes had begun to move slowly downhill. Several hundred of the larger islands were cut over during this time by crews who used horse teams or homemade tractors called skipjacks or jitterbugs to get the four-foot wood to shore. A skipjack, still used in the woods to some extent, is nothing more than an old truck (1½ to 2½ tons) stripped down to the frame and outfitted with welded log bunks, a two-speed rear end. Often a second transmission is mounted behind the original, facing the rear end and run in reverse to give the homemade vehicle a super-low gear to maneuver over uneven ground.

Probably no other island use did so much to generate the movement for island preservation than the wave of pulpwood cuttings of this period. A pulped piece of ground is unsightly, no question about it, but sensibilities had changed by this time, and the coast and islands were beginning to become important areas for summer recreation.

The Nature Conservancy, the largest private island owner on the Maine coast, acquired one of its first islands in 1964 by stepping in after the timber rights of a 150-acre island in Frenchman Bay had been sold and the harvest— a clear-cutting operation—had begun in earnest. In public discussions it is easy to get the impression that we want our forests to provide too many things for us: we want both inexpensive housing and uncut forests. But in the case of that island, an extraordinarily beautiful old-growth red spruce forest with an emerald carpeted understory of pleurocarpous mosses and fruticose lichens still stands, and within the high, knotty limbs of treetops in a corner of the island a heronry has recently been established. All things considered, it is a forest that rightly ought to be spared the woodsman's axe.

Island Farming: "Peculiar Sense of Proprietorship"

> Other islands have one house and one barn on them, this sole family being lords and rulers of all land and sea girds. The owner of such an island must have a peculiar sense of proprietorship and lordship; he must feel more like his own master than other people can.
>
> Henry Wadsworth Longfellow

It will come as no surprise that several hundred years of harvesting wood from islands has changed the composition, complexity, and diversity of the forests that cover the rocky isles today. It serves to confirm the low opinion many have of woodcutters. But if the truth be told, farmers also have had a hand in changing the face of island landscapes, and in some cases the changes they wrought have had more permanent and, in some ecological senses, more damaging effects; it is only because the effects of farming are more aesthetically pleasing that farmers are not more often called to account for their "management practices."

It somehow seems fitting that the first island cultivator was a sea-captain-turned-fisherman. In 1609 Captain John Smith planted a garden "on top of a rocky isle 4 leagues from the main [Monhegan] in May that grew so well that it served us for salads in June and July." But it is the farm on Richmond Island and the reports that Jonathon Winter faithfully wrote to Robert Trelawney that give the first and only detailed view of island farming in the early 1600s. In 1631 Winter wrote that "the island is a great priveledge to the plantation and at present very well stocked with all sorts of beasts that is needful. I take it to be the best plantation in the land, taking it every way both for sea and land."

One of the "sorts of beasts" with which this island (and very soon others like it) was well stocked was hogs. Pork was one of the most important sources of meat for the early colonial farms, but pig-raising on the mainland was slow to develop along the frontiers because of the practice of letting them forage in the woods during the warmer months. As often as not, they ended

Island farm.   *Rick Perry*

up as a fine pork dinner for wolves. However, if the hogs were set out on islands, particularly ones with oaks, the hogs could feed themselves in relative freedom, fattening on the fall acorn crop just before they were slaughtered. From Winter's account, it seems that hogs were also fed clams from the intertidal zone, and they soon learned how to dig out these truffle-like delicacies for themselves. After three years Richmond Island had 200 pigs. Along the coast of Maine there are 11 Hog Islands, and no doubt there were at one time many more.

On the subject of island names, we find the account of how Great and Little Hog were renamed Great and Little Diamond. For 2½ centuries they had been known as the Hog Islands, since they had been uniquely suited to raising pigs by having both clams for a staple and acorns for the fattening.

But when an association of Portlanders bought up Great Hog Island at the turn of the century and built cottages there, the matter of an appropriate name came up for discussion in a public meeting. Many favored retaining its original name, but according to one record the matter was finally settled after a well-fed, matronly resident rose and complained that her groceries delivered from the mainland always came labeled, "Mrs. So-and-So—Great Hog."

There are several advantages to island farms. One of the most important is that, owing to the influence of the surrounding waters, which act like a great thermostat, the growing season is extended later into the fall. Then there is the matter of the abundance of natural fertilizers. Seaweeds are always free for the taking, and although the early records are in dispute as to how widely rockweed, oarweed, and kelps were used, no doubt they had their proponents then as now. One island farmer in Muscongus Bay described his method of increasing his corn yield: he harvested mussels in the spring and set them in heaps along the upper edge of a cornfield to leach slowly over it during the growing season.

For those farmers who combined their farming with fishing, and most did, fish were used well into the 20th century as another source of marine fertilizer. The settlers all learned how to use fish in this way from the Indian cultivators, who probably figured that sharing information during growing season was preferable to sharing meager food supplies during the winter if crops failed. Trelawney, ever the interested patron, was told that Richmond Island farmers fertilized corn with menhaden or pogies—"1000 fish to the acre owing to their rich oil."

"One Acre in a Piece"

Island farming struggled inconclusively during the period of the long Indian Wars, but permanent family farms were as rare on islands as on the main. As soon as any island plantation got established during the brief years of peace, it was quickly snuffed out when hostilities were revived.

For almost a hundred years the eastern frontier of Maine was left in limbo as the population along the remainder of the eastern seaboard swelled to the bursting point, and land became scarce and expensive. At the end of the Revolutionary War, the eastern frontier reopened and young and old alike picked up stakes and moved to Maine. Two hundred and twenty-six towns were incorporated in Maine between 1783 and 1826, fully five times as many as before the Revolution. It was such a land rush that every available acre anywhere near the frail edge of civilization began to be cleared and turned under by rough horse-drawn plows as settlement pushed farther north and east into the wilds of Maine.

One of the chief attractions of an island farm, aside from the sense of proprietorship that Longfellow described, and the few ecological advantages that were, no doubt, lightly considered in any case, was that island titles were cloudy. There were many cases in which a persistent settler moved to an un-inhabited island, cleared the land, built a dwelling, and eventually, through one means or another, was awarded its title. The period after the Revolution was one of feverish land speculation, and often the cost of land was the chief limiting factor for would-be settlers. If a farm could be obtained cheaply or for free, it was all the more attractive, regardless of how poor a piece it was.

The census records of this period show that nearly every island greater than 10 or 15 acres (except for perhaps the completely "bald" islands) was settled for a short time, at least until wisdom became the better part of valor. Even the most bold, rugged, and steep-sided islands—which today seem dangerous to land on, let alone to attempt to farm—had their trees cut and the forests put to fields.

The original survey records of Islesboro, at the time when the island was divided up into approximately 100-acre lots, describe over and over again the condition of the ground that would bring this farm era to a relatively quick end: ". . . 40 acres ledgy, broken. Not more than one acre in a piece fit for plowing." The efforts of clearing the stones from the discontinuous patches of fields on islands made Yankee industriousness not just a virtue but a life-supporting necessity. You can imagine the effect of the descriptions of the new land that had just been opened up in Ohio on the folks back home on the island farm. Elisha Philbrook from Vinalhaven wrote back to the island that in Ohio he saw: "One hundred acres of corn in one field . . . so high that a man cannot hang his hat on them. Five acres of corn will cost not more labor than one acre will in Maine." And he added, "the land is free from stone." Hello, Ohio.

Hay and Potatoes

Hay was the first island cash crop that was shipped aboard just about any vessel at hand to feed the burgeoning livestock population in and around Boston. Since the principal means of transportation overland was the motive power of horse and oxen, prodigious quantities of feed were needed to keep things going. Massachusetts farmers who were raising livestock either for dairy products or to sell at market were no doubt reluctant to sell the crop on which their animals depended. Instead, at least in the early days, a good deal of it came from Maine's islands. On a reaching wind, Boston's famous Haymarket Square was not much more than a 24-hour passage.

One of the incidents that is still mentioned by residents of Matinicus Island was the murder of Ebenezer Hall by a group of Indians in 1724. It seems that Hall, a fisherman, was in the business of selling hay in Boston, and to stimulate a flush of new growth, he was in the habit of burning over nearby Green Island, then as now an important seabird colony. Green Island was particularly important for the Penobscot Indians, who used the island to collect eggs and young seabirds for meat. Unhappy with Hall's peremptory use of their traditional hunting grounds, they successfully peti-

Hay and potatoes declined after 1840, but island orchards continued to produce cash crops through this century. *George Putz*

tioned the distant Court of Massachusetts to enjoin him from burning over the island. When Hall burned Green again, a party of braves, no doubt angered over the delay in enforcement, settled matters by ambushing and scalping Hall.

There are about seven Burnt Islands so labeled on charts of Maine waters—a small percentage of the number of islands that were cleared either to raise a cash crop for Boston's Haymarket or later to pasture islanders' own stock. At least in the early days, all that was required to raise hay on a Maine island was an axe, hard labor, and a flintbox. Over the course of a year or two, depending on the size of the island, the trees were felled. Large, valuable timber may have been rafted to a nearby tidal mill, but as often as not, timber was left to dry out, awaiting a hot spell to be torched off.

Where and when the process of clearing and burning islands began seems to have been a matter of historical happenstance. On the early charts of the Maine coast, Swans Island was referred to as Burnt Coat, evidently a corruption of the French "Brûle Côte," or Burnt Coast. Some have attributed the early name of Swans to the hand of Champlain, although the name does not appear on any of his charts, yet it does appear on several of the other 17th century efforts. It's tempting to conclude that part of Swans was burned for pasturage by an early independent fisherman-trader who wished to leave a source of fresh meat on the island in antici-pation of his return. Champlain, in fact, mentions that wild bullock and sheep were left on Cape Sable by Portuguese fishermen in the 1540s.

The illuminating *Atlantic Neptune* series of charts calls Black Island in Casco Passage, "Grass Island." The *American Coast Pilot* presents this picture of eastern Muscongus Bay in 1804: "You may steer NE for Whitehead leaving George's Islands (which are three in number) on your larboard. The eastern island has no trees on it." The George's Islands are still three in number, but the eastern one, still called Burnt, has been reforested after a century and a half. Mosquito Island, which was described in the *Coast Pilot* as covered "with burnt trees," was described 60 years later by another eye as "a low rocky island covered with brush." The process of natural reforestation seems painfully slow.

Aside from the efforts to harvest hay, the sandy island soils produced little in the way of a cash crop other than potatoes. But by the early 1840s the potato blight had made its way to the shores of Maine, and the his-tories of both Deer Isle and Islesboro record the total failure of the islands' potato crops in 1845. Gradually blight-resistant strains of potato were reintroduced, but in 1874, those few farmers who had not moved west were plagued by the potato bug, which for several years ate up not only cash and profits but also what had come to serve as winter hog feed.

"Phantoms of Pursuit and the Almoner of Human Life"

During the initial period of Maine's settlement, farming was a distinctly less important occupation than fishing, lumbering, shipbuilding, or the Indian fur trade. The Englishman Sir Ferdinando Gorges, who was cheated out of immortality—as "The Father of Maine" (cheated out of really even being remembered when the Popham Colony which he financed fell apart after one brief winter)—was a planter at heart. He hoped to sow seeds of settlement in Maine not only out of loyalty to his King but also, it appears, out of an abiding belief that farming was a Good Way of Life. In a letter to one of his associates, he bemoaned the Maine settlers' interest in other pursuits: "Trading, fishing, lumber, these have been the phantoms of pursuit, while there has been a criminal neglect of husbandry, the true source of wealth and the almoner of human life." Though this sounds a little like a Masai tribesman who measures his wealth by the number of cattle he owns, Gorges had a point. Curiously enough, even after the attractions of farming for a living in Maine began to pale, husbandry continued to thrive, particularly on islands. Of the farm animals raised on island farms, none were more well adapted to the Maine archipelago than sheep.

In most of the colonies cows outnumbered sheep, since the settlers soon discovered that salt-marsh grass (*Spartina patens* and *S. alterniflora*)

made passably good winter fodder for cattle. The increase in cows for meat
and dairy purposes was slow to affect Maine for a number of reasons. Maine
had much less salt-marsh land to support cattle, cows were expensive, and
on the islands, they needed water and were hard to move around. In fact,
Hosmer's *History of Deer Isle* describes the death of a settler, his wife, three
children, and a neighbor when their gundalow overturned as they tried to
land a cow on Fog Island in Merchant Row. There are more Calf Islands
than Cow Islands off the coast of Maine, which makes one wonder whether
transportation wasn't another factor in limiting island cattle.

From the beginning, Maine islanders had little cause to interface with
Boston's cash economy, with the exception of their need for cloth. Import-
ing bolts of English cloth was an early necessity of life, but soon after sheep
were introduced, the idea of making homespun wool caught on, which no
doubt appealed to the isolated islanders.

According to Maine's agricultural historian, Clarence Day, the early
sheep were "long-legged, narrow-breasted, light-quartered, coarse-wooled,
roving and wild." After the Embargo Act of 1807 completely isolated the
young nation from the cloth trade abroad, sheep raising became more and
more significant to Maine's economy. For two generations, Maine was one
of the leading grazing states in the country. During this time, herds of the
famed and prized Spanish merino sheep were introduced into Maine's local
stock—in some cases selling for fabulous prices that only well-employed captains and merchants could afford.

The advantages of raising sheep on islands are almost too numerous
to list. First, there is the matter of fencing, which is time-consuming both
to build and maintain: none was needed for pasturing sheep on small or
middle-sized islands—say, up to 200 acres. Then there is the need to water

Metinic Island sheep. *Susan St. John*

other farm stock—a chore wasted on sheep, since they are perfectly capable of providing for their own needs on what they can get from dew or intermittent rains. Not only were they capable of getting their own water, but they supplemented their forage with seaweeds, notably kelps, from the islands' intertidal zones. Also, island sheep were relatively free of parasitic worms, which on the mainland took a continuous toll. Finally there was the matter of their wool. Wool from island sheep was highly prized and brought a better price at the local woolen mills. The exposure of the island sheep to cycles of sun, rain, and cold produced wool that did not shrink as much as other wool, was cleaner, and produced good staple or krinkle for easy spinning. The president of the Knox Woolen Mill declared that the long-stapled island wool was superior in every respect.

Perhaps the only drawback that could be charged against island sheep was described in Hosmer's Deer Isle history, published last century. The sheep on uninhabited islands were subject to "such depredations committed . . . by a worthless class who have opportunities for plunder, and were it not for that, those islands would be of more value than they are now." Free mutton and wool aside, it appears that islands were used then as now to settle scores among people: they were thrown together on isolated islands to divide up limited resources and settle feuds in the only manner possible. Slaughtering a man's sheep left on an island was one way.

It is true that the transporting of sheep back and forth to the island pastures was a considerable operation, and not without its dangers, but it was the kind of activity with which islanders were familiar and skillful: moving heavy items on and off rocky shores at the right time and tide. In flocks of 10 to 30, most sheep were taken to the peripheral islands from their winter quarters in May after they were sheared; if they were pastured before shearing, there was the risk of losing the long wool to bushes and brambles. In October the sheep were driven and captured to be returned to their winter ground, a more tricky and difficult enterprise than getting the sheep to the island. They were wilder in the fall, and a certain number were lost off the steep-sided islands' pastures. Stove-up leg of lamb and drowned wild sheep were trials of the trade.

Some Ecological Considerations

It is difficult to estimate the total number of sheep that were pastured on Maine islands when the industry was at its peak—1830–1840 was the peak for New England as a whole, but it did not occur until 1860 in Maine, and perhaps even later on the islands. In 1858 there were 2,000 sheep on North Haven, in contrast to approximately 250 cows and 25 horses. Kimball Island and Isle au Haut each had 400. In 1910 there were still 500 sheep on Great Duck Island south of Mount Desert; perhaps 1,200 on Monhegan and

The big trees of the original island forests have been cut.   *George Putz*

300 on Ragged Island—known as Criehaven—at the edge of Penobscot Bay. Even as late as 1960, there were 1,500 sheep pastured on Maine islands, according to a state agricultural department estimate.

When the great ranges opened up out West, and sheep vied with cattle (as well as sheep men with cattlemen), the science of range ecology developed. It determined, among other things, what came to be called the carrying capacity of the range; that is, how many animals of any sort can be grazed on a given piece of land without running it downhill and making it less able to support similar numbers in the future.

Along the Maine coast, as mentioned earlier, one of the management practices of early farmers was to burn islands periodically, since fires were known to stimulate new green growth. This practice, while practical and useful in some situations, usually has deleterious effects on island soils. In general, islands are not possessed of deep, loamy soils to begin with, and the cycles of burning and grazing gradually impaired their status over the course of a few generations.

The problem is chiefly related to nitrogen. Nitrogen, which is one of the most necessary but limited nutrients for plant and animal growth, is bound in soils mostly in organic compounds, which are released slowly to plant roots. The effect of burning is to oxidize the nitrogen, to produce nitrates—still one of the main commercial fertilizers. But nitrates are soluble in water, and while some of the fire-produced nitrate stays around to give a flush of new growth to undamaged roots, the greater amount of it, particularly on islands where rainfall and fog drip create high annual precipitation, is exported from the ecosystem. It leaches off the island into the Gulf of Maine, which is all well and good for marine growth but detrimental to island plant growth. The baldness and boniness of many islands today date from a period of burning sheep pastures over for a poor man's fertilizer.

The one situation in which the practice of burning seems to have been mitigated is on grassy islands that are also seabird nesting islands. On these islands the effects of the seabird excretions may have offset the loss of nitrogen in burning. Or at least the effects are less obvious, even to a practiced eye. Metinic Island in Penobscot Bay has had a herd of sheep on it continuously for 200 years, and, as the old expression goes, you cannot argue with success.

One of the other considerations about the mutual interdependence of sheep and birds has to do with the more subtle effect that sheep are likely to have on island ranges. They feed selectively on certain delicate species of island flora and can build up a tough grass-dominated turf that burrow-dwelling seabirds are unable to excavate. The rare Leach's storm petrel, which assembles or stages in the offshore waters of Maine and comes in under the cover of darkness to nest on Maine's outer islands, may have been restricted as a result of the "Golden Age of Sheep Raising." No one seems to know for sure.

Late 20th Century Island Farming and Forestry
Two Cases: "Ram" and Monhegan Islands

Nowhere are the dilemmas of how Maine's islands should be used more indicative of the state of environmental politics in the late 20th century than the discussion concerning proposals to reintroduce farming and forestry practices to two utterly different islands. One is a 60-acre uninhabited inshore island in Merchant Row south of Stonington. To preserve its anonymity, let's call it Ram Island. Monhegan is a large offshore island at the entrance to Muscongus Bay with a small year-round population of fishermen and a large summer artists' community. A pair of Stonington lobstermen want to graze a flock of sheep on the extensive meadows system of Ram Island, and some of the year-round residents of Monhegan would like to harvest some of the island's trees for firewood. These two islands seem to lie somewhere near the intersection of Nature and Philosophy.

Ram Island was settled at the end of the French and Indian Wars in 1760, and over the next century and a half, two-thirds of the island was cleared to become one of the most lovely and productive farms on the Maine coast. The Ram Island farm raised sheep, hay, and potatoes for the eastern market and supported three island families until around the turn of the 20th century. Even after the Ram Islanders moved onto the mainland, where schools were available and life not so isolated, sheep continued to graze in the meadows.

In 1972 Ram Island was donated to The Nature Conservancy, a private, nonprofit conservation organization established in 1948 to preserve examples of undisturbed ecosystems in an effort to protect plant and animal gene pools and generally maintain "biotic diversity." Since its establishment, The Nature Conservancy has come to own, either through donation or outright purchase, more than two million acres of ecologically significant land. It is widely considered to be the nation's leading land-protection organization. Like all national organizations, they have national policies, and one of these prohibits the grazing of domestic livestock on their preserves—and particularly on island preserves, which are considered to be more ecologically sensitive and fragile than any others they manage.

In the short time that The Nature Conservancy has owned Ram Island, the inevitable natural processes of reforestation have begun to encroach on the meadow system. The fields, which had been cleared by generations of human effort and maintained by countless more generations of island sheep, are beginning to revert to forest. If Nature is allowed to take her course, which is the general philosophical predisposition of The Nature Conservancy, there is no dispute about what will happen: within 15 years the meadows will have disappeared and will be replaced by a dense forest of young "cat" spruce, which will be all but impenetrable another 50 years later.

It is not surprising that the passing of this island's meadow system was not enthusiastically received by those members of The Nature Conservancy who at some time had stood near the top of the island and been able to survey, in one panoramic sweep, the view south to the church steeple on Isle au Haut and the outlook back across the Thorofare beyond the rusted granite derricks on Crotch Island, to Stonington. Although most Conservancy members are not professional ecologists, the idea of replacing 40 acres of open meadows interspersed with small conifer copses with an equal acreage of impenetrable cat spruce—especially when there are plenty of forested islands already preserved—somehow seemed wrong. They wondered what The Nature Conservancy was trying to protect: a unique man-made meadow or a typical spruce forest 100 years hence.

At the intersection of this dilemma, The Nature Conservancy decided to compromise. They would build a long fence from tideline to tideline across Ram Island and allow sheep to graze on one side to keep the meadows open and let nature take her headlong course on the other. Side by side, Nature and Philosophy will grow up, separated by thin galvanized wire, to show us what might be learned about forest and field and sheep and humans.

By all accounts, Monhegan is one of the oldest continuously inhabited pieces of land in America. At least two decades before Plymouth Colony was established, and several years before Jamestown was founded, Europeans of cloudy origin had established a fishing and trading station on Monhegan. For the next three centuries the population of this outer island rose and fell with the cycles of abundant winter groundfish and the hostilities between the inhabitants and the French, the Indians, and the British. When the hundreds of years of warfare had subsided, and the fish were still plentiful, Monhegan supported a year-round population of 145.

When the inshore groundfishery was exhausted, Monhegan's population began to decrease. During the 1940s, most of the island was purchased by the son of Thomas A. Edison and turned into a land trust. Beyond the edge of town, the outlying lands are today largely forested, and no trees can be cut unless they are obstructing a fire lane or a foot path through the woods.

It seems that nearly a century's worth of land-protection efforts on Monhegan would have helped create a complex and varied forest something like that described by both Rosier and Captain John Smith over 3½ centuries ago. But such is not the case. Nearly a hundred acres of Monhegan lie prostrate—an enormous jungle of twisted trunks blown down during the frequent windstorms that hit the island. It's all part of the natural processes that have been shaping island forests since they appeared at the end of the glacial epoch. But several centuries of exploitation of the island have left a forest quite different from the one described by the early explorers.

Monhegan's forest not only is dominated by a single tree species—spruce—but it is spruce of a single age class dating from the period when the sheep pastures that were abandoned around the turn of the century reverted to forest. There is every reason to believe that the original forest, aside from having an admixture of hardwoods, was composed of trees of many different age classes. When the older trees in such an *uneven-aged forest* fall victim to the agents of wind, disease, or old age, established trees of the younger age classes increase their crown and root growth to occupy the space vacated by the fallen monarchs. Uneven-aged forests are not only more stable, they are more aesthetically pleasing, because only a few trees per acre fall out of the overstory in any given year.

The trees in *even-aged forests,* on the other hand, reach an over-mature condition nearly simultaneously and are vulnerable to disturbances that level the forest all at once. Even though a new forest will replace the fallen one, it will also be even-aged, and it will remain so until the procession of the centuries changes the outline of the forests and ever so gradually replaces one part of the woods with trees of many different age classes.

Technical discussions aside, almost everyone who has taken a walk through an uneven-aged forest feels more comfortable. Not only is it more stable, it tends to be more aesthetically pleasing. For one thing, the walking is usually easier, since there is unlikely to be a tangle of wind-thrown trees and large, dense thickets. Monhegan is so exposed to the storm winds that slam into the island off the vast expanse of the Gulf of Maine that portions of her forest will always be young and even-aged. But there are enough protected sites within the forested interior to create impressive uneven-aged aggregations.

To think of Monhegan's forest as a wilderness, or even a wilderness in the making, misses the point. Its composition in the future will be greatly dependent on what happened in the past. If the objective of the land trust is to create a forest approximating the composition, structure, and condition of the original forest, more creative and energetic efforts will be necessary to redress some of the abuses of the past. These might include planting hardwood species mentioned in the early accounts of the vegetation, as well as selective removal of trees on some sites, to reduce the appalling fire danger, to re-create the uneven-aged forest on protected sites, and, incidentally, to generate a modest supply of firewood.

It's all well and good to let Nature take her course when she has never been disturbed by heavy hands in the past. But where offenses have been committed, even unknowingly, it's useless to suppose that they are quickly forgotten and that the original order will soon, if ever, be reestablished. Forests, and especially island forests, need to be courted carefully and kindly or they will continue to remain, like Monhegan's, tired and abused.

5

Birds of the Islands: Mews, Medricks, Hawks and Hernshaws

> The civilized people have lost the aptitude of stillness, and must take lessons in silence from the wild before they are accepted by it. The art of moving gently, without suddenness, is the first to be studied by the hunter, and more so by the hunter with the camera. Hunters cannot have their own way, they must fall in with the wind, and the colors and smells of the landscape, and they must make the tempo of the ensemble their own. Sometimes it repeats a movement over and over again, and they must follow up with it.
>
> Isak Dinesen, *Out of Africa*

WHY BIRDS? It's really quite simple: for all of the short island spring and long island summer, birds are It. To appreciate anything about the coast or the islands, you must take some time from what you are doing to observe the habits and behavior of birds. You'll be glad you did. This may sound categorical, but they are simply everywhere, doing everything. Birds aloft on wings or alight on water; birds beating their way north or south, soaring on silent feathers; wheeling in brilliant bursts of life, in tiny beating hearts, in huge wingspans; hatching out of grass- and down-lined nests or in craggy barren aeries: flying, dying, dancing, fishing, fighting, excreting, singing, mating, nesting, and making a living everyday all around you. There are few places on earth where the air is invested with such a palpable force of life. Most of us spend the greater part of our lives behind façades of glass and concrete, one step removed from the cycles of birth and death, which for creatures of the wild can be neither postponed nor avoided. For us, the creatures who walk upright, it is different.

One day—perhaps it is a doctor who breaks the news—we are given notice that we too are just another intricately designed, infinitely articulated machine to produce phosphates and free nitrogen. It always comes as a shock, but it needn't if we are attendant to the lessons of the wild. On the Maine coast, this instruction is provided tirelessly, day in and out; the price of admission is perhaps one pair of binoculars, until—well, until you have made the tempo of the ensemble your own—and even these become unnecessary encumbrances.

Like us and unlike most of the other species of mammals to whom we are more closely related, birds are diurnal, visual, and auditory. We find we share many of the same habits. Most mammals are nocturnal and olfactory. They leave scents for calling cards, rather than communicate through sight and sound. On the whole they are garbed in dark, drab colors and slink about by night. From the great number of these, our vague relations, we are estranged, probably an embarrassment to those whom we can neither smell nor track. Birds, on the other hand, are, occasionally, incomparably beautiful singers. I know of no one who can carry a tune, and many a one who cannot, who is not deeply touched by the liquid evening song of a thrush.

Several million pairs of birds nest on some 500 islands between Kittery and Eastport, Maine. Islands have always been their refuge: tiny pieces of rock, spruce, and turf where they rest, reproduce, raise their young, and return year after year to the edge of the bountiful, ever-giving sea. On the whole, through the efforts of many who have worked tirelessly for the last half century, the birds on the Maine coast are in good shape: there are as many as there ever were, and they are mostly well treated.

However, such was not always the case. Toward the close of the last century, during the period of the highest human populations on islands, populations of birds reached all-time lows—not just along the Maine coast, but throughout the East, as they became a source of everything from food to feathers and oil to eggs. Before the worst of the abuses were checked, several species were driven to extinction. These are gone forever, and our lives are poorer for it. Several others that used to nest there were hunted too remorselessly and no longer find the shores and islands of Maine to their liking—although they persist elsewhere. The greatest numbers, however, have recovered their original territory and populations, with only a few deleterious side effects. It could have been much worse, and for most of the rest of the coast from Massachusetts to Florida, it *was* much worse.

Indian Uses of Birds

The mainstays in the diets of Indian tribes who came to the Maine islands each spring were fish and fowl. Rosier describes the remnants of an Indian encampment on the shores of Allen Island in Muscongus Bay—where "fire

Island birds depend on different species of fish which they capture in a variety
of ways. Those which locate prey from the air must compensate
visually for the refraction of light in water. Clockwise from left: tern, gannet, gull,
cormorant and puffin. *Kate Fitzgerald*

had been made; and about the place were very great egg shells." The importance of birds to the Indians has already been alluded to in the previous chapter—in the serious matter of the burning of Large Green Island by an early Matinicus fisherman.

The Indians appear to have been concerned about the management of the bird resource. There is a record of an annual meeting held by Sagamores and Sachems one spring near Yarmouth to decide on which nesting islands in Casco Bay each group would concentrate their hunting. They would return to a given colony only once every three years.

Josselyn described how the Indians around Saco Bay harvested the cormorant (which he referred to as a shape or a shark). "Though I cannot commend them to our curious palates, the Indians will eat them when they are flayed. They roost in the night upon some rock that lies out in the sea; thither the Indian goes in his birch canoe when the moon shines clear." The Indian then quickly dispatched "the watchman," whereupon he was able, by "walking softly [to] take them as he pleaseth, still wringing off their heads; when he hath slain as many as his canoe can carry he gives a shout which awakens the surviving Cormorants, who are gone in an instant."

This remarkable description of Indian seabird hunting techniques compares closely with the methods employed for 600 years on the Outer Hebridean island of St. Kilda, the only European community that lived exclusively on the meat and eggs provided by the cliff-nesting concentrations of gannets, murres, puffins, and guillemots. An account from the 17th century describes the islanders' fowling methods:

> If the sentinel be awake at the approach of the creeping fowlers and hear a noise, it cries softly "grog, grog" at which the flock move not; but if this sentinel see the fowler approaching, it cries quickly, "bir, bir" which would seem to import danger, since immediately after, all the tribe take wing, leaving the fowler empty on the rock.

With the St. Kildans, as with the coastal Indians, if the seabird sentinel could be killed, it was comparatively easy to go through the remainder of the sleeping birds to collect a good store.

Fishermen and Birds: "As If They Had Been Stones"

Seabirds represented an important source of protein for the European fishermen and explorers, who often were suffering from scurvy by the time they made a landfall on this side of the Atlantic. Jacques Cartier described the harvest of the hapless and flightless great auk from Funk Island off the coast of Nova Scotia:

> We came to the Island of the Birds which was environed about with a bank of ice, but broken and crackt, whereof there is such plenty that un-

Otter Island cormorant nests, Penobscot Bay.   *Jim Kosinski*

less a man did see them, we would think it an incredible thing . . . they seemed to have been brought thither and sowed for the nonce. In less than two hours we filled two boats full of them as if they had been stones.

On the Maine coast the distribution and abundance of seabirds has more often been determined by the attitudes and habits and hunger of fishermen than by any other group. Good fishermen are nothing more than marine ecologists, just as prosperous farmers must be careful terrestrial ecologists. To catch fish, a captain must know where the seasonal concentrations of various species are likely to be at a given state of the tide, what they feed on, and how they migrate. But there is an important distinction to be drawn between the population dynamics of any commercially exploited species of fish and the birds that often feed on them. Food chains in the sea tend to be longer than on land, which is another way of saying that competition is intense in the relatively stable marine environment. It is a matter of eat-or-be-eaten. Most species of fish have developed the strategy of prolific reproduction to cope with the high mortality rates due to heavy predation. A gravid female cod will lay about two million eggs, which might produce two or three mature adults. Most fishermen, like other predators of finfish, gear up to exploit temporary concentrations of marine life, and even if 99 percent of a school of fish are caught, the reproductive potential of the remainder is enough to replace their losses.

When fishermen transfer sensible marine-oriented strategies to terrestrial systems, the results are often disastrous. The temporary concentrations of seabirds on their nesting grounds, for instance, are nothing like the fish in the sea in terms of their reproductive potential, and to harvest them as if they were fish results in serious and often irreparable damage—which is precisely what happened when bird management was one of the many sideline activities of Maine island fishermen.

Every visitor to the Maine coast who recorded his observations remarked on the concentrations of waterfowl and seabirds. Birds were one of the important reasons that the idea of permanent settlements could even be seriously entertained along the cold northern New England shoreline. Perhaps part of the attraction lay in the fact that hunting in England was a privilege restricted to the King and his attendants; one of the first colonial laws passed in the New World was the 1641 ordinance giving everyone the rights to "clamming and fowling."

Unlike fish, all birds apparently were considered edible. One colonist in the mid-19th century wrote: "There is nothing that swims the water, flies the air, crawls or walks the earth that I· have not served upon my table." He then goes on to describe the meals he has made of boiled owls and roasted crows. The directions for roast puffin were to slit the carcass down the back, open it flat like a kipper, then prop it upright on the hearth and grill it in front of the fire.

Seabirds were taken by shooting (which was expensive and inaccurate and inefficient before the percussion cap gun came into wide use) and by netting and driving. Netting seabirds involved setting stakes in the mud of a cove frequented by waterfowl and stretching a net between them to entangle diving birds as they swam away.

Without a doubt, the most devastating means of procuring eiders for the table, for the market, or for their feathers was through a "drive." Unlike most seabirds, which shed their feathers one by one to replace the worn-out flight suit, eiders molt, or shed, their feathers all at once. There is a period, usually toward the end of August, when they are flightless and raft up in extraordinary concentrations. When this occurred, a great number of boats would assemble from island and coastal settlements and station themselves so that the birds could be driven up on shore. Duck Harbor, on the southwest coast of Isle au Haut, was one of the places selected for such drives, since it is narrow at the mouth and extends a half mile into the land. Hosmer wrote that the drives would begin in Upper Penobscot Bay near Eagle Island, from where the flightless ducks would be driven south, "narrowing the flock. When the fowls reached shore they were taken and killed and everyone engaged could have all he needed."

A single drive on Vinalhaven took 2,100 birds, very close to the entire production of eiders for the West Bay that year. After the 1790s the drives became less and less successful as the eider population declined.

Fishermen at Gunning Rocks.   *Nineteenth century engraving*

Apart from the meat that the ducks provided, which could either be salted down or sent straightaway to market, feathers were an important commodity. Eider down, as well as the wing and tail coverts of geese, swans, and winter ducks, brought a ready market in the city for quilts and bedding. The bird world produces no better natural insulator than eider down, which fetched a premium price, but other species were hunted and sold as well. Charles Eliot's biography of the John Gilley family of Baker Island south of Mount Desert gives a good description of colonial island occupations. One winter Gilley's sons sold a hundredweight of feathers from winter sea ducks. It took six to eight duck skins for a pound of feathers, which gives an idea of the intensity of the hunting pressure placed on the ducks.

The other serious colonial pressure on the bird populations came from "egging," probably a harmless-enough activity when island populations were small, but more and more damaging when everyone got into the act. Islanders would row out to one of various Egg Rocks in the early spring after the birds had begun to nest. They were careful to take a bucket of fresh water, which would determine how far along toward hatching the herring gull, eider, or cormorant eggs were. If they floated, they had been incubated too long and were returned to the nest; if they sank, they were fresh enough to be sold and were taken back by the party. Farther east, the Halifax Eggers harvested 750,000 murre eggs in a single season—not what one could describe as a sustained-yield basis.

It is difficult to get an accurate description of how fast bird popula-

Herring gull eggs.   *Rick Perry*

tions declined along the coast of Maine. It was probably connected to the
increase in island populations, which accelerated rapidly until approximately 1830, leveled off, and hit a new peak with the beginning of the
labor-intensive quarrying era in the 1880s.

One glimpse into the state of affairs in the early part of the 19th century relates to what did *not* happen. John James Audubon, the aspiring
American ornithologist, had been traveling around the country collecting specimens for his exquisite eye to paint. After nearly a year in the
South, culminating in several feverish months of collecting and painting in
the Florida Keys and Everglades, Audubon returned to his wife, Lucy, in
Philadelphia and quickly planned another collecting trip. This time he
wanted to go north.

Audubon left Boston on August 14, 1832, aboard a steamer for Portland, intending to continue up into the Bay of Fundy. A week later he
wrote back from Eastport that, "Birds are very, very few and far between."
The next May Audubon returned, sailing down the prevailing wind for
Eastport again, where he arrived after a three-day passage. He chartered a
cutter and prepared an expedition, not to Maine waters but to the Canadian waters eastward. Among the islands off Grand Manan Island, Audubon searched hard for gulls. For gulls! It is obvious that in 1833 the Maine
coast was not what it is today. Today, an early May expedition would expect to sight, almost anywhere east of Cape Elizabeth, not just two or
three species of gulls, but terns, cormorants, eiders, guillemots, herons,
ospreys in great concentrations, and, with a little local knowledge, even
petrels, razorbills, and puffins, and perhaps an eagle. For several of these

species, Audubon had to go all the way to the desolate Labrador coast to find specimens to draw.

There are between 8,600 and 9,000 species of birds in the world, depending on how many subspecies you recognize. In the old days of taxonomic study, birds came in so many intermediate sizes, shapes, and colors that divisions developed between the "lumpers" and the "splitters"—those who combined as many birds as possible into one species and those who saw a new species in every color variation of wing or tail covert. Aside from the obvious humor of the situation, which has filtered down in diluted form to the present day among some ornithologists, it shows how dynamic, mutable, and rapid the process of evolution actually is. If we choose to look, species in the wild right now are being isolated from the rest of the members of the race with whom they share some genes, an isolation that, if complete enough, will produce over the course of many generations the expression of random non-lethal mutations—bona fide new species, regardless of whether you are a lumper or a splitter.

One easy way to understand the daily behavior of the birds of the islands of Maine is to consider their evolutionary relationship to each other. There are, to be sure, other ways to look at them. You could consider the birds that exploit similar prey species, or that look alike or that live together in the same habitat. But you would be missing a lot of the more subtle relationships between bird species of the islands. Besides, an evolutionary approach considers first those species that are represented earliest in the fossil record. It's another way of appreciating your elders.

Tube-Nosed Swimmers, Procellariiformes

The tube-noses, or albatrosses as they are more commonly known, belong to an ancient order of birds known in the fossil record as far back as 40 million years ago. They are all strictly pelagic—that is, oceanic—birds. To this

Tube-nosed greater shearwater.
Kate Fitzgerald

group belong the largest living species of bird in the world, the wandering albatross, whose awesome 12-foot wingspan far exceeds that of the next nearest competitor, as well as the smallest of seabirds, the swallow-sized petrels, who are seasonal residents of Maine's outer islands. This order of seabirds is distinguished by the hollow tube mounted on the top of the bill that functions, depending on which wholly unsatisfactory explanation you believe, as a means of excreting salt, of locating oily matter on which they feed, or as a directional wind sensor that allows them to sleep on the wing while riding out gales.

LEACH'S STORM PETREL, *Oceanodroma Leucorhoa*

If numbers were the only measure of such things, the Leach's storm petrel would be called both common and abundant in Maine. Though it nests in large colonies numbering in the thousands, it is rightly considered a rare species. Few people have ever seen this secretive and wholly delightful small seabird, which dances during the day like a butterfly over the sea's surface with its wings held aloft, while feeding on all matter of floating bits of marine life. To mariners of all sorts, pelagic birds are forever a source of mystery and revelation. How do they weather the fierce gales that can rip a vessel to open shreds, where do they rest when the sea gives no quarter, what do they eat in the huge, awful expanse of lifeless water far off the coasts?

In the Gulf of Maine these small petrels, no bigger than a robin, stage in the gathering darkness in unknown waters offshore and arrive under the cover of darkness on perhaps no more than a dozen barren lumps of rock at the outer fringes of the Maine archipelago. Here, after exuberant night-time mating flights, they crawl into a rocky crevice or perhaps a burrow they have excavated in the soft peat to lay and incubate eggs and raise a single, fat, downy chick. But there's much more drama and mystery to the lives of these grey and unassuming birds than this description suggests. First, they are nocturnal on their breeding grounds because they are altogether too easy prey for greedy gulls during the daylight hours. As many a gull pellet of tattered grey feathers and a pair of protruding webbed feet gives evidence, the life of a petrel can be quickly and wholly circumscribed by a single swallow of a great black-backed gull. Even moonlit nights are dangerous, as gulls are sharp-eyed hosts waiting, waiting for the dinner guests to arrive. Island nesting refuges are few and far enough between that mortal enemies must share the ground and pay the price.

But on dark nights, when the moon has set early or risen late or is new and therefore altogether faceless, it is a wholly different world for petrels on their remote breeding grounds. The air is suddenly filled with the sound of whirring flight as the petrels arrive from nowhere to relieve their mates in the burrows. Wings whirring in dark air. And then the songs. Like nothing you have ever heard. It is a low, faintly musical sound that moves by in waves, in winged waves, and is in a moment answered, at first softly and then with more insistence, maybe relief, from the burrow. The air and the ground become alive with the song of the night-time seabird. In the early part of the season the flights will last for hours in the large colonies, building to a crescendo—an ode to joy.

Surely it is unscientific and suspicious to impart these sounds with human meanings, and yet, in times like these, science fails us. It is true that we can have no idea what a petrel feels, if anything at all, at such ritual reunions. But to a human ear, it has the distinct sound of joy, exaltation, mirth, and a momentary mystic disregard for all the ills of the petrel's world. It is night, mates are together for a while, underground and safe. They have neither become meals for the serious sentry gulls nor fallen victim hundreds of miles away at sea. Tonight all is well.

SHEARWATERS, *Puffinus gravis, P. griseus*

Shearwaters are not common tube-nosed birds among the islands, and they are rarely seen, unless you are in the habit of riding the Bluenose Ferry back and forth to Nova Scotia. They are birds of the outer offshore waters that occasionally stray in near places like Matinicus and Mount Desert Rocks.

If you see a shearwater stray close, chances are it is either a greater shearwater or a sooty shearwater, both of which are most easily identified from their distinctive habit of flying low over the water between wave troughs, almost as if there were a special layer of denser air here that makes their flight more effortless.

They are among the most ambitious of oceanic voyagers, coming north to the Gulf of Maine from May through October to winter. To winter? Shearwaters breed in November and December in the Southern Hemisphere's summer, and they turn the tables on us by coming north to winter during our hemisphere's summer. Seems a little unfair to confound matters so. About 90 percent of the world's entire population of shearwaters breed on one South Atlantic island, Tristan da Cunha, near 60° south latitude. From there they cross the enormous expanse of northern and southern oceans that serves as a migration barrier for the greatest numbers of other birds great and small.

Full-Webbed Swimmers, Pelecaniformes

Among ornithologists, this order of less than fully seagoing birds is chiefly distinguished by their four toes united by a single web. To bird watchers, they are better known for their gaudy throat pouches, called gular sacs. These pouches are most colorfully developed in tropic birds and frigate birds, where they serve not only for transporting fish but also for elaborate sexual displays. Most members of the order have large wings, short legs, and large bills. They are known to be strong flyers, but they are rather ungainly on land.

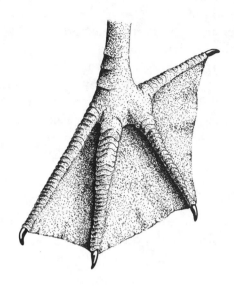

Species of this order have all four toes
joined by a single web.   *Kate Fitzgerald*

DOUBLE-CRESTED CORMORANT, *Phalacrocorax auritus*

It's not easy to like a cormorant unless you overflow with the milk of
human kindness for all living creatures. After all, a bird that was known
since colonial times as a shark, or to fishermen as a shag, for its habit of
pilfering fish weirs, hardly inspires feelings of respect. It's not a matter of
the reasonably small number of fish that cormorants could consume that
would make otherwise reasonable men think nothing of shooting them at
each and every opportunity; it is their habit, when entering a weir, to chase
(or shag) the fish, which breaks up the school and allows the fish, in their
confusion, to find the way out.

The fisherman-sponsored pogrom directed against the cormorant grew
in intensity as coastal fisheries became commercially more important than
the bank fisheries. The fairly detailed descriptions of the period between
1880 and 1925 indicate no records of any cormorants nesting in Maine.
They were simply eliminated as a breeding species for 45 years.

In more recent times the wardens of the U.S. Fish and Wildlife Service
have participated in the vendetta. Salmon smolt are stocked in some of the
estuaries of the state's major rivers in an attempt to augment natural pop-

ulations or reestablish them where they have been driven off by the Long March of civilization. This usually happens during the second week of April—which, as it happens, is when the cormorants descend on Maine, voracious after their long flights north to their nesting grounds. What ensues, as anyone could have predicted, is that the sluggish hatchery-raised smolt are consumed in great numbers until the larger, more desirable alewives arrive, thus angering not only the far-away salmon fishermen, who will come to Vacationland to catch fish and spend money, but also the hatchery personnel, who have taken great pains to raise these temperamental fish. The effort to control Maine's cormorants seems almost timeless; it is at least as old as Indians paddling canoes out to cormorant colonies, or bank fishermen collecting them for bait. For bait, indeed! Surely these large, dark birds are less pestiferous than to be salted in barrels for fish bait. Nowadays, wardens motor out to the various Shag, Pulpit, or Smutty Nose Rocks and have a field day blowing the big birds out of the sky. It's an expensive and time-consuming method of control, but apparently it does not lack for enthusiastic volunteers. One of the wardens, who is head of the Pest Control Division of the Wildlife Service, has been an actor in this drama, although he has no great love of visiting the offshore colonies for the hunt (which never worked anyway, for no matter how many breeders were slain, there seemed always to be enough nonbreeders to take their place immediately). He found that patrolling a short section of the river where the sluggish salmon smolt were dropped was enough to discourage the greatest number of cormorants from their estuarine easy street; he actually became quite fond of the birds, who seemed day by day determined to make his work easier. All he had to do was arrive in the morning towing the same outboard-powered boat behind the same station wagon and the cormorants would take immediate flight and be gone all day. When you think about it, cormorants are a lot harder to dislike.

During most of the season, cormorants feed on the less-desirable sculpin, cunner, and gunnel, which they dive for in waters of less than 30 feet. Of a more primitive stock than other diving birds, cormorants have fewer oil glands to keep their feathers dried, which explains their habit of standing with wings outspread on buoys or ledges as if they are drying out their laundry. They build nests on the most exposed, least desirable pieces of colonial seabird real estate, nesting frequently on the same rocks with gulls, eiders, and guillemots. Occasionally they nest in trees, but their habit of fouling their nests spills over onto the trees and strips them of needles. Many a treeless Maine island has the double-crested cormorant to thank for its green, grassy look, but before the trees fall, arboreal rookeries look like ghost towns in the making.

The cormorant young are born without feathers; in fact, they are covered with reptilian-like scales and have a distinct tailbone protruding from their sterns. They look for all the world like little black lizards until they

Cormorant-killed trees on Nightcap Island, Pleasant Bay. *Jed Horne*

grow a juvenile plumage. Anyone who has doubted the truth of Darwin's theory of evolution should have a closer look at the homely young of the cormorant before insisting that birds are not descended from reptiles.

GANNET, *Morus bassanus*

Gannets are extraordinarily large-bodied, yellow-headed seabirds that nest in great colonies in the waters to the east of Maine. They have probably never nested here, insofar as historical records are concerned, but the young, brownish nonbreeders regularly show up in Maine, quite lost after days of fog have hidden land and sea in a shroud, or after a terrific gale has beaten the coast. Along the outer islands in September and October, the white-feathered adults, not normally gregarious after the breeding season, will occasionally gather in goodly numbers when one of their kind has located fish. The gannet is chiefly noted for folding its wings close into its body and not checking its flight in the least before hitting the water in an enormous, violent splash from 60 to 80 feet overhead. Fortunately, they have evolved adaptations in their breasts to cushion the shock.

Herons and Their Allies, Ciconiiformes

The Ciconiiformes are the long-necked, long-legged wading birds that inhabit every ice-free coast of the world. Their telltale toes are long, slightly

Young cormorants in nest.   *Kate Fitzgerald*

webbed, and arranged three in front and one at the rear. The flight of most wading birds is lumbering and strenuous, but they travel great distances in migration once they get airborne. Almost all of the 114 species belonging to the Ciconiiformes have long and often peculiarly shaped bills that are adapted in some way to persecute finny creatures swimming in shallow waters.

Great Blue Heron, *Ardea herodias*

The great blue heron, measured tip to toe, is the largest bird of the Maine coast, though it relinquishes its primacy to the bald eagle when the measurement is taken wingtip to wingtip. Herons are colonial nesters, which of course does not mean that they have been here since colonial times (though this is also true), but that they are in the habit of nesting in squawking, honking, flapping concentrations of their own kind and their near relatives.

To see a heron take flight or land at the end of a branch that can just barely take its weight, its long legs stabbing about for some purchase or trailing out behind, and its neck curled back between its shoulders, is to be reminded of its antiquity as a species. It would be difficult to think of a common bird of the United States that looks more primitive, that lumbers through the air as if flight were a habit just acquired, or that makes a noise that, if we did not know better, we would associate with the roar of a terrifying flying lizard.

Great blue heron over Mark Island, Penobscot Bay. *Rick Perry*

There are perhaps a half-dozen Maine islands with the name of Heron, and the birds have been part of the coastal scene since the white man arrived—and for a time long before, no doubt, since herons are known in the fossil record for 40 million years. Rosier and Josselyn both mentioned them, calling them "Hernshaws," a more polite name than "shitpoke," which is what fishermen call them. However impolite, it is a good description of the condition of the 20-odd large heronries found on islands between Saco and Machias Bays. The adults build ridiculously small nests of sticks in the tops of trees, where their wings won't be damaged as they fly in and out. They prefer deciduous trees, which are stronger-limbed than the spindle-topped spruces they are often forced to inhabit. It seems likely that the short-term effect of their copious droppings is to fertilize the island forests where they become established in colonies that range from 15 to 200 nests. But the longer-term effect—over, say, a decade—is to kill the leaves and needles of the trees in which they nest, forcing them to evacuate

Great blue heron on roost. *Philip Conkling*

to another island, a process that happens more quickly when they have been nesting in spruces.

Before the feather-seeking milliners arrived on the Maine coast in the 1880s, the population of this large heron was already declining from what appeared to be wanton human vandalism, particularly within mainland colonies, which have all but disappeared. But the decline was also due to the indiscriminate habits of fishermen, who used anything they could get their hands on for bait. By 1850, great blues were already scarce, which helps explain why the plume hunters, who were so relentless in their exploitation of herons and egrets elsewhere, were not even more destructive to Maine colonies.

One of the most remarkable annual bird spectacles is the mating ritual of the great blues. They are somewhat ungainly birds on the ground or on their nests, and really only look majestic either flying ponderously from inshore tidal flat to offshore nesting island or standing motionless in shallow waters before striking their lightninglike necks to catch a fish. But when the mating season comes around, they cast away all pretense of majesty for a dance they perform for the benefit of each other. They alight on the ground in small groups and begin walking around in circles, slowly raising and lowering their wings while an occasional male breaks rank to engage in a mock sword battle with the bill of a rival male. It's all been taking place for eons and will continue to be a secret spectacle as long as their breeding grounds are protected from disturbance—no less real when it results from the interested eyes of bird watchers in tennis shoes, hip boots, or otherwise.

Egrets and Ibises and Other Herons

Many of the ecological habits and much of the history of the great blue heron apply equally well to other members of the wading bird clan. One of the most interesting behavioral adaptations of herons and their allies is what ornithologists call post-breeding dispersion. Most birds raise their young and then, keyed to the changing length of day and night, begin to get restless in late summer. Ducks and geese, as well as cormorants, terns, and some gulls, begin staging in bays and protected waters in anticipation of the day when they will all of a sudden get up and go south. But at the end of the summer, wading birds fly off in all directions to all points of the compass; many fly hundreds of miles north, and the young in particular often pay for this behavior when frozen flats cause starvation. But the advantage of this behavior is the discovery of new breeding habitats by those who go off prospecting.

In recent years the Maine coast has benefited from the dramatic and sudden northward shift of the breeding range of snowy egret and glossy ibis. Before 1970 these birds were rare visitors to the Maine coast, but in 1972 not only did they show up on the islands in Saco Bay, they settled down and raised young in multispecied heronries. In an era when we have become used to the sad litany of human incursions into the number and diversity of wild creatures, it is reassuring to realize that Nature is still quite capable of striking back with a pleasant surprise.

Waterfowl, Anseriformes

The birds we call waterfowl and lump together into a single order are called wildfowl by the British. Both names are an indication of the service they have rendered to mankind. It seems likely that no other group of birds has provided as many meals to as many different societies as the ducks, geese, and swans, which together compose the greatest number of this order's members. These birds were among the first to be domesticated, although the most meritorious service in this regard now rests with the relatives of the Asian guinea fowl, whose chicken descendants make it the most abundant species of bird on earth.

Ducks, geese, swans, and their relatives are semiaquatic birds that are strong divers and flyers, have well-developed oil glands that protect their plumage from becoming waterlogged, and possess for the most part downy feathers for insulation.

COMMON EIDER, *Somateria mollissima*

The eider is the second-most common species of nesting bird of the coastal islands of Maine, after the common herring gull. This is remarkable, since a census of breeding birds on Maine islands in 1904 turned up only four eider adults, and those were only at the extreme eastern end of the coast, on Old Man Island off Cutler. Thirty years later there were still only two dozen nesting pairs. Today, on some 300 to 400 Maine islands, approximately 50,000 eiders pair off to mate in April, and this number does not even include the immature or nonbreeding adults.

Like most other ducks, the male and female eiders are sexually dimorphic, which is an elaborate way of saying that the males are brilliantly colored. Male eiders are a stunning black and white with a faint green crown; the females are uniformly dull brown, presumably a protective coloration, since they do all the incubating on the nesting islands. Once the brief mating period is over in early May, the brightly colored males raft up and hang about the edges of the nesting islands, cooing and moaning at their now totally disinterested mates until they give up, swim off, and form bachelor groups.

The hen eiders eat little during their month-long vigil over the eggs, although on sunny days they occasionally will mound up the down they have earlier plucked from their breasts to line the nest and arrange it quiltlike over the eggs while they take a break. More often than not, the nesting islands chosen by the eiders are inhabited by black-backed and herring gulls. This seems somewhat curious, since the gulls are the most relentless predators of young eider chicks. Nor are the gulls above gorging on the eggs of a temporarily vacated nest. Part of the explanation for the tenuous arrangement is that nesting space is limited, even on the innumerable islands of the Maine coast. It is also true that the aggressive gulls are more effective in driving off other predators, such as crows, mink, and raccoon, which occasionally show up on a nesting island looking for a quick meal. But there is another, more interesting hypothesis that might suggest itself more readily if we did tend to view predation in such monochromatic terms.

The dynamics of the relationship of gulls to eiders is illustrated in dramatic terms during the early weeks of June, when the greatest number of downy eider chicks hatch. Although the four to seven eggs are laid over a period of as long as a week, the sounds or sympathetic vibrations of early-hatching chicks stimulate the whole brood into a feverish attempt to break through their calcium incubators, such that they all will normally emerge

within minutes of each other. Without this synchrony, the losses to predation would not permit many eiders to survive. Within a few hours after the
hatching, the chicks are mobile enough to be shepherded by the hens down
to the water, where they are much safer from the attacks of gulls. The opportunistic gulls are intimately aware that a procession of duck dinners will
be attempting to make its way through the nesting ground. They watch
and wait. The eiders also know this, and a fair number of them use the
cover of darkness to make their way through the gauntlet. With the hen
in the lead and the chicks keeping close behind, constantly peeping and
cheeping, which seems certain to give away their location, the family makes
its way down to the sea. Some 25 percent are lost or stranded in the under-
brush or in the gullets of gulls before the first day of their life is over. In
sheer numbers, the mortality is immense. There are on the order of 25,000
nesting hen eiders in Maine, which together produce something like 100,000
to 150,000 chicks within perhaps a three-week period. It is literally a field
day for the gulls, who will prune these numbers down to between, say,
75,000 and 125,000 chicks within a few days.

Once the chicks and hens have reached the water, the losses are fewer,
since the young are precocious; they can dive and feed themselves from
birth and are afforded protection from the cruising gulls by their response
of disappearing underwater when a shadow passes close by. Gulls can still
pick the unwary young out of the water, and it is in this selection of the
unwary that gulls and eiders seem to coexist for each other's benefit. The
eiders produce enough young to supply part of the diet of the gulls with
whom they share nesting space, and the gulls prevent the least well-
adapted chicks from reaching the age when they might otherwise pass
unfit genes on into the next generation. It's not a very noble or sentimental
arrangement, but it seems to work spectacularly well.

An Invidious Proposal. Eider down is the best insulator that Nature
has yet made known to us, as anyone lucky enough to own a down vest or
sleeping bag will tell you. The feather collectors of the 19th century also
knew this, since eiders fetched the highest price of any duck skins sold for
bedding or quilting. The down that we use primarily for recreational
equipment comes from Iceland and Greenland, where eiders are raised
for this purpose. This is a happy enough circumstance for these distant,
impoverished island communities until you look at the resource-based
economies nearer to home.

Managing the eiders for feathers doesn't involve the killing of any
birds, since the down is collected from new nests, not from live birds. Although it is probably true that collecting down would place the hens under
some increased stress, the stress of buckshot is much more real.

The idea that some of Maine's eiders might support a home-grown island
industry is not likely to impress the Fish and Wildlife Department, which

Down-lined eider nest. *Rick Perry*

is primarily interested in raising ducks for hunters; or Audubon members, for whom there can never be enough birds; or environmentalists, who think that enough of the natural world already serves the rapacious needs of mankind. But the fact of the matter is that eider down is one of the islands' renewable resources, which, if managed wisely, could support a few more island families.

WINTER DUCKS

Maine's nesting eiders start to move south in late September and October, and though some of their species are present in the winter, they are the breeders from farther north. These northern eiders arrive with squadrons of other migratory waterfowl, including Canadian and blue geese, brant, and teal, to name a few. These are birds of passage that are mostly headed for the salt-marsh estuaries of the Massachusetts coast and farther south that have not been filled in by a generation's worth of commercial development of so-called "wasteland."

Along with the passersby come the winter ducks, which will spread themselves out along the protected coastlines of every island shore from Stratton on the west to Old Man on the east. Among other places, they con-

Winter ducks. Left: drake bufflehead; right:
drake old squaw.   *Jamien Morehouse*

gregate around the offshore ledges where the pounding surf loosens the
holds of a variety of marine creatures on which they feed. Goldeneye, buf-
fleheads, scoters, scaup, and old squaw—known to hunters as whistlers,
butterballs, coots, bluehills, and pintails—swim in and about the various
Gunning Rocks from October to April.

Of all the winter ducks that have been residents of the coast during
the bitter months, none is more rare and beautiful than the harlequin duck,
which inhabits one of the most violent ecological niches of the bird kingdom. The incomparably colored and appropriately named harlequin feeds
on the small crustaceans and marine snails kicked up by violent surf breaking on a half-tide ledge. For the last 80 years at least, these uncommon
northern ducks have been arriving and wintering off the Brandies and
Roaring Bull Ledges surrounding Isle au Haut. Locally they are called
squeakers and are in the habit of scurrying in the "gutters" or guzzles
formed just in front of a breaking wave, and reappearing in its train. One
19th century hunter remarked that he had collected no other species that
showed more mended broken bones than the harlequin duck. Bless their
turbulent souls.

Birds of Prey, Falconiformes

One of the inexplicable distinguishing features of birds of prey, the order
to which hawks, eagles, and falcons belong, is that the females are all larger
than the males. There are many possible explanations for the adaptive advantages this arrangement might convey, but none of them are quite able
to explain why a larger female body size hasn't arisen in any other orders
of birds. Aside from matriarchal predominance of body size, birds of prey
are also distinguished by their diurnal habits, keen vision, sharp talons, opposable hind toe (useful for grasping prey), and a strongly hooked bill. Up
close, the bills look imposing and threatening, but they are less lethal than

Osprey talon with opposable hind toe.
Kate Fitzgerald

the talons, which are strong enough in the eagle, for instance, to break a human neck—not that this has ever happened.

NORTHERN BALD EAGLE, *Haliaeetus leucocephalus*

In 1979 there were 48 nesting pairs of eagles in Maine, a pathetically small number, except that their numbers are greater here than in any other state east of Mississippi (with the possible exception of Virginia and Maryland, whose eagles move back and forth across state lines often enough to confuse the issue). Two-thirds of Maine's eagles nest on the coast rather than on the large inland lakes, and most of the coastal population maintain their aeries on islands where they are less likely to be disturbed.

Estimates of precolonial eagle numbers vary, but it is likely that there were perhaps 400 or 500 pairs before the Europeans arrived. Josselyn reported that in 1668 a great shoal of eels was stranded in upper Casco Bay, and that an "infinite number of Gripes (eagles) . . . thither resorted insomuch that, being shot by the inhabitants, they fed their hogs with them for some weeks."

Sheepmen throughout the world consistently have a dim view of eagles, national bird or no, and by the mid-1800s the great increase in the flocks of island sheep could only mean trouble for eagles, which have an appetite for dead, dying, small, and newborn lambs. In 1806 the town meeting on Vinalhaven placed a bounty of 20 cents on eagles.

By the 1830s eagles were all but gone from Casco Bay, where one naturalist had a few years earlier described being surrounded by a flight of 13 of them as he climbed a nest tree on Peaks Island. In the early 1800s there were 15 occupied nests on the Kennebec River below Bath, but they were gone by 1908. By the 1940s the population for the entire state was estimated at 60 pairs, and the numbers have steadily declined since then. If the decline has been slower than for other persecuted species, it is because eagles live 25 to 40 years in the wild, but it seems clear that for the past 25 years, though protected by law, they have not been reproducing at a rate sufficient to offset the annual mortality.

Because eagles, like humans, eat at the top of a food chain, they tend to concentrate environmental poisons that have been introduced in trace

Immature bald eagle.   *Philip Conkling*

amounts to their food supplies. In the 19th century, island sheepmen realized that a measure of eagle population control could be accomplished by
lacing the carcasses of dead animals with strychnine. In the latter part of
the present century, eagles have suffered from the introduction of persistent
pesticides into food chains that, in the case of DDT, interfere with their
calcium metabolism such that in the worst cases, eggs are laid in jellylike
masses. As DDT has begun to decline in tissue samples, polychlorinated bi-
phenyls, known as PCBs, have begun to show up in alarming concentrations
in the bodies of dead eagles.

The purpose of describing the sad state of affairs regarding our national bird is not to repeat the points made better elsewhere concerning
the progressive pollution of our environment, but to point out that Maine's
eagles have been intently persecuted for upwards of a century and a half,
and that we now find, ironically, though it is our intention to protect what
we had earlier neglected, it is not going to be an easy task. In 1970 there
were still five or six nests left along the Kennebec River, and a progressively
greater representation at least of this largest of birds of prey in the coastal
waters eastward. A decade later, the westernmost concentration of breeding
pairs is found in and around Mount Desert Island. Quite aside from the
chronic physiological stress attendant upon a contaminated food supply,
eagles don't like to live near us, even though we like to live near them. Unless they make some astounding evolutionary accommodation in the immediate future, it is likely that Canada will become the sanctuary for
America's national bird.

In the bays where this rugged bird of prey still maintains a nest, and suffers our human curiosity in silence, spectacles of their strength and majesty will present themselves. One pair has taken up a nest in a heronry in Narraguagus Bay, which must present all sorts of uneasy dilemmas for the great blues, whose defenseless and ungainly young are almost too easy a target for the pair of eagles that stare at them daily out of unsentimental eyes. Because the eagles maintain an awesome presence there, scavenging gulls, crows, ravens, and their kind are less likely to cause mischief, but the herons apparently pay for this protection, if the picked bones of young heron found in the eagle nest are any indication. This almost sounds like the custom of sacrificing virgins to propitiate the hungry gods.

Eagles return to one of several nests they have built within a limited territory and construct a new floor of sticks cemented together with guano. Over the course of years, these nests can assume enormous dimensions, as one energetic ornithologist discovered by weighing a nest that had finally broken the branches that had held it up. It weighed more than a ton.

The adults start breeding even before winter is fully over in March. The young hatch often as early as April and are fed by the adults into July, when one day the free ride is over. Huge, fat nestlings begin gradually to lose weight. Before the feeding stops, the unfledged young are larger than the adults. Driven to the edge by hunger, they must one day launch themselves into the thin ether or starve. Many of the eagles will stay together in loose family groups into the winter, searching far and wide for food, but returning to favorite trees to roost for the night. In their search they learn what is worth the price of hunger. A friend once came upon a dark brown immature eagle that had discovered a great black-backed gull along the shore with a broken wing. The eagle dropped out of the sky, but there was no deft ending. A slow, violent, agonized, and brutal struggle ensued. She did not stay to watch.

AMERICAN OSPREY, *Pandion haliaetus*

Perhaps no other bird is so characteristic of the Maine coast as the osprey, whose numbers, unlike those of the eagles, have recently increased after their bout with DDT. Ospreys inhabit every continent of the world except Antarctica and nest up and down the East Coast. But somehow their brilliant brown and white plumage and harsh *kree-kree-kree* cry is a more appropriate addition to the dark contours of a spruce-lined cove. Captain John Smith thought so when he visited these rocky isles 3½ centuries ago: "Yet you shall see the wild hawks [who] give pleasure in seeing them stoop 6 or 7 after one another, at the schools of fish in the fair harbors."

Although the osprey is large, it is not exceptionally strong for a hawk. Most of the time they have no particular need for strength, since they feed on relatively small fish, which they catch by dropping out of the sky and into the water feet first. However, eagles are in the habit of intercepting

Adult osprey returning to nest.   *Kate Fitzgerald*

these slightly smaller cousins returning with a fish to share with mate or young. When this happens there is no contest: eagles win, wings down.

Ospreys have never been persecuted to the same extent as eagles. To most fishermen, it is bad luck to kill an osprey that has to make a living in the same unpredictable way. During the quarrying years, however, the superstition from which ospreys had benefited did not deter the coast's new immigrants. The late Arthur Norton, founder and curator of the Portland Museum of Natural History, reports that after Hurricane Island Granite Company fell on hard times in 1890, nine of the 12 pairs of ospreys nesting across Hurricane Sound on Green Island were shot by unemployed quarrymen "whose primitive conception of hunting was abetted by an abundance of cheap fowling pieces and ammunition."

Most of Maine's ospreys migrate to Central and South America for the winter and return to this rocky coast during the first week of April. Either they reoccupy the same nest used in previous years, or—if winter gales have wreaked havoc on their platforms of sticks, potwarp, and seaweed—they begin anew. Most build nests in the tops of shoreside spruce, but some birds appear to prefer nesting on the ground. One population of eight or 10 pairs in northern Penobscot Bay nests exclusively on inaccessible rocky shores. This population, which has increased over the past decade, occupies needle-shaped ledges characteristic of the volcanic rocks of the northern end of the bay. A good number of these ground-nesting pairs are no doubt related to untold generations of the ospreys who for a century and a quarter occupied a nest on a ledge at the entrance to Pulpit Harbor on North Haven. Since 1975, however, this nest has been abandoned, and we have had to make do with the story rather than the reality of the persistence of Pulpit Harbor osprey.

OTHER HAWKS AND FALCONS

The coastal islands of Maine form an important part of the flyway for northern-nesting hawks. The fall migration is more spectacular than the spring arrival, since hawk and falcon movements are closely tied to changes in the weather. When the wind veers into the northwest after a September gale, cold, clear air pours in over the ribbon of land and water, bringing high pressure, which means flying time. Suddenly every variety of winged creatures seems to be slicing southwest, and the hawks are close behind to pick up the pieces. The soaring hawks, such as the red-tailed hawk and the broad-winged hawk, avoid the islands and the water in between, but the accipiters, the mid-sized Cooper's hawk and the smaller sharp-shinned hawk, will fly by your head all day if you stand on a high hill where the wind rises up and over. During the fall migration of the accipiters (low-flyers), no other species of bird is as self-sacrificing as the ponderous, ant-eating flicker. Small piles of yellow-shafted flight feathers mark the spots here and there along the islands where they have become fuel for hawks flying farther south.

Along the outer rim of the islands, if you have sharp eyes and sit still, it is possible to see merlins, magical falcons that stoop to conquer the slow of wit and wing. In an earlier era the merlins would have been accompanied by a smaller number of peregrines, the fastest bird on wings, which is known to dive out of the sky at speeds approaching 200 m.p.h. If you are young enough, it is possible that you will live to see their shadow darken your retina for an instant, since their numbers are increasing along the islands where they used to nest.

Gulls, Terns, Auks, and Shorebirds, Charadriiformes

It is maybe a little unfair to put shorebirds at the end of the list of birds that make up the order Charadriiformes, since they account for most of its species. But a great many of the shorebirds—the plovers and sandpipers that nest on the wide expanse of Arctic tundra—fly directly across the mouth of the Gulf of Maine on north–south trips and are most typical on the vast mudflats fringing Cape Cod and the embayments farther south. Maine gets a fair representation of turnstone, dunlin, curlew, willet, and godwit flocks —to mention a few of the larger shorebirds—but along our coast they are on the move, toward either their northerly breeding grounds or sandy southern beaches. When they stop on a half-tide ledge or an indented muddy cove, it is often just for a quick periwinkle and go.

Gulls, terns, and auks, on the other hand, are more comfortable in and around Maine waters and have been associated with the Gulf of Maine in mariners' minds ever since the first Biscay shallop whitened the horizon. These birds are divided into two families, the laridae and the alcidae, or alcids. They are colonial breeders, which means their reproductive hormonal balance is synced to a group critical mass; they don't really get into the mood to pair, mate, and incubate until the air is full of their darting shapes.

GREAT BLACK-BACKED GULL, *Larus marinus*

The black-backed gull is the largest member of its family in the world. Though now an archetypal feature of the Maine coast, this gull is a comparatively recent addition to the state's register of breeding birds. The greatest concentrations of black-backs are found in Arctic waters, along the barren coast of southern Labrador. In Maine the first 20th century breeding records of this huge black and white bird are from the early 1930s, and it was not until another 15 years later that their density among the nesting islands had reached a large enough number to enable them to extend their breeding range rapidly into all Maine bays. It is one of the most surprising and rapid range extensions recorded in this century.

The black-backed gulls nest in mixed colonies with herring gulls, cormorants, and a variety of other seabirds, but they always command the highest ground on an island. They are generally not as gregarious as other gulls and terns. Their breeding numbers seldom exceed 50 pairs on an island that may support several hundred pairs of herring gulls and perhaps 500 or 1,000 pairs of terns. In flight a black-back resembles the bald eagle as it soars and wheels in great circles, showing a brilliant white head and tail at either end of its great dark back. It's a good enough resemblance to carry over to its habits in and around a colony. No other bird exerts so strong a presence or is so aggressive a predator of other birds. Black-backs can swallow whole the young of gulls or eiders that are big enough to be immune from the harassment of all other appetites, with the single exception of eagles.

One of the more resourceful feeding habits of the black-back steals a page from an ancient Chinese method of fishing. For thousands of years the Chinese have used a species of cormorant to catch fish. They tie a piece of leather around the long, snaky neck of a tame cormorant and take it out to dive for fish. When the bird surfaces, it is unable to swallow the catch, which is promptly removed from the cormorant's maw, thank you very much. In a variation of this highly efficient operation, you will often see the black-back seemingly carelessly watching a diving double-crested cormorant. If the cormorant surfaces with a fish large enough to require some time and effort to swallow, the black-back drops into the water next to the gagging cormorant, which obligingly and quickly regurgitates the fish for the big gull. Thank you very much.

Great black-backed gulls, Seal Island.   *Philip Conkling*

Gulls at dump.

HERRING GULL, *Larus argentatus*

Life was not always as fat for herring gulls as it has been for the past several decades, and there are signs that some new hard times may lie ahead. For the last 20 years their numbers have been exploding on the breeding islands off the Maine coast, and they are the most universally distributed species of gull, not only in Maine but in the rest of the Northern Hemisphere. Recently, however, with the closing of open-burning town dumps, herring gulls are denied the important source of food that has helped maintain large populations. Although the data are not yet complete, it appears that Maine islands might hatch as many young gulls as ever, but that increasing numbers of their young are being forced to move southward to search for food. While it may be unfair to suggest that places like Massachusetts, New York, and New Jersey have more garbage to offer (since these states now also have laws against open dumps), the increasing numbers of tagged Maine gulls that end up along their shores suggest that some kind of population shift is in the making. As far as the herring gull is concerned, we may have seen their high-water mark along the Maine coast.

It is hard for many ornithologists to embrace wholeheartedly this opportunistic feeder that hangs around fish-packing plants, lobsterboats, and garbage dumps getting fed on and occasionally entangled in the excess of our throwaway lifestyle. It's not just a case of familiarity breeding contempt; there is a resentment against a species that has driven some of the smaller and rarer of terns and laughing gulls out of places where they were once common. Even though the herring gulls now nest just about everywhere and eat just about anything, a century of egging and a few decades of feather collecting had reduced their breeding territory to a handful of Maine islands. For a period of time around the turn of the century, their southern breeding limit along the entire eastern seaboard was No Man's Land, at the outer edge of Penobscot Bay.

In recent years the herring gull has been immortalized in popular culture in a thin volume about one *Jonathan Livingston Seagull,* a story that unaccountably remained on the best-seller list for well over a year. No doubt some bird watchers would have preferred that the country be given a best seller about a more discreet, less rapacious species. I confess that this more nearly expressed my own sentiments until a recent experience with the gulls (or mewes, as they used to be called) enlightened me. One summer morning, the waters of a small cove whose shores make a most pleasant walk began to fill with a large shoal of elvers. The few herring gulls that happened to be standing around or sitting idly in the water soon stirred to action, and within a few short minutes more gulls appeared, and then more, until there were several hundred of them feeding in desperate haste before the movable feast disappeared. In the midst of the horde, or along its changing edges, was a scattered handful of gulls that took absolutely no notice of the mad tumult around them. They sat preening themselves, stood on the decks of the few moored lobsterboats, and stared distractedly out to sea. Perhaps they were not hungry or had just eaten. There may be a good and sufficient explanation for their lack of concern, but it had all the look, to one schooled in the traditions of western liberalism, of unfettered, unrestrained Free Will, which, harking back to Jonathan Livingston Seagull, was his claim to fame.

TERNS—COMMON, ARCTIC, AND ROSEATE, *Sterna hirundo, S. paradisaea, S. dougalli*

Terns, or sea swallows or medricks, are Maine birds that have never fully recovered from the effects of the millinery trade during the brief, brutal years that their feathers fetched a fine price in the garment district of New York. Hunting of winter ducks for feathers had been an important way of generating cash for islanders during the 19th century, but collecting feathers for ladies' hats was an entirely new business. Terns were the chief objects of interest when the collecting began in earnest on Maine seabird islands in 1886. By 1896, after terns had been virtually exterminated on their nesting grounds, the breast and wing feathers of gulls were collected. Keen competition among the milliners drove the price of a dozen pieces from $4 to $12. The few tern colonies that were not exterminated were located on lighthouse islands, such as Matinicus Rock, where keepers and

Protective coloration of herring gull chicks.   *Jim Kosinski*

their families protected the creatures that were often their only company from early May to September.

The excesses of the millinery trade generated the first widespread public outcry against the habits of those who thoughtlessly exploited wildlife resources for personal profit. Overhunting had been a serious problem for several decades in America, particularly for species such as the passenger pigeon, which migrated in compact flocks and made attractive targets for market hunters. The slaughter of birds, not to eat but to decorate ladies' heads, was simply insupportable to many who were willing to overlook the excesses of hunters. Suddenly it was possible to prick the consciences of enough people not only to stop the milliners in their tracks but to initiate a spate of national bird protection laws. The lobbying was brief and intense. Frank Chapman, the distinguished American ornithologist, conducted a survey during the course of two afternoon walks through the streets of New York. Five hundred and forty-two heads out of a total of 700 had been decorated with feathered hats from 20-odd species, including terns, grackle, owl, grouse, and green heron.

In 1898 William Dutcher of the American Ornithological Union hired several Maine fishermen and lighthouse keepers to protect terns and gulls from the milliners. The same year, Dutcher reported that he had ex-

Hovering tern.   *Kate Fitzgerald*

tracted an agreement from New York City milliners that they would not buy the skins of any birds shot after 1899. Two years later, the Maine Legislature passed a model bird law, making it a crime to sell or ship bird skins. By 1902, Dutcher, who had personally seen to the protection of Maine bird colonies on Great and Little Duck, No Man's Land, and Stratton Islands became the chairman of the newly formed National Association of Audubon Societies. Fait gradually accompli.

Before the widespread slaughter of terns was initiated in 1886, Norton had counted 75 tern colonies on the islands of Maine. After the turn of the century, their numbers continued to decline, even though they enjoyed protection. In 1900 there were 23 colonies between Saco and Machias Bays; 30 years later Norton found a total of 21 colonies. The most recent (1977) count of the number of Maine tern colonies was 28.

It appears that herring gulls, whose numbers were equally reduced during the plume-hunting years, recovered more quickly and have increased at the expense of terns. In a mixed gull and tern colony, terns are forced to occupy smaller and smaller territories, and in some cases they have been driven off nesting islands altogether.

Arctic terns, which are slightly larger than their more southerly cousins, the common and roseate terns, are distinguished by their 25,000-mile round-trip flight to and from their breeding grounds. The northernmost-nesting birds travel from near the Arctic Circle across the North Atlantic to Africa, back across the Atlantic to the coast of North America, and down to Patagonia and Tierra del Fuego before turning around and retracing their flight path. In the process, many of these small birds see more hours of sunlight than any other creature. For four months during the breeding season near their northern limit, the sun never sets. For another four months on their winter grounds, the sun shines at midnight, and during the months in between, they still get more than their share. With all this light, it is easy to understand why these birds are so high-strung.

THE ALCIDS

The alcids, or the auks, puffins, and guillemots that are at the southern end of their breeding range on Maine's offshore islands, are the Northern Hemisphere's equivalent of penguins. They even look like penguins in their formal black and white plumage, and one of their extinct numbers that stood three feet high was, like all Southern Hemisphere penguins, flightless. The processes by which similar ecological habits and habitats channel evolutionary change into a limited number of morphological options is called convergent evolution. Auks and penguins look alike because they prey on the same kinds of species, live in the same kinds of habitats—in other words, they occupy similar ecological niches, such that the demands that their environment imposes upon them, even though they come from different ancestral stocks, cause the same kinds of random genetic traits to be naturally selected. Favorable traits in later generations frequently show the species looking more like one another.

GREAT AUK

The great auk was the first species to become extinct in the New World. It is still an open question whether these flightless black and white seabirds nested on Maine's islands, but they were most certainly regular visitors. They swarm along the outer islands diving for fish on their way south to winter along the barrier islands of Cape Hatteras or on their way north to mate on the coasts of Labrador, Newfoundland, and Iceland. Their bones have shown up in Indian shell middens with enough regularity that the arrival of this bird full of oil and meat must have been an important event for coastal tribes.

Awkward on land, the great auk was the fastest and most powerful diving bird in the evolutionary record of life. They used their short, tapered wings to propel themselves down to 40 fathoms in pursuit of schools of smelt, herring, or capelin. The few observations of their fishing techniques made by naturalists before the auks disappeared described rafts of 20 to 50 birds that would dive to surround a large school of herring, actually driving the fish to the surface. This would feed not only the young and less adept of their species, but also the flocks of gannets, murres, kittiwakes, and puffins that would gather for a piece of the action.

For several hundred years after the Funk Island colony was discovered by early Newfoundland fishermen, the great auk provided one of the few reliable sources of fresh meat that an expedition could expect to find after a North Atlantic crossing. After the turn of the 19th century, the ease with which these large feathered birds could be driven down to the shore and clubbed to death made them attractive targets for those who had a market

Great auks and puffins. *Kate Fitzgerald*

for their oil, meat, and feathers. The tiny islands of Hamilton Inlet off the coast of Labrador, for instance, supported a colony of some 500,000 great auks that was virtually wiped out in one season.

The adults mated for life, an apparently common trait for many of the world's large birds, but if one of the pair died, the other would neither pursue nor accept another mate. As exemplary a behavior pattern as this loyalty might seem, it no doubt hastened their downfall. The one egg that the mated birds produced could never replace the loss of those two, and the single birds whose mates had fallen victim to the market hunters' clubs no longer contributed to the population. In 1844, the last known great auk was collected by a naturalist for a museum collection.

ATLANTIC PUFFIN, *Fratercula arctica*

The Atlantic puffin is one of the most common birds of the North Atlantic, with a total population of perhaps 15 million birds, but it is now, and has always been, a rare bird on the coast of Maine. Before some of the excesses of hunting, egging, and feathering were halted at the end of the last century, puffin colonies were eliminated from four or five islands where they had once nested. The largest of these colonies, on barren Seal Island at the entrance to Penobscot Bay, supported some 1,500 pairs of puffins. Sometime during the 1860s they disappeared from Seal. Their numbers were decimated by herring fishermen, who draped nets over their burrows at night to catch them in the morning. Matinicus Rock, the 30-acre dome of granite 30 miles offshore, is the location of Maine's only puffin colony. One of the minor historical ironies surrounding this colony is that it survived the millinery years not so much because people were fond of this little seabird filled with the look of preposterous self-importance but because the rock supported one of the few protected tern colonies at the end of the century. Without the protection of the terns by the lighthouse keepers, it is anyone's guess whether Maine's puffin population would exist at all.

Like other members of the alcid family, the puffin has wings that are a hopeless compromise between the conflicting morphological demands that flight through both air and water imposes. When puffins fly toward Matinicus Rock, they look like "toy doodlebugs," but their lack of grace in the air is more than made up for when they beat their wings through the denser medium of seawater to catch darting schools of fish. Someone has taken the time to count the most fish ever seen hanging out of a puffin's bill: 28. This is quite a feat, since they catch them one at a time and must figure out how to hold 27 slippery, squirming bodies while they try to snare the 28th.

On a mostly bare eight-acre piece of granite at the outer edge of Muscongus Bay, an unlikely group of interns recruited from all walks of life, funded through the patronage of the National Audubon Society, and directed by a witty, thirtyish traveling ornithologist, is trying to reintroduce puffins to one of their former colonies. Stephen Kress is the man and Eastern Egg is the rock.

The effort to reestablish puffins in Muscongus Bay is one of the most likable research projects ever conceived. You cannot look at a puffin, or even a picture of a puffin—with its ludicrous posture and its most magnificent bill—without liking it immediately and, unreservedly.

For five years, Kress and his odd collection of housewives, artists, serious ornithologists, accountants, and what-nots have been collecting eight-day-old puffin chicks from Whitless Bay, Newfoundland, then flying them to Owl's Head, driving them to Bremen, loading them in a boat bound for Eastern Egg Rock, and placing their charges in specially constructed burrows to which a few may one day return to breed. Quite aside from the issue of whether the effort will be successful (and there are many reasons why it may not be), these young bird people have developed an important, perhaps *very* important technique: how to transport and rear wild seabird chicks. In this their success has been impressive: 95 percent of the 654 chicks they have handled have been successfully fledged—that is, they have gone off of their own accord as teenagers to make their own way in the world.

The reason that this effort may one day prove so important has to do with oil and water. For the rest of this century, anyway, it appears we are committed to finding the few remaining oil deposits at almost any cost. Exploration and drilling for oil will increasingly be done in the oceans, which, after all, cover three-quarters of the earth's surface. For seabirds whose plumage loses its insulating qualities when exposed to oil—not to mention that their food supplies are smothered by contact with oil—the future is hardly rosy. We have only to recall that the oil slick from the *Torrey Canyon* tanker spill exacted its fiercest toll on the puffins and other seabirds that used to nest along the coast of Brittany. Unless we give up the notion that such losses are unacceptable, we are going to have to learn how to manipulate our environment even more finely—to undo with our right hand the damage that we did with our left.

In the matter of the politics of energy, the puffin-rearing project on Eastern Egg Rock takes on a different tone. For the last few years, the interns marooned on this wave-swept piece of rock have trained their eyes for sights of banded puffins returning. To make these wayward puffin sons and daughters feel more at home and get into the mating mood—maybe even the family way—when they land upon the Rock, there are painted decoys and recorded seabird noises played over loudspeakers to regale the five-year-old puffins who return as young adults. It will all require a leap of faith, not only for the returning puffins, but for Kress and his band of interns, who must wonder if they are really fooling these bright-billed birds with their decoys. But from here, it seems worth all the effort that has gone into that lonely piece of granite.

RAZOR-BILLED AUK, *Alca torda*

Razor-bills are the rarest nesting bird on the Maine coast. They live in two widely separated island colonies—one on Matinicus Rock and the other

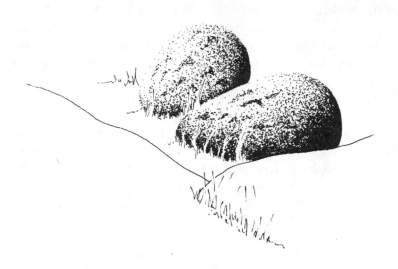

Razor-bills lay eggs highly tapered at one end.   *Kate Fitzgerald*

off Cutler. They number, the last time they were counted, approximately 40 pairs. They are a smaller version of the great auk, look like Adelie penguins, and have never been abundant enough to have been hunted for their meat, eggs, or feathers, except when they were in the range of fire of those who shot anything that moved.

Throughout most of their range in the North Atlantic, they nest on rocky cliff faces and lay eggs that are highly tapered at one end. If a returning adult happens to kick them upon landing on the ledge, the eggs roll around in a circle and not off the cliff. Once the young have hatched and been fed for a period of a month or so, the parents abandon them on the nesting island. Shortly afterward—usually at night when they are less likely to become a quick meal for a black-backed gull—they slip down to the edge of the sea and swim off into the darkness. They will spend the winter at sea, as well as the next several years, after which a restlessness stirs them to head for some isolated island, as often as not the one on which they hatched, to participate in the same reproductive mysteries through which their lives began.

BLACK GUILLEMOT, *Cepphus grylle*

The black guillemot is the most abundant alcid found on and around the coastal islands of Maine; unlike their cousins, they are here year-round.

Hummingbird temporarily paralyzed by sudden temperature drop during fall migration. *George Putz*

Unlike the razor-bills and puffins, the small, round guillemot nests quite readily on inshore islands. However, when they nest close to land, they lay two eggs instead of the single egg that is customarily found in the nests of offshore island colonies. The two-egg strategy is probably an adaptation to protect against the higher losses to predation that inshore colonies must suffer from the closer proximity to egg-eating mammals.

Guillemots—or sea pigeons, as they are called—feed almost exclusively on rock eels, which are small, thin fish and not eels at all. Rock eels have never had any commercial significance, and therefore sea pigeons have never been persecuted to any degree by fishermen. Guillemots are among the most difficult of all seabirds to count, but the best estimates put their numbers at around 2,000 pairs on the Maine coast.

Passeriformes

The passerines, the order to which swallows, wrens, robins, and wood warblers belong, are the most numerous and the most intricately speciated group of birds in the world. Of the 8,000-odd avian species scattered across the globe, about 5,000, or 60 percent of them, are passerines. This means, among other things, that no matter where you are, if you see a small, colorful bird and identify it as a passerine, you will be right more often than you are wrong (a highly comforting happenstance in an age of uncertainty).

Another distinction accorded passerines is that the great majority of

Swallow nest.   *Rick Perry*

their species have only recently diverged from ancestral types—as recently, in many cases, as the Pleistocene, a few thousand years ago.

The wood warblers of North America are perhaps the best example of bona-fide new species to appear in the recent record of life. The prodigious intercontinental migratory flight of the tiny black-and-white warbler that wings between northern conifer forests and South American tropical forests has demonstrated to evolutionary biologists how difficult a task it can be to maintain a species gene pool. If some subtle change should reduce its food supply so that the warbler wintered in Florida, rather than completing its spectacular annual journey to the Amazon River basin, it would be isolated from its congeners in the Southern Hemisphere and would slowly diverge to become a new species.

Apparently processes similar to this have been occurring over the past few thousand years (and surely for many thousands before that)—which in part explains the wonderful proliferation of gaudy-colored warblers that annually nest in northern spruce forests.

The myriad spruce-clad islands of Maine provide convenient resting and feeding spots during the semiannual migrations for what seems like every small bird that uses the Atlantic Flyway. They also provide nesting habitats for the bewildering variety of warblers that would confuse us with their subtle wing-bar and eye-stripe markings: the black and white, the black poll, the yellow, the Cape May, the myrtle (or yellow-rumped), the black-throated green, the parula, the bay-breasted, the pine, and the Canada —to name just the common species.

When the first waves of these passerine fellow-traveling swallows, thrushes, sparrows, and warblers hit the islands in late April or early May, the spring air is suddenly charged with new tones and pitches and with the million possibilities of new life. Soon they will be settling in amid the lichen loft of spruce limbs (if they are warblers), or in the banks of some soft island side (if they are swallows), or in bushes and shrubs around an abandoned field or homestead (if they are redstarts or hummingbirds), and begin to sing as if their lives depended on it. In fact, not only do their lives depend upon it, since mate selection is a function of their sonority, but certainly ours do too.

Tweet-Tweet

What are we to make of the history of our relationships with birds along the coast of Maine? One thing is apparent: in sheer numbers there are now more nesting birds on the islands than there have been at any time since shortly after 1800. As in the rest of the country, the past has left a mixed legacy. It is true that we will never again see the likes of the Labrador duck or the great auk, which disappeared from the earth before we knew what hit them. Other species, such as the cranes (either whoopers or sandhills, according to Rosier, nested in Muscongus Bay) and the Eskimo curlew, may or may not have been rescued from the brink of an irreversible genetic event: extinction. Their fate is still hanging from an excruciatingly thin thread.

The pesticide dilemma still shadows the fate of eagles and peregrines, but there is wider public recognition that in ecological matters there are no free lunches: protecting the forests from an endemic insect known as the spruce budworm also contaminates food supplies and eventually the health of those that eat at the top of food chains. And you don't have to have feathers to be a target. This much is true. But it is not the whole truth. The most silent spring, to use Rachel Carson's worrisome phrase, as far as the songs of birds on Maine islands have been concerned, happened before the turn of the century, and the springs for 20 or 30 years afterward were pretty quiet.

But we are headed toward the next century in much better shape. Many of the most wonderful birds that totally disappeared from our shores have returned to nest in great numbers. For others, such as the puffins, we may actually be able to leave them a better world than they have known for several centuries. It could be better, but it also could be a lot worse. If we do not admit this, we will continue to fight battles that were won and lost in the past and not only risk credibility with a skeptical public but may also fail to perceive the dimensions of future confrontations that inevitably will be played for much higher stakes.

6

Mammals of the Islands: Stags, Polecats, Coney, and Dogs Like Wolves

MOST OF THE INDIGENOUS MAMMALS of Maine sport fur linings, which is well enough for keeping warm, but they become heavy and sodden when wet. For the greater number of them, long-distance water travel is not a great temptation. Those mammals that have moved back into the sea, such as whales and seals, or have learned to negotiate the tricky channels of the air, such as bats, have found vacant ecological niches in and around the coastal islands of Maine and are represented in great numbers.

Aside from the finned and winged exceptions, most of Maine's island ecosystems support depauperate mammal populations, which means that common mainland species are missing from the islands. From the point of view of nesting birds, whose lives are quite solitary, poor, nasty, brutish, and short enough anyway, the limited variety of omnivorous mammals found on islands makes their lives more secure. It could be said that there are so many birds on the islands simply because there are so few mammals.

James Rosier, the observant 17th century naturalist, compiled the first species list of Maine mammals during a two-month exploration of the islands and coast with Weymouth's expeditions. On his list of "Beasts We Saw the Country Yield in the Small Time of our Stay there," Rosier included Reindeer, Stags, Fallow Deer, Wild Great Cats, Dogs—some like Wolves, some like Spaniels, Coney, Hedgehogs, and Polecats; as well as the expected Bear, Beaver, Otter, and Hare.

Unfortunately, Rosier does not describe which species they sighted on the islands and which they saw on the mainland, but it is possible to piece together some of the original picture.

Beavers are one of the 'missing' species on most Maine islands.   *Jim Kosinski*

Canids

WOLF, *Canis lupus*

It is only within the last 10 years that anything like a significant minority of public opinion has warmed to the wiles of wolves. Almost from Day One of settlement in Maine, wolves were a problem. "Their hideous howling made night terrible to the settlers," Edward Trelawney wrote back to his brother in England. Since the early mainland settlements were huddled along the coastline, the colonists in effect had placed themselves between the deep forest where the eastern timber wolf sought cover and the shores where it sought food. The outlying pastures where land was cleared for livestock became increasingly tempting targets for these meat-eaters. One of the chief reasons that Casco Bay islands were cleared for pasturage was that hogs and cattle were less subject to depredations from wolves. Throughout eight or nine months of the year, a colonial farmer who pastured livestock on the islands lying offshore could rest easier at night in the knowledge that none had provided a wolf its dinner. But come the winter and the freezing of the Bay out to the islands, the peace was broken.

According to several accounts, the wolves possessed a sixth sense about the ice. Year after discouraging year, Casco Bay farmers waited for an early spring breakup to get even with wolves trapped on the islands when the ice gave out. But no matter what day, week, or month the ice bridge was

Island sheep were safe from the depredations of wolves.

lifted, the farmers would find tracks of the wolves that left the islands at the last moment, depriving them of certain revenge.

"The wolves are of divers colors," writes John Josselyn in his usual informative manner, "some sandy colored, some griseled, and some black." Since the diet of the wolf had a more immediate and direct effect on the fortunes of colonial farmers, they were hunted down more intently than were bears. In 1739 a bounty of £5 was paid for a dead wolf; a few years later it was £8, and then £16, "if a man should kill three." These figures, almost unheard-of sums in colonial New England, illustrate how diligently the colonists tried to eliminate the wolf from its domain.

Several of the town histories of coastal Maine relate the story of a settler returning home, usually in the winter after dark. At some point this individual realizes he or she (and they were as often as not women returning from some neighborly chore) is being trailed by a wolf or a pack of wolves, which begin to close on their quarry. The terrified human figure begins walking faster, breaks into a trot and finally into headlong flight, sometimes dropping a piece of clothing, to interrupt the wolves' pursuit for a few moments. No doubt these events took place much as they are related. But what is interesting in these accounts is that no one actually gets eaten; they just get chased—often right to the farmhouse door, which they close just as the wolves hurl themselves against it. From the wolves' point of view, you cannot help but wonder whether the chase isn't the point; it evens the score a bit to chalk up a moral victory for the canines, which more frequently end up on the losing side in an encounter with the two-leggeds.

Cyrus Eaton, the historian for the St. George River Valley, describes the last wolf hunt along the shores of West Penobscot Bay. In the spring of 1815 a she-wolf and five whelps were spotted. The alarm went up, and soon some 20 men and their dogs took up the chase, which lasted three days and ranged through Waldoboro, Thomaston, and St. George. At the end of it, the last wolf, one of the pups, took to the water and headed out toward the islands of the Muscle Ridge. Whether the pup made it, we are not told, but no wolves were ever seen again in the area.

BEAR, *Ursus americanus*

The problem with bears is that they are large and therefore have large appetites, particularly when they emerge from their winter dens. The expression, "hungry as a bear" gives the right idea. When they subsist on fruits, nuts, seeds, roots, insects, fish, rodents, and carrion, as they do in the few wild and mountainous areas to which they have been restricted in Maine, they are not greatly persecuted. However, because they also have a fondness for the tender meat of wild and domestic ungulates (fawns and lambs, in our part of the world), they were never very popular with the settlers.

Bears completely disappeared from island ecosystems in the early decades of the 1800s, when serious island settlement began. Isolated and rugged islands no doubt furnished more than a few secure denning sites. Both Marshall Island in Jericho Bay and Bradbury Island in North Penobscot Bay were originally called Bear Island. On today's charts, an island adjacent to Bradbury is still called Bear, as is a smaller island in the passage known as Western Way off Mount Desert, but neither of these islands has recorded the massive paw print of this mammal in more than 150 years. Various island histories record the dates when the last bears were shot, as if, like the Indians who fell before, their deaths meant the community was safe from evil. Two bears were shot on Swans Island before the turn of the 19th century, and no others arrived to take their place. On Vinalhaven, a solitary bear persisted within the confines of the large swampland northeast of Carver's Pond until 1825, when it, too, was shot.

Maine's islands appear to have been ideally suited to these individualistic, somewhat ornery, and antisocial creatures. Since bears find their meals lower on the food chain than do wolves—which is another way of saying that they do not rely chiefly on meat, as do their canine associates—bears do not need as much operating space. Within forested areas they can sustain themselves on a range of between one and five square miles of territory, a figure that need not be so great on an island, since they have the benefit of the intertidal zone, where they can supplement their largely vegetarian diet. Writing of his experiences on the coast of Maine in the mid-1600s, Josselyn describes bears fishing for lobsters, which were plentiful enough to be stranded in tide pools: "The bear is a tyrant at a lobster and at low water will go down to the rocks and grope after them with great diligence."

In addition to having the availability of food, bears are strong and single-minded enough to swim the waters between most of the forested islands of Maine. Except for a few weeks in the fall, when they are captive to the fury of their hormones, which trigger a brief mating season, bears do not seek out each other's company. It is easy to imagine Papa Bear retiring to the peace and solitude of an island shore for the winter, grumbling and lumbering around until he gives in to a long winter's sleep.

Maine supports the East's largest population of black bears, but most of these are found in the northern woods. However, Cross Island, a 1,500-acre forested island in Machias Bay, supports at least one shy bear—or else someone has gone to a lot of trouble to make bear prints around several of the island's waterholes. If they are here on Cross Island, they are likely to appear elsewhere on the islands sooner or later.

Fox, *Vulpes vulpes*

Almost everyone who has taken a moment to listen to the history or folklore of the islands knows that the Fox Islands—now Vinalhaven and North Haven—were named for the sly canids that were sighted on their shores by an English explorer, Martin Pring, in 1603. Pring's voyage was underwritten by a wealthy group of London merchants who were eager to get their hands on a load of sassafras, a tree whose medicinal qualities could supposedly cure all that ailed. They made their landfall at 43° north latitude on the Maine coast and rode at anchor on the southwest side of Vinalhaven, probably in what is now Old Harbor. They found the shores "pleasant to behold, adorned with goodly grass and sundry sorts of trees," and named the largest two islands for "those kinds of beasts [we saw] thereon."

Somewhere along the way, the foxes that Pring saw came to be called silver foxes, although they were not so described in the original account of the voyage Pring wrote for Richard Hakluyt, England's compiler of New World discoveries. Silver foxes make a better story, and it is certainly possible that the tree-climbing grey fox (*Urocyon cinereoargenteus*), which had a more southerly distribution throughout the United States, could have thrived on Maine's larger islands. It is also remotely possible that a population of red foxes had been genetically isolated on Vinalhaven and North Haven for a long enough period of evolutionary time that their pelage changed from a reddish-brown to a silver-grey. Apparently such a situation has occurred on the Channel Islands off Santa Barbara, California, where a dwarf species, the island fox (*Urocyon littoralis*), now lives.

The possibility of a separate species on Vinalhaven and North Haven seems a little unlikely, since even these islands, which lie 8 to 12 miles out to sea, are periodically connected to the mainland by ice in the winter.

We are told by various island historians that 1816 was the first time in 35 years that West Penobscot Bay was completely frozen over. Again in 1835, by early February the Bay froze to the outer islands. Horses and sleighs crossed the bay until mid-March to transport hay to island livestock in danger of starvation, although few undertook the dangerous trip with any relish.

No doubt the foxes, whatever their precise lineage, used the same arteries of winter travel, following the trails of rabbit, hare, and small rodents, which struck off into the white unknown looking for better things to eat. When and if our climate grows gradually colder so that the islands are again briefly connected by frozen seawater, we may expect to find small populations of foxes on the larger islands that they once inhabited. Until such random climatic events occur, foxes are unlikely to make island voyages, since there is quite enough for them to eat around their mainland hideouts.

MINK (AND MINKHOLERS), *Mustela vison*

The mink belongs to a distinctive group of carnivores called mustelids, all of which possess specialized anal scent glands that serve primarily as a means of olfactory communication either among individuals of their species or close competitors. Just a squirt on a rock or a stump; it's so much easier than a nasty confrontation. In the case of the ponderous skunk— called a polecat by Rosier and Josselyn after a similar species common in the Old World—these scent glands can convey a particularly emphatic message to a harassing predator: don't bother, it's not worth it.

Mink are the most common carnivore and the only mustelid or fur-bearer found on the islands of Maine. They are almost as quick on land as in the water, where they can swim fast enough to catch small fish. In their diets they are both opportunistic and omnivorous, as even a casual examination of one of their other calling cards, a scat or dropping, will confirm: raspberry and strawberry seeds mixed with bits of crab and egg-shell, rodent hairs, and even small feathers. There is at least one record that a mink climbed the trunk of an osprey nesting tree and carried off a helpless nestling.

A slightly larger and presumably separate species, called the sea mink, was known only to the coast of Maine, and the various Otter Islands lying off the main must have been named for this creature, since Maine's real otter is restricted to a fresh-water habitat. The Otter Ponds on several of the larger islands, however, have been inhabited from time to time with real otters, which must have succumbed to wanderlust as they looked out across the water to Maine's islands. The sea mink disappeared by about 1860, probably a casualty of overtrapping, and its north woods relative moved into the vacant niche.

The island niche occupied by the small, agile mink appears to have

Mink on granite talus shore.   *Kate Fitzgerald*

benefited significantly from the effects of the quarrying era. The huge piles of granite tailings on the quarried islands provide literally thousands of opportunities to pull a disappearing act, as well as hundreds of miles of underground tunnels and innumerable burrow sites to raise young. Mink swim about from island to island looking for food, but no islands are quite as hospitable as those that have been cut up for granite. Occasionally you can find fresh mink scat on a seabird nesting island, but this situation is rare enough to intimidate even this highly aggressive package of speed and stealth.

During the rash of strikes that shut down operations on many of the granite islands just before the turn of the century, the derogatory term "minkholer" was coined and applied to scab labor brought in to break strikes. No doubt the furtive and opportunistic activities of this breed of men resembled in the minds of union men the habits of the mink, which today still emerge hungrily from tailing piles and scurry about the shore when a granite island falls to silence.

Rabbits and Raccoons: Island Introductions

These creatures belong to quite separate families of mammals, occupy different niches, and have evolved from quite different ancestral stocks. In

Racoons do not relish salt-water swimming.   *Kate Fitzgerald*

fact, they have little in common except that they are about equally uncommon on Maine islands.

Raccoons are quite handy at fishing in fresh-water streams, and are
often seen along salt-water shores foraging for crabs, clams, and mussels,
but this is all very deceptive, since they avoid at all costs any water that
is deeper than they can wade in. With good reason, one might add, since
they are poor swimmers. If hunger drives them to it, raccoons may be able
to negotiate the narrow channels that separate them from islands just off
the mainland, but for the most part, they are found on larger islands only
because someone thought they were improving island fauna through their
importation. Several years ago a sporting club on Vinalhaven did just that,
with the idea that hunting raccoons with dogs in the winter would be good
fun. After a season or two of such winter diversion, the sport has died away,
and now partridge or grouse are nearly unknown on Vinalhaven, and farm
fowl disappear in ones and twos over the winter.

Among the many terrors of a rabbit's life, water must rank near the
top. Every once in a while a population of rabbits or hares (which are a
different species) appears on islands near the mainland, but their access
routes must certainly be over a temporary ice bridge that forms in a quiet
channel. There is a lot more to be discovered about the lives of rabbits,
but not much that relates to islands. They are like people who simply will

Hypothetical island hybrid.   *Jamien Morehouse*

not set foot on a boat, and therefore appear on islands only in unusual circumstances. One of these circumstances that deserves passing mention is their presence on quarried islands. During the granite years on islands such as Vinalhaven, rabbits were raised as an additional and inexpensive source of red meat. The Italian stone carvers, in particular, were in the habit of setting up hutches to raise rabbits for Sunday dinner. Over the years some of these Sunday dinners wandered off and have intermixed with other rabbits introduced for the wilder purpose of hunting. Someday an energetic soul will conduct a study of Maine island rabbit blood and be surprised at the number of exotic strains that are commingled within the island populations.

Since the subject has turned to island introductions, it is appropriate to mention that there is a record of a population of red foxes released on the 30-acre No Man's Land in 1916, probably by a Matinicus fisherman. Though the record does not indicate the purpose, if any, one imagines they were to be raised for their pelts. Whether or not the foxes were a successful business enterprise can only be guessed. It is certain, however, that the effect was felt chiefly by the burrow-nesting Leach's storm petrels, which apparently provided the foxes with most of their food until the colony was exterminated.

Rodents and the Theory of Island Biogeography

Although it seems very unlikely, voles—the country cousins of city mice—are the most common mammal on the islands of Maine. It is unlikely because they are so small, can usually fit in the curve of a tablespoon, don't regularly take to water, and are usually thought of (to the extent that we think of them at all) as timid and unassuming. There can be little truth to this prejudice once one realizes that voles come to Maine's islands either as clever stowaways or, when a particularly high tide catches them unaware, as castaways on little wooden boats otherwise known as driftwood. It's what ecologists call the "sweepstakes route."

No one has ever thought to introduce meadow mice or voles to an island to raise fur or to hunt—no one, that is, except for an individual

Meadow vole. *Kate Fitzgerald*

named Ken Crowell, who did it almost 20 years ago. As a zoology student, Crowell wondered what kinds of small mammals were distributed among the scattering of Maine's islands, and from this modest wonderment over the course of many years came a very elegant idea that helped lay the basis for what has come to be known among evolutionary biologists as the theory of island biogeography.

Crowell began trapping small animals on Deer Isle and the smaller islands of Merchant Row and soon discovered that of the three species commonly encountered on the larger island, only one, the ubiquitous meadow vole or field mouse (*Microtus*), inhabited the smaller offshore islands. The species that were "missing" from the other islands were the deer mouse (*Peromyscus*), recognized by its large ears and long tail, and the red-backed vole (*Clethrionomys*), which has a rusty red back, as its name suggests. The fact that both of these forest-dwelling species were absent from the islands where the field mouse had arrived and maintained itself led Crowell to speculate on one of the most fundamental questions of ecology: what determines the number of species living together in a natural community?

Over the next 15 years Crowell introduced the missing species to various Merchant Row islands and recorded their fates. One by one, most of the introduced populations of deer mice and red-backed voles slipped into extinction. Through patient observation, Crowell discovered that the reason for the extinctions boiled down to the specialized feeding habits of the deer mice and the low reproductive potential of the red-backed voles. While *Microtus* is one of the most prolific rodents—producing 6 or 8 young every two weeks—*Clethrionomys* is one of the slowest rodent reproducers. In the time that *Microtus* could produce 233 offspring, *Clethrionomys* would leave only 25. In the matter of the roulette probability of survival, *Microtus* populations had a greater chance of pulling through simply by virtue of their greater numbers. *Peromyscus*, however, has as impressive a reproductive potential as *Microtus,* and their disappearance seems to be a matter of a preference for seeds and fruits of plants rather than stems and vegetable parts, which *Microtus* eats. Since there are fewer meals of seeds and fruits per acre than there are of stems, the deer mouse needs more space on islands. With a less abundant and more unreliable food supply than *Microtus, Peromyscus* becomes extinct on the smaller islands, but it is able to maintain itself on the larger islands—even if they are farther offshore.

Research by Crowell and others has recently been translated into a predictive mathematical model by E. O. Wilson and Robert MacArthur. The reading gets pretty thick unless differential equations make diverting reading for you, but Wilson and MacArthur's theory of island biogeography suggests that the number of species that inhabit islands is a balance between the colonization and extinction rates that populations naturally undergo. Because larger islands have more niches, extinction rates are lower and more species are found; and because islands closer to the mainland have higher colonization rates, more species are likely to be found there also. In recent years, the theory has been extended to predict the number of species likely to be found in any discontinuous habitat. For, ecologically speaking, mountaintops, caves, and ponds are really islands in space and time, and the numbers of species that make up these communities can be predicted with some accuracy on the basis of the same mathematical model. When you boil down all the mathematics, it gets down to something like this: the number of species on any island is proportional to the cube root of its area divided by the distance to the mainland. Maybe so, but it took a lot of Ken Crowell's mice to put this information into an elegant quantitative framework over which a new generation of theoretical ecologists can ooh and aah.

Moose, *Alces americanus*

It seems significant that Rosier mentions both fallow deer and stags in his list of mammals of the New World, since in the 17th century many naturalists did not recognize males and females as belonging to the same species. It is possible that Rosier was just confusing bucks and does of the white-tailed deer, but since his exploration of the new land was conducted during the early summer, when the antlers of bucks are just beginning to appear, it seems more likely that stags refer to the moose. A few decades later, Josselyn describes the moose or elk as "a monster of superfluity," and the tips of their antlers "are sometimes found to be two fathoms asunder."

Rockland's and Thomaston's historian, Cyrus Eaton, writes that in 1750 a group of six moose were sighted on an island in North Penobscot Bay. One feeble calf was captured and made into a pet. Evidently moose were not strangers to islands—after all, they swim well and move about

Young moose on the shore of Vinalhaven.

considerably in search of browse—but they make such obvious targets and provide so much meat that it is likely that they disappeared quite early. In the last 40 years since the moose-hunting season has been in abeyance, their numbers have increased noticeably along the coast, and they have once again begun to appear on the large forested islands. In the summer of 1977, we tracked a two- or three-year-old moose on Hog Island in western Muscongus Bay, which has been an Audubon Wildlife Preserve since 1936. Even on this 330-acre forested island, there is not enough browse to support a young moose for very long, but a few weeks later, one of the Audubon Society's summer guests spotted the "monster of superfluity" early one morning in the low, thick woods of the island's interior.

Moose have reappeared on the islands in smaller numbers than in the Maine north woods, where the combination of 40 years of protection from hunting and the increased timber harvesting (which produces browse species they favor) has created something of a moose boom. The Maine Fish and Wildlife Department conservatively estimates moose numbers to be 25,000 —enough, in their opinion, to support a limited hunting season. The extent to which moose might become occasional island visitors again will be determined by the reaction of the coastal public to the experimental hunting season conducted in the sparsely populated northern woods, where livelihoods and larders still depend, in part, on the success of the season's hunt for hoofed ungulates.

Deer, *Odocoileus virginianus*

Virtually every forested island along the Maine coast shows signs of occasional visits by deer. To some of us, it is hard to believe that deer can get around among the islands as well as they do, but it should not come as

Deer crossing. *Kate Fitzgerald*

a great surprise. Healthy deer are reasonably good swimmers, perhaps not as strong as moose in the water, but certainly capable of the across-the-bay marathons they occasionally undertake. Their center of buoyancy in the water is slightly forward of their center of gravity, which has the effect of allowing their front quarters to ride a little higher as they swim, and their long necks then make it easy for them to keep their heads in the air. Like all mammals without long fur coats, they also float naturally without any great effort. The only part of their body that leaves a bit to be desired in terms of water travel is their set of tiny hooves, which provide their modest propulsion. The splayed feet of the moose allow these beasts to swim a little faster; deer must be slow and steady, but they do get around.

Several summers ago, in a boat off Bluff Head, a granitic promontory on the shore of Vinalhaven, we saw what we assumed was a speck of a bird with a broken wing making its way toward us from the middle of Isle au Haut Bay. It turned out to be a young buck, which set itself ashore unsteadily after what must have been a six-mile marathon from the shores of Acadia National Park's offshore island.

No doubt it is the young bucks that, as in other mammalian groups, do the greatest amount of traveling. In summer when food is plentiful, the younger bucks are looking not so much for adequate forage as for a population of does to impress. They abandon those places where the talent is too scarce and the competition too keen, since in deer societies a few big bucks have all the fun in the fall. The young bucks look for those places where an aging monarch can be successfully challenged during the strut-your-stuff fall rut, when their necks swell, when they rub the velvet off their antlers and generally get aggressive. If they find such a place, they will stay there until one day they themselves are challenged for part of the action.

Deer also move back and forth between the mainland and the nearby islands. There are islands Downeast where the local hunters swear that groups of four or five move out to the large, dense islands for the duration of the hunting season and then return to the mainland either at the onset of colder weather or when the ice builds them a temporary bridge.

Farther off the main, the greater number of deer choose an island on which to spend the winter. Island winters may be more raw, but they are less severe in terms of the degree of cold and the depth of snow. Snow is the great winter killer in a food-stressed deer herd. An accumulation of snow higher than 18 inches effectively limits their movements in search of food. In all but the tallest, it catches them just below the brisket and causes them to "yard up" and wait it out. If you've ever traveled in the woods without snowshoes when the snow depth is over your knees, you know how exhausting it is to try to move about. Once the food is gone from the yard, the grim starvation dance begins, since it takes more energy to go in search of food than the deer have in reserve.

The problem for deer in island winters is that after a certain point in December they are isolated by the frigid water. In the winter, deer need six or eight pounds of woody vegetation per day for food; once that supply is exhausted, they cannot withstand a frigid interisland swim to find a better supply. It is true that island deer are able to supplement their diets with kelps and other seaweeds from the intertidal zone, but in the less severe winters, and in the absence of predation or significant hunting pressure, their populations gradually increase even as their food supplies remain constant or decrease.

Starvation can occur over the course of a severe winter, but the cumulative effects of food stress usually take several years to become acute. One of the first responses of chronic food stress is that does drop a single fawn instead of the usual set of twins in the spring. Fewer fawns survive, disease increases, and the average size of the younger individuals declines. Where these effects continue for years, islands produce herds of tiny deer, adults not much bigger than dogs.

Ultimately, all populations are limited by the supply of food that is available to them; it is a question, however, of how quickly the natural controls intervene to bring a population back in line with its food supply. In short-lived species with high reproductive potential, the interaction happens relatively quickly. A population of rabbits or lemmings, which are the classic example, can peak, then crash, then increase again over the course of a few years, without anyone much noticing—except a few of their predators, which must switch temporarily to other prey species.

Deer, on the other hand, are not so finely tuned with their food supplies. They can put off the inevitable for much longer periods of time, during which they have much greater impact on their range and on the capacity for the range to support future populations.

In a limited island gene pool, where the increased competition and habitat specialization create a trend toward smaller and smaller deer, it is questionable whether blanket prohibitions against hunting make good sense. Even on Isle au Haut, where, as part of the National Park system, deer are meant to be enjoyed, overpopulation may lead ultimately to a crash and to a reduced capacity to support future populations. Sometimes you have to ask yourself some hard questions about hunting. This kind of dilemma is quickly reduced to a discussion of conservation of a resource versus preservation of a theory about the infinitely modulated and feedback systems we believe are inherent to undisturbed nature. We tend to ignore the fact that the world has been greatly modified by our heavy hand in the past. In the case of island deer herds, we have eliminated their predators. Blanket prohibitions often turn out to be ill-conceived efforts to freeze the present systems that are constantly changing in nature. Sooner or later something has to give. On isolated islands with an overpopulation of protected deer, the deer starve in massive numbers.

Marine Mammals

Ever since amphibians first wriggled out of a warm, epicontinental sea, a general progression of life forms has followed them onto land. In some ways this migration is surprising, since life on land is certainly more harsh; temperature extremes are greater from day to night and from season to season; and in the early days of life before a thick atmospheric shield had evolved, ultraviolet light was an intense stress to which land animals had to adapt. But there was a huge variety of niches to occupy once successful strategies had evolved for coping with these wildly fluctuating environmental conditions. One of the most significant of these strategies is warm-bloodedness, which allows animals to regulate their body temperatures rather than be regulated by the whims of the weather. Some people have recently introduced the intriguing notion that even dinosaurs were warm-blooded, and this idea promises to become one of the most heated of paleontological debates for the next generation.

In comparison to life on land, the environment of the sea is stable. It is not surprising, therefore, that some mammals have moved back into the sea, having acquired the advantages of live birth and regulation of body temperature. In fact, four different groups have reversed their ancestors' sea-to-land voyage and now live primarily or exclusively in the salty sea. Sea otters completed the marine transition approximately two million years ago; the sirenians (manatees and dugongs), from whom tales of mermen and mermaids have developed, reentered the sea almost 80 million years ago; and the cetaceans (whales and dolphins) almost 100 million years ago— scarcely after they became warm-blooded mammals in the first place. No doubt the ancestral stocks of these groups first became coastal dabblers, jumping into the water to look for food and climbing back out to eat it or rest. But gradually they began to exploit food resources farther and farther from land. The oldest marine mammals, the whales and dolphins, are full-fledged seagoing creatures, while the youngest—the sea otters—go ashore to rest and bear their young. The seals are somewhere in between; a few are truly seagoing, the rest occasionally have to come ashore. It seems to be a matter of how much evolutionary time they have had to adapt to their watery environs.

Pinnipeds

HARBOR SEAL, *Phoca vitulina*

If you like dogs, particularly water dogs like Labrador retrievers, you are likely to be an easy touch for seals. Because their eyes have almost no iris, their foreheads are decorated with a pair of large, liquid brown eyes, which make them one of the chief attractions at zoos and aquariums, where they entertain for hours on end. The analogy with dogs goes quite a bit further, since the young seals are called pups and their vocalizations are best described as barks. But the adult seals, which are awkward on land, apparently remind naturalists more of farmyard bovines, since they are known as cows and bulls.

Harbor seals are the most widely distributed of the 33 species of seals in the world. They inhabit the waters and half-tide ledges of the shores of Japan and China in the Pacific; the west coast of North America from the Bering Sea to Southern California; and both sides of the North Atlantic. The minimal world population is on the order of 150,000, although there may be twice as many as that.

To the extent that scientific minds have any adequate means of measuring nonhuman intelligence (it seems to be a kind of interspecific insecurity that we are forever trying to figure out how "smart" other mammals are), harbor seals are said to be highly intelligent. They are capable of recognizing individual boats from which people have shot at them in the past; they often "know" whether a fisherman has a gun before they can see it, and they can judge rifle range more accurately than most other quarry. In fact, in the Gulf of Maine, one of the reasons that some fishermen still shoot at them is that harbor seals apparently test their marksmanship to the limit.

The shores of Maine host between 5,000 and 6,000 members of this species of true seal. They are true seals since their hind flippers drag out aft, whereas the eared or walking seals have theirs turned forward so that they are more mobile on land. Although a portion of the population are year-round residents and do not swim to more southerly shores for the winter, it is in the summer that harbor seals are the most numerous and noticeable on the Maine coast. The harbor seals mate in the spring of the year, along about May, either in the water or, on sunny days, when the mood is right, on half-tide ledges. They are not faithful to one single ledge, particularly where they are persecuted, but they have group ranges that a bull and his harem and their pups use throughout the summer. The whelping ledges onto which cows crawl in June to give birth to shiny-eyed 10- to 20-pound pups are generally tucked up into the inner reaches of the bays, where the waters are more protected. There is some evidence that seals can control the timing of their parturition, particularly when a storm makes it difficult and dangerous to crawl onto a ledge. If harbor seals are born in the water, the cows can sometimes cradle the pups between the flippers, but they must get them to land quickly or the youngsters will drown.

The pups suckle from mom's retractable teats and totally depend on their supply of fat-rich milk for the first several weeks of life. If the pups are separated from their mothers during this time, they normally starve, because they have not yet learned how to catch fish. Mortality is high among seal pups. Storm seas and tides often come between mothers and pups, disease strikes others, and angry bulls defending the rights of access to the harem cows will crush a few more in their clumsy fury. After the pups are capable of feeding themselves, they make all the mistakes that young chil-

Stranded seal pup.   *Jim Kosinski*

dren make; annual mortality figures during the first year are on the order of 60 percent.

Year in and year out, boatmen along inshore waters pick up stranded harbor seal pups, which are one of the few species of mammals that can be raised successfully by humans and reintroduced to the wild. It's an arduous and expensive process, but it has been done, and fairly often.

A friend and I had an agonizing opportunity to consider the moral ins and outs of our relationship to seals one evening a few summers ago as we rounded up into a cove in northern Penobscot Bay in late May. Mixed in with the cries of the gulls and the slow lap of the waves on the shore, we could hear the barely audible whines and moans of something else. At the head of the sloping, 30-foot beach, a single silver form began inching toward the water, whining all the while. We rowed ashore and discovered the pup pictured here, small and helpless enough to have seven inches of umbilical cord still attached. What should we do? Bring it aboard and take it ashore to be raised by someone with the proper facilities? (New England Aquarium in Boston and College of the Atlantic in Bar Harbor accept stranded seals.) We struggled with this one for a while, but uncertain of whether a captive life was better than a natural death, we just stared into the big brown eyes as the pup circled our sloop begging for food. The sun set and the rising tide eventually carried it off and away; its cries in the descending curtain of fog finally blended in with the sounds of the night-time sea. We turned in, feeling awful, but then woke to a clear day. The fog had scaled, and just a quarter of a mile north, perhaps a half hour's ride away on a flooding tide, lay a major haulout ledge occupied by 20 or 30 barking seals. (The barks are the means that seals use to let each other know their movements, since cows "imprint" on the voices of their pups, and vice versa.) The chances are that the silver pup had been carried away from its mother on the ebbing tide and been stranded high on the beach, where we had found it exhausted. The chances were better than even that the same pup had been carried back, barking, past the group's haulout site, where it had been rescued by its mother. Anyway, we chose to think so. One of the hardest lessons for our kind to learn—so successful are we with manipulating objects with which we come into contact—is that sometimes doing nothing is better than doing something.

GRAY SEAL, *Halichoerus grypus*

The larger, horse-faced gray seals are much less social than harbor seals. They confine themselves to the outer ledges of offshore islands such as Matinicus Rock, Frenchboro, and Great and Little Duck. Gray seals are at the southern end of their range in Maine and are a rare sight for all but a few lobstermen who haul in these waters. It is thought that no more than 125 of these occasionally gigantic marine mammals—the bulls of which weigh upwards of 800 pounds—inhabit the Gulf of Maine. They are not just uncommon in Maine; their total worldwide population probably does not much exceed 100,000, which makes them one of the rarer mammals on our globe.

One of the reasons, if we can speak of nature as rational, that gray seals are rare is simply that they are less gregarious than harbor seals. They do not fish cooperatively in groups, which is one means by which wild species can reduce their unit level of energy output in relation to the food they eat. It's a matter of efficiency of effort. It's the same with a pack of wolves or African hunting dogs, which can chase down moose or zebra that are both larger and faster than they are. One or two take the lead in a chase, burning up all available energy until they drop to the rear, and another pair that has been loping along moves up—sometimes transecting the arc of the fleeing quarry until predator and prey arrive exhausted at a standoff, where the superior numbers prevail.

Since they are less common, and confine themselves to out-of-the-way ledges that they are unwilling to share with great tribes of their own kind, gray seal populations have never been greatly affected by fishermen. You do not hear the same horror stories from herring fishermen about these enormous seals getting into the nets of fish weirs and wreaking havoc. Nor have their members been, like harbor seals, rendered into oil that, when mixed with red ocher, will make a barn paint defy the elements for years. Maybe individualistic, uncooperative, and antisocial behavior is not such a bad trait after all.

Cetaceans

Unless international events take a sharp turn for the worse and we are all thrown back to a primitive reliance on inexpensive animal oil and protein, many of us will live to watch the end of an era. For a thousand years at least, and probably a lot longer, men of some courage and daring have been paddling or rowing small boats offshore to chase and spear the largest living creatures in the evolutionary record of life—the great whales. Now there is an international moratorium on the taking of all species of great whales. The few smaller species that continue to be killed are the price that the great whaling nations of the world (Japan, Norway, and the USSR) have exacted to ease their moribund industry into its long-overdue grave.

In an ecological sense, whales do something no other creatures can: they transform tiny plants and animals that float around in a nutrient broth of the sea into complex and compact animal proteins and oils. A single calf of one of these grazing whales—called baleen whales from their comblike modified teeth that strain sealife from a single 5,000-gallon gulp—will put on 15,000 to 20,000 pounds in a single year. When you compare this to the time and effort of raising grain or forage for beef, which convert plant life into animal protein at a ratio of 10 pounds of vegetable to one pound of meat, it's easy to understand one reason why many whales have been hunted

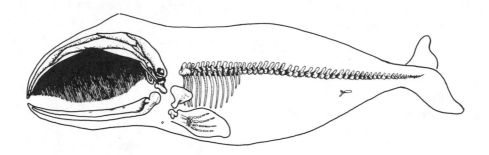

Baleen and skeleton of a right whale.   *Kate Fitzgerald*

to near-extinction. They are too successful at the way they make their living.

James Rosier has given us one of the few eyewitness accounts of how Maine's Indians captured whales:

> He bloweth up the water and . . . is 12 fathoms long; they go in company of their king with a multitude of their boats and strike him with a bone made in the fashion of a harping iron fastened to a rope, which they make great and strong of the bark of trees. . . . Then all their boats come about him, and as he riseth above water, with their arrows they shoot him to death.

The species of whale that the Indians most likely hunted were right whales and humpbacks. Compared with the swift rorqual whales (finbacks, seis, and minkes), both are rather slow in the water. They move along the inshore waters of the Gulf of Maine, appearing in late April or early May. Captain John Smith describes them as appearing in great numbers and "easy of approach," though he turned aside from his original intention of taking whales to catch cod, which were even easier of approach.

John Josselyn writes that the Indians and colonists alike hunted dolphins and porpoises, species of small whales that inhabit Maine waters. Called sea hogs by the English, they were cut into thin pieces and fried. "It tastes like rusty bacon or hung beef, if not worse, but the liver boiled and soused with vinegar is more grateful to the palate." Perhaps so, but it is a little harder to trust Josselyn's judgment on marine mammal matters after reading his description of ambergris, the waxy substance formed within

Harpooned humpbacks. *Penobscot Marine Museum*

sperm whales and occasionally found washed ashore on the Maine coast. Josselyn took it "to be a mushroom . . . that riseth out of certain clammy and bituminous earth under the seas, the billows casting up part of it on land and fish devour the rest." Maybe it's unfair to pick on Mr. Josselyn's ambergris mushroom, since almost no one else at the time had any idea where this valuable substance, used as a perfume fixative, came from. Nor would anyone else be able to say for sure until New England ships had harpooned and slit open enough sperm whales on their Indian and Antarctic feeding grounds to lay that particular mystery to rest.

By the time that New England towns such as New Bedford and Nantucket had established themselves as the centers of the world's first great whaling empire, the costs of fitting out a whaling voyage had become prohibitively expensive for other coastal towns that wanted to get into the trade. Even wealthy Wiscasset shipowners were reluctant to refit their ships with all the costly and specialized equipment necessary to capture and render whales into everything from candles to corset stays. A few expeditions were sent out from Bath and Wiscasset in the 1830s, but they were not overwhelmingly successful, and Maine passed out of the whaling era almost before it began. Occasionally, someone would gear up from an island town such as Vinalhaven to hunt whales in the Gulf of Maine, but until the harpoon with an explosive head was invented in Norway in 1925, and fast steamships were designed, it was not very easy to catch whales from these shore stations.

One of the unanticipated benefits of the few and irregular efforts to capture whales in the Gulf of Maine has been to preserve stocks of the great whales in this corner of the North Atlantic at something close to their original numbers. It has also meant something else far more important. As we learn more about the habits and behavior of these long-lived marine mammals, we have come to realize that they are not just large, dull creatures; nor are they dumb. In fact, they all have elaborate means of communicating with one another in forms and terms that are indistinguishable from language and song. The fact that they have been so rarely hunted from Maine's shores means that many of those individuals that appear year in and year out in coastal waters are not as "paranoid" (to use a human term that seems appropriate) as they are where they have been persecuted more mercilessly. In simple terms, they are approachable.

The toothed whales—dolphins, porpoises, pilot whales, and orcas (the so-called killer whales)—are here too, but they are all smaller than the baleen whales and usually travel about in a great hurry while trying to locate their food—schools of elusive fish. The filter-feeding baleen whales are rarely short of food, since they utilize smaller and more abundant forms of marine life, so they are in general less hurried than their flesh-eating relatives. Another way to look at it is that humpbacks, finbacks, seis, and right whales, to mention the baleen whales (*Mysticeti*) that are common in Maine waters, eat lower on the food chain than the toothed whales (or *Odontoceti*). Two levels lower, in fact. In an ecological sense, you are not so much what you eat but where you eat in relation to the different energy levels of a food chain. Since there is only a 10 percent efficiency of energy conversion as you move up from one level of the food chain to the next—for instance, from copepods to herring—the size and numbers of a predatory species are limited by this ecological principle. Baleen whales strain out tiny but abundant forms of life and can therefore be larger and more numerous than their fish-eating relatives.

It is difficult to overestimate the effect of seeing a whale for the first time. The familiar large land animals are chiefly interesting to us because of their fearlessness, at least where they are not intently hunted. Back in the days when it was still possible to watch grizzly bears feeding at the Yellowstone National Park dump, I remember the shock of seeing one walk past our parked VW bug at dusk, its shoulder filling the window for a shuddering moment. It was obvious from its taut, edgy demeanor that this creature was capable of doing a lot of damage in a very short time.

The baleen whales are different, although it is difficult to convey this to people who have never seen them. Fear is a reaction wholly alien to an

Humpback whale and calf in outer Penobscot Bay. *Jack Morton*

encounter with a great whale—whether you are in a kayak, a large boat, or in the water with them. They are absolutely graceful in their movements—which is difficult to believe, given their size—and they move effortlessly through the water. A slight wave of their flukes and they are 30 to 50 yards away. They appear from below or out of nowhere, changing buoyancy like a living submarine—or, rather, a submarine in the best of circumstances can approximate the movements of a living whale.

If it is a humpback playing with you because all is right with the world for this moment, a large, long, white flipper might break the surface and stretch toward the sky. Ah, sun, sea, and whale between. Ever after worlds without ends. Hundred-million-year-old cetaceans: the two-million-year-old *Homo sapiens* have finally agreed to take their fingers off the triggers of cannons that explode into your great dark backs churning into a sea of red froth. Emotions boil into fury at the spectacle, but now we will leave you in peace and turn the barrels of our long dark cannons at each other, ever after, world to an end.

Looking back over 350 years of our relations with the island mammals, the record could have been much worse. Bears are back; moose, too. Cats and caribou were never enthusiastic islanders. Porcupines, skunks, and groundhogs have never crossed the waters to islands. The deer live on islands occasionally in numbers too great for their own good. Now and again rabbits and raccoons have made the trip out to the islands, often helped by the two-leggeds who want them around for sport or food. The slightly weasely mink has moved into the habitat once occupied by a separate species of sea mink and has been provided additional good accommodations through the efforts of the now-deceased quarrymen. Voles, mice, and muskrats continue to stow away or become cast away on island shores—and provide, in their unknowing way, the meat of scientific inquiry. Seals still haul out on ledges to watch us from a safe distance and to raise their bewhiskered pups. In the rich waters of the Gulf of Maine, the most ancient, and some say most highly developed, mammals of the world sing, splash, and dance in the blue-green water column.

Of the families of island-dwelling mammals, only the canids—wolves and foxes—have seen better times. Wolves have disappeared from everywhere in New England, although recent evidence suggests that they may be returning disguised as large coyotes, which have been relentlessly pushing their range eastward to fill the niche vacated by the wolves. We'll never know whether the original island foxes were red, grey, or silver, but as long as the islands host voles, mice, and birds for food, a few will walk out in cold winters when the ice bridges the worlds of the main and the islands, or will get caught on an ice flow and drift to an offshore home. All things considered, there is a greater diversity of island fauna than I, for one, would have dared to hope.

The Beast that Walks Upright: Island Endemics

The process by which isolated populations adapted to local conditions gradually diverge from the main concentrations of their own kind to form subspecies and eventually true species has been studied since Darwin's time. On far-flung oceanic islands, land birds like Darwin's finches have provided insights into this process called speciation. On coastal islands it is often the mammals whose colonization by the "sweepstakes route" provides clues about the rate at which local adaptations are evolved. The populations of island mammals that most clearly exhibit endemic behavioral characteristics are those warm-blooded animals that walk upright on two legs, after a stage during their initial development when they characteristically crawl around on all fours.

Homo rusticans humorus

The subspecies of two-legged mammals known as *Homo rusticans humorus* is highly migratory on Maine islands, usually arriving on or before the Fourth of July and leaving shortly after the first Monday in September. The adult females of this subspecies commonly arrive before the adult males to set up housekeeping units known as cottages. Although this description of their dwellings implies modest burrows, they are more often than not

The Casco Bay islands, served by ferries like *Abenaki*, are at the cutting edge of tourist development. *Peter M. Ralston.*

large and elegant and command the heights of land on an island or the isolated and protected coves of the shore. In their habitat preferences on Maine islands, *Homo rusticans* might be compared to the black-backs of a gull colony.

During the months of their island stay, they are highly gregarious with other individuals of *H. rusticans* but are not notably sociable with other hominid subspecies. While not often physically imposing, the *rusticans* males have large empires of industrious workers at their beck and call in the metropolitan habitats of the eastern seaboard, where they spend the major portion of each year, and to which they must often return to keep a firm handle on their interests. The young of *Homo rusticans humorus* are strikingly similar to each other in outward appearance, but without more careful anatomical study, it is difficult to determine whether this resemblance is based on a kind of temporary protective coloration in a new and threatening habitat or is the result of a carefully controlled breeding program.

It is difficult to pin down precisely when the initial dispersal of *H. rusticans humorus* to Maine's islands occurred. Appledore House in the Isles of Shoals opened its doors to the public in 1848 and began drawing such distinguished guests as Nathaniel Hawthorne, James Greenleaf Whittier, James Russell Lowell, Sarah Orne Jewett, Richard Henry Dana, and William Dean Howells. It seems that 1870 was the first year that summer visitors were put up in farmhouses on Great Chebeague Island in Casco Bay. In Penobscot Bay, the first summer islander was David Sears III, who had inherited what was then called Brigadier's Island off Searsport from his father. In an attempt to escape from the pace of summer life in Newport, Sears built a large summer cottage at the southern tip of the island sometime before 1870. David Sears' son, David Sears IV, upon graduating from Harvard College in 1874, described himself in his yearbook as residing at "Boston and Brigadier's Island near Bangor, Maine."

Mount Desert Island has often been described as the first island colonized by *H. rusticans humorus*. While a few artists may have thrived in the 1850s, serious rustication did not occur until such men as the President of Harvard and the Episcopal Bishop of Boston arrived in the 1870s. One member of this community, a Supreme Court Justice, Oliver Wendell Holmes, would later write about his Bar Harbor contemporaries:

> We are forming . . . a de facto upper stratum of being which floats over the turbid waves of common life like iridescent film you may have seen spreading over the water about our wharves—very splendid though its origin may have been tar, tallow, train oil, or other such unctuous commodities.

Recent generations of *Homo rusticans* appear to be less tolerant of individuals of unctuous origins.

In 1875 the United States Coast Guard began to buoy the Maine coast, and some of the first cruising yachtsmen appeared in Maine waters. About the same time, steamship companies began making regular runs from Boston to Portland, Bath, and Bangor. Rockland, Deer Isle, and Mount Desert were added when the 244-foot sidewheeler, the *Star of the East,* joined the fleet. With the emergence of efficient water transportation to Maine's islands, several large boarding houses were built to accommodate the growing numbers of *H. rusticans*. In Penobscot Bay, the Quinn House on Eagle Island and the Casino on nearby Butter Island were the most well-known island boarding houses after 1900. The Quinn House flourished until 1931, almost twice as long as the Casino on Butter Island, which had been renamed, for the purposes of tourism, Dirigo Island, after the Maine State motto. The Casino ceased to operate after 1915 when word got around that the advertised swimming pool was actually a shallow duck pond where the feathered dabblers were separated from the hairless bathers only by a wire partition.

In 1929 a virulent economic malady spread through the ranks of *H. rusticans* and their numbers declined dramatically up and down the Maine coast. A few islands continued to support relict populations of the subspecies where they formed homogeneous associations and dominated a single island, but elsewhere they disappeared. For the next 30-odd years, *rusticans* were a rare subspecies on the Maine islands. The virulent epidemic of 1929 caused the initial decline, and the increased use of the automobile in the 1950s made it unnecessary for *H. rusticans* to go somewhere by boat or train and stay for an entire summer season. Instead, they scattered in all directions and explored new habitats.

In the last 10 or 15 years, the numbers of *H. rusticans* have begun to approach pre-epidemic levels, following several decades of favorable economic conditions, which have allowed many to build their own boats and purchase their own islands. The competition for island cottaging space has occasionally been intense and has been reflected in the prices that *H. rusticans* are willing to pay for exclusive use of rocky and exposed coast and islands. Most ecologists believe that the proliferation of *rusticans* cannot last much longer. They are part of the 5 percent (soon to be 4 percent) of

Populations of *H. rusticans* have recently increased on the islands of Maine.   *Jan Erik Pierson*

the world's population that consumes 35 percent of the world's resources, and they have reached, or perhaps exceeded, the carrying capacity of the environments that they frequent.

Homo maritimus humorus

> A community narrows down and grows dreadful ignorant when it is shut up to its own affairs and gets no knowledge of the outside world. . . . In the old days, a good part of the best men here knew a hundred ports and something of the way people lived in them. . . . Shipping's a terrible loss to this part of New England from a social point of view, ma'am.
>
> *The Country of the Pointed Firs,* Sarah Orne Jewett

On most of the larger islands, *Homo rusticans* shares the limited island space with *Homo maritimus humorus,* a subspecies that has been declining over most of the present century but that used to be the dominant mammalian presence on Maine islands. In 1860 there were 11,375 mariners in the state of Maine—a fifth of the population. Although most of the individuals of this subspecies have changed their fishing habits in recent decades and no longer rely on sailing craft, they used to be regarded as among the finest sailors of the world. The entire crew of the America's Cup Race was recruited from the fishing port of Deer Isle when the challenge was first initiated.

The history of the relationship between *H. maritimus* and a mainland species, *Homo officinalis,* has been fraught with misunderstanding and hostility for more than two centuries. In the early years of the Republic, when Maine's merchant marine was recovering from the destructive privateering attacks of the Revolutionary War, the domestic fleet was crippled by an act sponsored by the nation's farm-oriented president, Thomas Jefferson. As France and Britain drifted toward war with each other, Jefferson was determined to avoid being drawn into the hostilities. When England blockaded France, Napoleon responded by blockading German ports on the North Sea, and Jefferson passed the Embargo Act, making it illegal for any American vessel to clear for a foreign port. During the two years the Embargo was in effect after 1807, coastal shipping towns such as Wiscasset were virtually wiped out, as whole cargoes of fish and lumber rotted on the wharves and in the holds of ships.

Jefferson's act immediately created an illicit smuggling trade that was headquartered in, but by no means confined to, Eastport, and all manner of sailing and rowing craft carried cargoes across the border into British-controlled Canada. Captain Samuel Hadlock of Little Cranberry Island off Mount Desert dried his catch of cod on the coast of Labrador and sailed directly for Portugal, where he sold it for a high price and returned with salt and lemons. Hadlock made out so well on the enterprise that he ordered a new schooner, which he named *Hazard*—what else? In the future,

Anatomy of a kitchen of *H. maritimus*. *George Putz*

whenever there was money to be made in an illicit trade, some of the sub-species of *H. maritimus* would be at hand to take advantage of quick profits to be made by those who knew the waters.

Some of the behavioral characteristics of *H. maritimus* date to their earliest days on the Maine coast. John Josselyn described Maine's fishermen as "walking taverns." A master mariner from Islesboro, writing his town's history two centuries later, described *H. maritimus* individuals as super-stitious: "They firmly believe in witches and will not enter an under-taking on Friday."

During the salt cod era, tremendous amounts of shorefront land were necessary for flake yards to dry the catches, and *H. maritimus* continues to operate as if the 1729 colonial ordinance reserving the first 40 feet of the shore for fishermen were still in effect. It is in this conception of property rights that they most often come into conflict with *H. rusticans*, who dom-inate island shores for two months out of the year before returning to more comfortable fastnesses. Among populations of *H. maritimus*, an intri-cate web of ownership rights is enforced by rules based on kinship, resi-dence, and only then upon actual ownership of property. Unresolved con-flicts between these two island subspecies have in the past occasionally degenerated into unselective vandalism and arson.

Whatever the causes and results of subspecific competition between

Homo rusticans and *Homo maritimus,* it pales beside the highly territorial behavior between neighboring populations of *H. maritimus.* "Lobster wars" occur when an aging or declining population of one island's fishermen loses control over traditional waters. Boundaries on the water are fluid, and they are maintained by informal agreements until one group can no longer adequately defend its territory. When this situation arises, traps are cut in an escalating confrontation, which has from time to time involved gunplay.

Populations of *Homo maritimus* tend to follow their own laws rather than those of landsmen, partly because they know the local waters better than anyone else and can exercise their authority as they see fit. Recently the appearance of electronic navigation equipment has greatly improved the ability of both *H. rusticans* and *H. officinalis* to get around in thick weather, which to some extent threatens the independence and traditional authority of *maritimus* populations, though lately even the new vessels of the latter are similarly equipped, at the insistence of the banks, who now

Homo maritimus.   *George Putz*

Fourth of July on Vinalhaven; part of the traditional patriotic,
celebratory sensibility of island town life. *George Putz*

own a great percentage of any fleet. In the days of sail, however, a fisherman could define his position and navigate among the islands and ledges
by identifying the "rote," or the sound of the sea breaking upon a rocky
shore. These days, the number of individuals of *Homo maritimus* who can
navigate out of their own local waters by dead reckoning is so small that
rusticans are able to challenge them for superiority in this respect.

By having lived an existence of making do with the materials at hand,
H. maritimus has a well-deserved reputation for being supremely inventive.
It was a Maine islander who invented the mackerel jig in the 1820s; another developed the seine for the mackerel fishery; a third islander figured
out how to keep a huge catch alive long enough so they wouldn't rot before
packing or pickling in salt brine. None of these advances, though, matches
the creative energy that Clarence Howard of Eagle Island in northern
Penobscot Bay brought to the lobster fishery. He was the first to use a brass
rudderpost and packing box in place of the iron pipe through the hull,
which often leaked badly when boats were loaded. He was the first to use
an automobile steering box rather than rely on slack tiller ropes, which
could break on a hard turn. He was the first to use a jury-rigged Ford rear
axle for a lobster-pot hauler, and when he turned his attention to the herring fishery, he was the first to set seine nets off a stern roll and the first
in the area to use a depth recorder as a fishfinder.

Talents such as these are rare enough anywhere, but on Maine's islands, they are at least partially maintained by the islanders' habit of producing large families whose offspring marry within island communities. In the genealogy of one Islesboro clan, a settler who moved to the island had five children, four of whom found spouses on Rackliff, Leadbetter, South Fox (Vinalhaven), and Matinicus Islands, respectively. The fifth moved away to Ohio. One of the patriarchs of Matinicus Island last century married three times and produced 28 children. Even today, within island communities, sooner or later almost everyone is vaguely related to everyone else. It may be anathema to some, but it is an ecological arrangement that ensures that those traits that convey high survival value are well represented in future generations.

Epilogue

FROM WHATEVER INDISTINCT POINT in biological time that *Homo sapiens* became one of the earth's newest species, we have been radiating into all kinds of unlikely environments, from the frozen polar tundras to the blazing equatorial deserts, and recently even into the black void of space. But we occupy no habitat more densely or tenaciously than the shores of the earth's major bodies of water: the oceans and the banks of the rivers that empty into them. In ecological terms we are, more than anything else, a littoral species.

In the western world, coastal island cultures have grown up, flourished, and all but disappeared in historic times. The earliest Neolithic settlers in the British Isles evidently preferred the small Orkney and Shetland Islands to the island-continents of Great Britain. Tiny St. Kilda Island, at the outer rim of the Hebrides, was an intact insular community whose economy for a millennium was based on harvesting of seabird oil, eggs, feathers, and meat. During the 6th and 7th centuries the uninhabited islands off the coasts of Ireland and England were settled by Christian ascetics who chose these remote rocks to live the life of their resurrection. In Maine the first half-dozen unsuccessful settlements were located on islands, and the first permanent settlement was successfully established on Damariscove Island in 1622. The motives behind these island settlements have varied, but the ecological underpinnings for them haven't. Islands are surrounded by sinuous and productive littoral zones that shelter edible marine life nourished by nutrients washing off the land and circulated by tidal rhythms. The coastal marshes and intervales provided ideal natural livestock pasturage from whose shores small homemade fishing vessels were easily launched on expeditions to supplement the agricultural efforts.

In the early decades of the 20th century, the entire coast of Maine fell on hard times because of a combination of overfishing, overcutting, poor soil management, the eclipse of merchant sail, the disappearance of markets for such products as salt cod and granite, and the withdrawal of government support for the offshore fisheries. Those communities on the islands at the edge of the coast, which depended most heavily on fishing and shipping, fell into a decline more rapid and more serious than occurred in similar communities on the mainland, where shifts to other means of earning a living were possible. Along with this decline, an independent, thrifty, hardworking, self-reliant, and vigilant way of life was eclipsed. If it were not for the modest development of the luxury lobster fishery, it is doubtful whether much of a seafaring tradition would have persisted in the state where the sea has historically been the most vital economic and social asset. As with all tragedies, this decline has all too human a face. An insular community that loses its economic identity comes to resent any outsiders and turns more and more on itself, like a snake swallowing its tail. Disillusionment and demoralization are expressed in accelerated rates of alcoholism and drug abuse and the institutionalized dependence of a welfare economy.

After nearly a century of neglect, Maine's coastal islands have again become important. Although issues such as the siting of an oil refinery on Moose Island in Eastport have been churning public discussions for more than a decade, the real conflicts—between those who wish to see the unique natural features of the islands and the Maine coast managed and those who wish to protect them as they are now—have not fully emerged. The issue of the Eastport refinery, for example, is more a dress rehearsal for the real conflicts to come, simply because the Pittston Company's proposal has so few friends in court. The company that was responsible for the collapse of the dredge spoil dam that destroyed the West Virginia coal mining town of Buffalo Creek has convinced very few people that it is capable of guiding huge supertankers through the tricky and narrow Head Harbor Passage without a serious mishap.

Pittston aside, the issue of turning the Maine coast's deep water and adjacent island land bases into economic assets will surface again and again in the near future. The siting of a power plant on Sears Island in Penobscot Bay and the drilling for oil on Georges Bank are two matters that have recently arrived on the public docket. The development of islands for recreation and summer homes and the management of island forests for timber are hovering in the background. There will be more schemes and dreams to come.

These issues are both large and small—large as the sea itself and small as a ledge whose nesting seabirds may be imperiled by the contamination of oil; large as the possibility of Maine's becoming an energy source for the rest of New England and small as the confrontations between individuals

Winter crossing on Vinalhaven ferry.   *Jim Kosinski*

who seek to maintain traditional rights of access to islands and those who have recently purchased the same for solitude.

An anthropologist friend who used to write environmental impact statements, when he could find no other work, is fond of describing how he used to read report after report that devoted long chapters to analyses of how a certain project would affect wildlife, but just a few pages to the effects on the elderly. In fact, it seems a curious myopia that in the decade following Earth Day, most environmentalists who have made a career of protecting the furred, feathered, and flowered have rarely extended the same umbrella of concern to the scruffy lot of the rest of humankind. The delaying politics of the environmental lobby have served the greatest number of us very well in the last decade. They have given us, among other things, time to survey the damage of unprecedented growth of industrial society, to repair some of the worst of its excesses, to educate an increasingly concerned public, and to develop skills and techniques to guide future development.

The success of the environmental movement in slowing down our headlong flight into ever-larger development projects with increasingly large and hidden environmental costs would have been hard to predict 10 years ago. But it is much easier to rest on the victories of the past than it is to plan whether and where to compromise in the future. All development entails some risk, but all risks are not doomed to failure. The fear is

Marine railway on an island farm.   *Rick Perry*

that public confidence in, and support of, the environmental movement
will begin to erode unless its adherents are able to allay the growing suspicion that they are against everything and for nothing.

The fate of whether and to what extent Maine's islands will be developed for commercial or individual purposes hangs in the balance between
various state and federal agencies (which have recently asserted an interest
in the management of coastal resources) and the private, nonprofit conservation groups (which own an increasing number of most significant islands). The wild cards in this equation are the residents of year-round
island communities whose opinions and interests are often ignored but
whose behavior toward these groups is likely to be the final arbiter. It is
difficult to imagine how a conservation group's effort to protect nesting
seabirds can succeed without the support of the inhabitants who have tra-

Sunset. *Jim Kosinski*

ditionally used the birds as an additional food source; or how a summer cabin can be built on an island that has traditionally been regarded as a semipublic resource without an assurance that the new owner intends to honor such use; or how some of the islands might again be developed for sheep pasturage without the support of a community that is not above muttoning during deer season.

Few islanders oppose the gradual development of specific islands by individuals or groups who help financially to support hard-pressed island businesses, schools, and clinics; who favor the expansion of the fisheries; or who support the kinds of proposals that enable island residents to earn an honest living. To the extent that environmental decisions on island resource use are made on the basis of the *total* community—which includes the human community—the environmental movement will remain a viable and healthy political force. To the extent that human communities are excluded from the decision-making calculus, environmental policies will come to serve narrow, relatively privileged special interests. If the environmental movement should then collapse, it takes no great prescience to predict that well-financed development interests will quickly move into the vacuum and divide up the spoils for their own benefit.

Sources and Resources

Albion, R. G. *Forests and Seapower*. Cambridge, Massachusetts: Harvard University Press, 1926.

Authoritative study of the British interest in the settlement of Maine from the point of view of their drive to control the supply of masts of white pine from the coast and islands.

Apollonio, Spencer. *The Gulf of Maine*. Rockland, Maine: Courier-Gazette, 1979.

A highly informative, technical book on the physical and chemical oceanography of Maine waters written by Maine's Commissioner of Marine Resources.

Atkins, C. G. *Sixth Report of the Commission of Fisheries of the State of Maine*. Augusta, Maine, 1872.

Useful for its line drawings of the various types of fish weirs used at the time.

Audubon, Maria R. *Audubon and His Journals*. New York: Scribner's, 1897.

Audubon's letters describing his voyages to Eastport, Maine, where he fitted out for his Labrador expedition.

Babcock, Charles. *Along the Shores from Boston to Mount Desert*. (pamphlet) 1865.

A description of the coast of Maine from deckside, with a few descriptions of the islands.

Baird, John C. "Some Ecological Aspects of the White-Tailed Deer on Isle au Haut, Maine." University of Maine, Orono, Master's Thesis, 1966.

Documents island deer use of intertidal seaweeds.

Barbour, M. G., et al. *Coastal Ecology*. Berkeley: University of California Press, 1973.

Basic ecological characteristics of coastal plant habitats.

Baxter, James P. (ed.). *The Trelawney Papers,* in *Collections of Maine Historical Society,* Second Series, Documentary, Vol. III. Portland, Maine, 1884.

The letters of Jonathon Winter giving the best early description of island living, including accounts of fishing, farming and lumbering on Richmond Island and Casco Bay islands, 1632–1645.

—————————. *Sir Ferdinando Gorges and His Province of Maine.* Boston, 1890.

Description of the Popham Colony on Georgetown Island and references to later settlements on Damariscove and Monhegan.

—————————. *Christopher Levett of York.* Portland, Maine, 1893.

Levett's account of his voyage to the Maine coast is one of the best sources of ecological information on the presettlement forests. Nicely edited by Baxter.

—————————. *George Cleeve of Casco.* Portland, Maine, 1885.

Like the rest of Baxter's work, this is a highly readable account of early Maine history that provides ecological details omitted in many histories.

Belknap, Jeremy. *History of New Hampshire.* Vol. I, 1784; Vols. II and III, later.

One of the few contemporary accounts of the white pine masting industry conducted along the coasts of Maine and New Hampshire.

Bent, Arthur C. *Life Histories of North American Diving Birds.* Washington, D.C.: *Bulletin,* Smithsonian Institution, 1919. Reprinted by Dover Press.

Descriptions of behavior, feeding, breeding range, and food of auks, puffins, and guillemots by one of America's great field ornithologists. Because so much of Bent's data was collected on Maine island nesting colonies, this series is an important source of information on the distribution of various species during the first two decades of this century.

—————————. *Life Histories of North American Gulls and Terns.* Washington, D.C.: *Bulletin,* Smithsonian Institution, 1921. Reprinted by Dover Press.

Same information as above for the six common nesting species of gulls and terns on Maine islands.

—————————. *Life Histories of North American Petrels and Pelicans and Their Allies.* Washington, D.C.: *Bulletin,* Smithsonian Institution, 1922. Reprinted by Dover Press.

Breeding information on Leach's storm petrels on Maine islands.

—————————. *Life Histories of North American Wildfowl, Part II.* Washington, D.C.: *Bulletin,* Smithsonian Institution, 1925. Reprinted by Dover Press.

Eiders, and the winter ducks.

—————————. *Life Histories of North American Birds of Prey, Parts I and II.* Washington, D.C.: *Bulletin,* Smithsonian Institution, 1937 and 1938. Reprinted by Dover Press.

Accounts of the distribution of ospreys and eagles on Maine's islands.

Beveridge, Norwood P. *The North Island: Early Times to Yesterday*. North Haven, Maine, 1976.

A Bicentennial history with informative descriptions of North Haven's farming and shipbuilding history.

Bigelow, Henry B., and William C. Schroeder. *Fishes of the Gulf of Maine*. Fishery Bulletin No. 74. U. S. Fish and Wildlife Service. Washington, D.C.: Government Printing Office, 1953.

Wonderfully descriptive species accounts of all the commercial and noncommercial fish found in Maine waters. Bigelow was probably the most famous and knowledge-able oceanographer of Maine waters; he was one of the few scientists who had the respect of both his colleagues and a great many fishermen, because he was an ex-cellent seaman.

Bishop, W. H. "Fish and Men in the Maine Islands." *Harpers New Monthly Magazine,* 1880. Reprinted by Lillian Berliawsky Books, Camden, Maine.

Blunt, Edmund M. *The American Coastal Pilot, Containing Directions for the Principal Harbors, Capes and Headlands on the Coasts of North and South America*. 1800, with revised editions every few years.

The navigational directions into several Maine harbors give detailed descriptions of the conditions of various islands. It is a useful volume to help reconstruct the composition of original island forests.

Bolton, Charles K. *The Real Founders of New England; The Stories of Their Life Along the Coast, 1602–1628*. Boston, 1929.

Firsthand accounts of the techniques of mackereling, haking, longlining, salting, drying, lobstering, canning, etc., conducted on and around the Maine islands at the height of the fishing industry. Very fine and revealing drawings.

Bourque, Bruce. "Aboriginal Settlement and Subsistence on the Maine Coast." *Man in the Northeast*. No. 6. Fall 1973.

——————. "Fishing in the Gulf of Maine: A 5,000-Year History." *Blackberry Reader,* Gary Lawless (ed.), Brunswick, Maine.

These two articles give one of the most recent reviews of Indian use of the re-sources of the islands of Maine. Much of the information is based on artifacts ex-cavated from North Haven. Bourque is the Maine State Archaeologist.

Bureau of Industrial and Labor Statistics of Maine. *The Granite Industry of Maine*. 16th Annual Report. Augusta, Maine, 1902.

A listing of all the major island and inland quarries and a summary of the major projects for which each supplied stone.

Burrage, Henry S. (ed.). *Early English and French Voyages, Chiefly from Hakluyt, 1534–1608*. New York, 1906.

One of the places to read annotated accounts of Rosier's Relation of Weymouth's exploration of the St. George Islands in Muscongus Bay. Also, Pring's discovery of the Fox Islands and the Relation of the Voyage to Sagadahoc (the account of the failure of the Popham Colony).

Carleton, W. M. "Masts and the King's Navy." *New England Quarterly*, 12, pp. 4–18, 1939.

Centennial Committee. *Brief Historical Sketch of the Town of Vinalhaven*. Rockland, Maine, 1900.

One of the few early histories of Vinalhaven, mostly reconstructed out of the town records, with a few important pieces of information.

Chadbourne, Ava H. *Maine Place Names and the Peopling of Its Towns*. Freeport, Maine: Bond Wheelwright Co., 1955.

Town-by-town summaries of the dates of incorporation, with important facts about the establishment of island communities. Reissued in 1970 by counties.

Chapman, Carleton A. *Geology of Acadia National Park*. Greenwich, Connecticut: Chatham Press, 1970.

The best single source of technical information on Maine coast geology, emphasizing the granite belt, and written for a nontechnical audience. Also includes self-guided tours of Mount Desert and Schoodic—which is the best way to teach yourself geology.

Clifford, Harold. *The Boothbay Harbor Region 1906–1960*. Freeport, Maine: Bond Wheelwright Co., 1960.

Some interesting detail of the fishing industry at the beginning of 1900 and hard times.

Colby, A. H. *Colby's Atlas*. Portland, Maine, 1881.

Shows the numbers of dwellings and commercial establishments on islands, particularly around Vinalhaven, Deer Isle, and Mount Desert.

Conkling, Philip W. *Green Islands, Green Sea*. Rockland, Maine: Hurricane Island Outward Bound School, 1980.

A guide to foraging on the islands of Maine. Good drawings by Kate Fitzgerald.

Crowell, Kenneth L. "Downeast Mice." *Natural History*, October 1975.

Describes Crowell's experiments with mice on Maine islands.

——————. "Experimental zoogeography: introductions of mice to small islands." *American Naturalist*, Vol. 107, No. 956, 1973.

Same information for the technical audience.

Daughters of Liberty. *Historical Researches of Gouldsboro, Maine*. Bar Harbor, Maine, 1904.

A few bits of information on Stave and Ironbound Islands in Frenchman Bay.

Davis, Ronald B. "Spruce-Fir Forests of the Coast of Maine." *Ecological Monographs,* Vol. 36, Spring 1966.

The best technical introduction to the vascular flora of coastal spruce forests.

Day, Clarence A. *A History of Maine Agriculture 1604–1865.* Orono, Maine: University of Maine Study Series No. 68, 1954.

A comprehensive account of farming methods from the earliest settlement to the Civil War, with a surprising amount of interesting ecological detail.

——————. *Farming in Maine 1860–1940.* Orono, Maine: University of Maine Study Series No. 78, 1963.

Primarily useful for the description of island sheep farms.

Diamond Island Association. *Great Diamond Island.* Portland, Maine, 1972.

Mostly late 19th and 20th century history of this Casco Bay island.

Dow, Robert L. "The Need for a Technological Revolution in the Methods of Catching Marine Fish and Shellfish." *Marine Technology Society Journal,* December 1979–January 1980.

Useful summary of the recent history of commercial fishing in the Gulf of Maine, with some summaries of landings for the 1960s.

Drury, William H. "Rare Species." *Biological Conservation.* Vol. 6, pp. 162–168.

A theoretical discussion of the importance of islands for maintaining sources of genetic diversity.

——————. "Population Changes in New England Seabirds." *Bird Banding.* Vol. 44, pp. 267–313, and Vol. 45, pp. 1–15. 1973–1974.

A definitive study of the breeding ecology of the major species of seabirds nesting on the Maine and New England coasts, and an account of how their numbers fluctuate over time.

Eastman, Joel W. *A History of Sears Island, Searsport, Maine.* Searsport Historical Society, 1976.

Well-researched history of this north Penobscot Bay island mostly from the Knox Papers. The study was financed by Central Maine Power Company, which has proposed in recent years to build either a nuclear or a coal-fired power plant on this island.

Eaton, Cyrus L. *History of Thomaston, Rockland and South Thomaston.* Hallowell, Maine, 1865. Reprinted by Courier-Gazette, Rockland, Maine, 1972.

Good early history of the islands off these towns, with some interesting detail on animal life.

——————. *Annals of the Town of Warren, etc.* Hallowell, Maine, 1872.

Good details of early shipbuilding along the upper reaches of the St. George River.

Eckert, Allan W. *Great Auk*. Boston: Little, Brown, 1963.

The story of the extinction of this giant seabird, told from the point of view of the auk with a great deal of ecological detail.

Eckstorm, Fannie Hardy. *Indian Place Names of the Penobscot Valley and Maine Coast*. Orono, Maine: University of Maine Study Series No. 55, 1941.

A compendium of definitive information and carefully documented research on the meaning of Indian place names.

Eliot, Charles. *John Gilley, Maine Farmer and Fisherman*. Boston: Beacon Press, 1899.

An admiring portrait of the *pater familias* of Baker's Island by one of Mount Desert Island's early summer people—who was, incidentally, President of Harvard College.

Enk, John C. *A Family Island in Penobscot: The Story of Eagle Island*. Rockland, Maine: Courier-Gazette, 1953.

Mostly the recollections of Captain Erland Quinn of the four generations of Quinns who inhabited Eagle Island and the various occupations they pursued.

Fairburn, William A. *Merchant Sail*. 6 vols. Center Lovell, Maine: Fairburn Marine Educational Foundation, 1945.

A unique work of everything anyone will ever want to know about the days of merchant sail. The section on Maine boats is as comprehensive as any work in print.

Farrow, John P. *History of Islesborough, Maine*. Bangor, Maine, 1893.

Mostly genealogies of the early settlers, some of whom settled on the smaller surrounding islands. The written descriptions of original lots on the island give a surprisingly detailed look at the composition of the original forest.

——————. *The Romantic Story of David Robertson Among the Islands, Off and On the Coast of Maine*. Belfast, Maine, 1898.

This story might not be as interesting if it hadn't been written by a historian. With great attention to detail, it describes the life of the original settler of Lime Island in Penobscot Bay.

Fillmore, Robert B. *Gems of the Ocean*. Privately published, 1914. Available from Maine State Library.

Various facts about turn-of-the-century life on Matinicus and Ragged Islands and Matinicus Rock.

Goode, George Brown. "Fishery Industries of the United States." U. S. 47th Congress, 1st Session (1881–1882), *Miscellaneous Documents,* Vol. 7, Section II, 1882.

A valuable source of information on American fishing near its height; compiled by regions.

Goold, Nathan. *A History of Peaks Island and Its People*. Portland, Maine, 1897.

A smattering of useful historical details.

Graham, Frank. *Gulls—A Social History*. New York, 1975.

A complete history of the relationship of gulls and men from the mid-19th century through the present. The majority of it focuses on Maine nesting islands. Also, lovely photography by Chris Ayres.

Grant, W. L. *Voyages of Samuel de Champlain, 1604–1618*. New York: Scribner's, 1907.

Descriptions of Champlain's two voyages along the Maine coast, reconstructed and annotated from Champlain's detailed notebooks.

Greene, Francis B. *History of Boothbay, Southport and Boothbay Harbor, Maine. 1623–1905*. Portland, Maine, 1906.

A standard and comprehensive history.

Greenleaf, Moses. *A Survey of the State of Maine (in Reference to its Geographical Features, Statistics and Political Economy)*. Portland, Maine, 1829.

Greenleaf was the man hired to survey the publicly owned islands after Maine became a state. Lots of original hard data.

Grindle, Roger. *Quarry and Kiln, The Story of Maine's Lime Industry*. Rockland, Maine: Courier-Gazette, 1971.

Grindle grew up in Rockland and has provided a look at the lime industry mostly gleaned through old newspaper accounts.

——————. *Tombstones and Paving Blocks, The History of the Maine Granite Industry*. Rockland, Maine: Courier of Maine, 1977.

Provides useful background information on the operations on Vinalhaven, Hurricane Island, Clark Island, and Dix Island.

Gross, A. O. "The Present Status of the Double-Crested Cormorant on the Coast of Maine." *Auk,* Vol. 62, pp. 513–537.

Valuable historical review of the fortunes of the cormorant.

——————. "The Present Status of the Great Black-Backed Gull on the Coast of Maine." *Auk,* Vol. 62, pp. 241–256.

Describes the range extension of this Arctic species of gull.

Gross, Clayton. *Island Chronicles. Accounts of Days Past in Deer Isle and Stonington*. Stonington, Maine: Penobscot Bay Press, 1977.

Some interesting information on the fishing industry of Deer Isle around the turn of the century; by a resident.

Halle, Louis J. *The Storm Petrel and the Owl of Athena*. Princeton: Princeton University Press, 1970.

A delightful series of essays about pelagic seabirds written by a gifted amateur naturalist.

Hill, A. F. "The Vegetation of the Penobscot Bay Region, Maine." *Proceedings of the Portland Society of Natural History*. Vol. 3, Part 3, pp. 305–438, 1923.

Comprehensive and useful description of island vegetation in Penobscot Bay; written by a botanist of the old school (i.e., someone who went out and identified plants in the field and arranged them according to habitat).

Hosmer, George L. *An Historical Sketch of the Town of Deer Isle, Maine; with Notices of Its Settlers and Early Inhabitants*. Boston, 1886.

Hosmer's is the definitive history of Deer Isle, and it contains a great deal of interesting detail about this island and the smaller ones in Merchant Row.

Jenney, Charles F. *The Fortunate Island of Monhegan, A Historical Monograph*. Proceedings of the American Antiquarian Society, Vol. 31.

A useful summary of Monhegan's history compiled from secondary sources.

Jewett, Sarah Orne. *The Country of the Pointed Firs*. New York: Houghton Mifflin Co., 1910.

Sketches of coastal life and the inhabitants of a small fishing village. Includes one or two island characters.

Johnson, Douglas W. *The New England Acadian Shoreline*. New York: Hafner, 1925.

A classic study of the physiography of the New England coast; it describes why regions look like they do.

Johnston, John. *A History of Bristol and Bremen*. Albany, New York, 1873.

This work was most useful for its descriptions of the various Indian tribes that influenced the early history of Maine.

Jones, Herbert G. *The Isles of Casco Bay in Fact and Fancy*. Portland, Maine, 1946.

Mostly fancy.

Josselyn, John. *An Account of Two Voyages to New England*. William Veazie (ed.). Boston, 1865.

An excellent source of contemporary descriptions of everything from fishing and fishermen to black flies, Indians, lobsters, and wolves around his brother's plantation in Saco during the 1630s and 1640s.

————. *New England Rarities Discovered*. Edward Tuckerman (ed.). Boston, 1865.

Josselyn's second volume from his recollections of his stay in the New World. It is a source of descriptions of native grasses and wildflowers. His species accounts of New England wildlife, while entertaining, are sometimes fantastic and at other times misleading.

Joy, Barbara E. *Historical Notes on Mount Desert Island*. Bar Harbor, Maine, 1975.

A compendium of historical facts that provide some interesting details not available in the standard histories of the area.

Kingsbury, John M. *The Rocky Shore*. Greenwich, Connecticut: Chatham Press, 1970.

One of the best introductions available to the life found in the rocky intertidal by the former director of the Isles of Shoals Marine Laboratory. Fine drawings by Marcia and Edward Norman allow it to be used as a field guide.

Kobbe, Gustow. "Heroism in the Lighthouse Service. A description of life on Matinicus Rock." *Century Magazine*, 1897.

A few useful tidbits.

Kohl, J. G. *History of the Discovery of Maine*. Collections of Maine Historical Society. Documentary History. 1869.

A good introduction to the geography of the coast and the waters of the Gulf of Maine by an authoritative German geographer.

Korschgan, Carl E. *Coastal Waterbird Colonies: Maine*. U. S. Fish and Wildlife Service, Biological Services Program, 1979.

A listing of the number and distribution of the various waterbirds that breed on the Maine coast. Also includes a useful summary of historical changes and a good bibliography.

Kress, Stephen W. "The History and Future of North Atlantic Seabird Populations."

Unpublished pamphlet. Available from National Audubon Society.

Lewis, J. R. *The Ecology of Rocky Shores*. London: Hodder and Stoughton, 1964.

A British text that gives the most comprehensive account of the dominant plant and animal communities of rocky shores.

Lockely, R. M. *Gray Seal, Common Seal*. New York: October House, 1966.

Detailed species accounts of these two seals common to Maine waters. Written in informative, nontechnical language.

Loomis, Alfred F. *Ranging the Maine Coast*. New York: Norton, 1939.

A classic by one of *Yachting* magazine's great writers. Lots of interesting historical information woven into the narrative of his voyages aboard the *Hotspur*.

Lunt, Vivian. *A History of Frenchboro, Long Island Plantation, Hancock County, Maine*.

Typed manuscript, 1976. Available from the Maine State Library.

Valuable addition to the local island histories.

MacGinitie, G. E., and Nettie MacGinitie. *Natural History of Marine Animals.* New York: McGraw-Hill, 1968.

Another husband-and-wife team who obviously spend their spare time together collecting creatures from California's rocky intertidal. This volume was most useful for its introductory chapters on marine food webs.

McLane, Charles B. *Islands of the Mid-Maine Coast: Penobscot and Blue Hill Bays.* Privately published, 1980.

McLane has written individual histories of 275 islands from Port Clyde to Bass Harbor, which will undoubtedly be a significant contribution to island history.

Manley, Sean and Robert. *Islands: Their Lives, Legends and Lore.* Philadelphia: Chilton, 1970.

For the hard-core island buffs.

Manville, Richard H. "The Vertebrate Fauna of Isle au Haut, Maine." *American Midland Naturalist,* Vol. 72, 1964.

One of the few accurate accounts of mammalian species found on an offshore island of Maine.

May, R. M. "Island Biogeography and the Design of Wildlife Preserves." *Nature,* Vol. 254, pp. 177–178.

Interesting theoretical discussion that bears on the preservation issues confronting Maine islands.

Mendall, H. L. "The Home-Life and Economic Status of the Double-Crested Cormorant, *Phalacrocorax auritus auritus.*" Orono, Maine: University of Maine Study Series, 2nd Series, No. 38, 1936.

Detailed history and biology of the cormorant.

——————. "Eider Ducks, Islands and People." *Maine Fish and Wildlife.* Vol. 18, No. 2, pp. 4–7, 1976.

Presents the author's hypotheses on the disturbance to nesting eiders posed by human visitation to islands.

Merrill, John and Suzanne (eds.). *Squirrel Island, Maine. The First Hundred Years.* Freeport, Maine: Bond Wheelwright, 1973.

The story of the island's summer colony.

Monks, John P. *History of Roque Island, Maine.* Boston: The Colonial Society of Massachusetts, 1967.

A good history of this unique island.

Morison, Samuel E. *The Story of Mount Desert Island, Maine.* Boston: Little, Brown, 1960.

A colorful and amusing history by one of Mount Desert's most respected summer residents.

——————. *The European Discovery of America: The Northern Voyages.* Boston: Little, Brown, 1971.

What makes Morison such an excellent naval historian is that he has cruised much of the same area as the original explorers. Also, few other historians have such a graceful prose style.

——————. *Samuel de Champlain: Father of New France.* Boston: Little, Brown, 1972.

Morison on Morison's favorite explorer. Includes a good description of Champlain's two expeditions along the Maine coast.

Morse, Ivan. *Friendship Long Island.* Middletown, New York: Whitlock Press, 1974.

The recollections of one of the island's oldest residents, whose memory stretches back to before the turn of this century. A good oral history.

Norton, Arthur H. "Some Noteworthy Plants from the Islands and Coast of Maine." *Rhodora*, Vol. 15, No. 176, 1913.

Norton was the backbone of the Portland Museum of Natural History for almost three decades and traveled extensively along the Maine coast visiting nesting islands and collecting plants.

Palmer, Ralph S. "Maine Birds." *Bulletin of the Museum of Comparative Zoology.* Cambridge, Massachusetts: Harvard College, 1949.

Palmer graciously acknowledges that this volume is "based largely on data gathered by Arthur Herbert Norton." It provides a unique look at the breeding colonies of the Maine islands with many notes on the condition of the vegetation.

Porter, Eliot. *Summer Island.* Sierra Club.

A lovely book about a Penobscot Bay island by the man who nearly invented color nature photography.

·Raisz, Edwin J. "The Scenery of Mount Desert Island, Its Origin and Development." New York Academy of Sciences, Vol. 31, 1929.

Good description of the glacial epoch and its effects in shaping landscapes.

Richardson, David T. "Final Report, Assessment of Harbor and Gray Seal Populations in Maine." Augusta, Maine: Department of Marine Resources, 1975.

Solid research.

————————. "Final Report, Feeding Habits and Population Studies of Maine's Harbor and Gray Seals." Augusta, Maine: Department of Sea and Shore Fisheries, 1973.

The only original research on the feeding habits of seals on the Maine coast.

Rowe, William H. *The Maritime History of Maine: Three Centuries of Shipbuilding and Seafaring*. Freeport, Maine: Bond Wheelwright Co., 1948.

Particularly useful for the accounts of forest cutting for shipbuilding.

————————. *Shipbuilding Days on Casco Bay*. Portland, Maine, 1946.

The forerunner of the volume described above.

Russell, Howard S. *A Long Deep Furrow, Three Centuries of Farming in New England*. Hanover, New Hampshire: University Press of New England, 1976.

A one-of-a-kind book that is both an encyclopedic historical reference and a good treatment of the ecology of farming.

St. Pierre, James A. "Maine's Coastal Islands: Recreation and Conservation." Augusta, Maine: Bureau of Parks and Recreation, 1978.

A listing of the significant resources attached to Maine islands. Also a comprehensive bibliography.

Sauer, Carl O. *Northern Mists*. San Francisco: Turtle Island Foundation, 1968.

One of the only serious histories of European exploration of the New World to research the question of whether early unrecorded fishing voyages visited the New England coast.

Schemnitz, Sanford D. "Marine island-mainland movements of white-tailed deer." *Journal of Mammalogy*, Vol. 56, 1975.

Documents the swimming abilities and migratory habits of white-tailed deer.

Simmons, M. H. "Report on Island Titles Along the Coast of Maine, under the Resolve of 1913, Chapter 180." *Report of the Maine Forest Commissioner*. Augusta, Maine, 1914.

A listing of the islands that were found to be in the public domain in 1913.

Simpson, Dorothy. *The Maine Islands in Story and Legend*. Philadelphia: J. B. Lippincott, 1960.

Research material compiled from the Maine Writers Research Club.

Small, H. W. *A History of Swan's Island, Maine*. Ellsworth, Maine, 1898.

A thorough history of the island compiled by a resident and based on many first-hand recollections of the island's old people.

Smalley, Albert J. *St. George, Maine.* Typewritten manuscript available from Maine State Library, Augusta, Maine.

An informative history of everything from the design of tidal sawmills to a description of the methods of quarrying granite. A first-rate piece of work.

Smith, George Otis. "Description of the Penobscot Bay Quadrangle, Maine." *Geologic Atlas Folio,* 149. Washington, D.C.: Government Printing Office.

Smith, John (Captain). *A Description of New England: or the Observations and Discoveries of Captain John Smith (Admiral of that Country) in the North of America in the Year of Our Lord 1614.* London, 1614.

Smith's account of his voyage to the coast of Maine, which, together with Rosier's and Levett's accounts, give us the best look at the condition of Maine's forest and fishing resources.

Snow, Wilbert. *Collected Poems.* Middletown, Connecticut: Wesleyan University Press, 1963.

Snow was born on Whitehead Island in the Muscle Ridge, where his father was part of the lifesaving-station crew. His poetry reflects a great deal of the flavor of Maine island living—from fishing to quarrying to hunting.

Sterling, Robert T. *Lighthouses of the Maine Coast.* Brattleboro, Vermont: Stephen Greene Press, 1935.

The dates of the construction (and often the automation) of every lighthouse on the Maine coast, with a short anecdote from its history.

Stern, William L. (ed.). *Adaptive Aspects of Insular Evolution.* Bellingham, Washington: Washington State University Press, 1974.

Theoretical discussion of the effect of isolation of small gene pools.

Tinbergen, Niko. *The Herring Gull's World. A Study of the Social Behavior of Birds.* New York: Harper and Row, 1960.

The classic account of the behavior of this highly social bird by the man who helped define and later won the Nobel Prize for ethology.

Tyler, Harry. "Common Terns, Arctic Terns and Roseate Terns in Maine." Augusta, Maine: State Planning Office.

This is one of a continuing series of pamphlets describing Maine's bird life and other unique natural features. All are written for a general audience and are good educational tools.

Varney, George J. *Gazetteer of the State of Maine.* Boston, 1882.

A valuable source of odd pieces of historical data for island towns.

Wasson, George S. *Sailing Days on the Penobscot: The Story of the River and the Bay in the Old Days*. New York: Norton, 1932.

Description of the coasting world in the 1870–1880s with an interesting chapter on Isle au Haut.

Wheeler, George A. and Henry W. *History of Brunswick, Topsham and Harpswell*. Boston, 1878.

Dates of early settlement for the islands on this side of Casco Bay.

Whipple, J. M. *A Geographical Review of the District of Maine*. Bangor, Maine, 1816.

Interesting listing of the timber products that were commercially valuable at the time, with notes on their distributions.

Williamson, William D. *The History of the State of Maine 1602–1820*. 2 volumes. Hallowell, Maine, 1832.

Good coverage of the Indian Wars. Volume 1 has a section on the islands.

Winship, G. P. *Sailors' Narratives of Voyages Along the New England Coast 1524–1624*. New York, 1905.

A good place to find descriptions and accounts of little-known voyages to Maine.

Winslow, Sidney L. *Fish Scales and Stone Chips*. Portland, Maine: Machigone Press, 1952.

The closest thing to a history of Vinalhaven by a man whose father was part of the quarry era.

Wise, David A. "The Flora of Isle au Haut, Maine." *Rhodora*, Vol. 72, 1970.

A detailed description of the vegetation of a forested outer island.

Woodbury, Charles L. *The Relation of the Fisheries to the Settlement of North America*. Boston, 1880.

Other historians have discussed the connection between fishing and exploration, but no other writer has made it the central thesis of a book.

——————. *Pemaquid and Monhegan*. Hyde Park, New York: Hyde Park Historical Society, 1891.

More on the winter fishery.

Wroth, Lawrence. *The Voyages of Giovanni da Verrazano*. New Haven, Connecticut: Yale University Press, 1970.

A new translation of Verrazano's journals.

Young, Hazel. *Islands of New England*. Boston: Little, Brown, 1945.

Except for the last chapter, this book is really about the islands of Maine, written by the daughter of a Matinicus lobsterman.

Rick Perry

About the Author

Over the past ten years Philip W. Conkling has visited more than 800 Maine islands, collecting ecological information for Hurricane Island Outward Bound School, the Nature Conservancy, the Maine Coast Heritage Trust, and individual island owners.

In 1984 he founded the Island Institute, a membership-based resource-management information service for the island owners and communities along the Maine coast. The institute publishes *Island Journal*, an annual book-format publication that examines the ways humans have interacted with the Maine islands for over four centuries.

Mr. Conkling lives in Rockport, Maine, with his wife, Jamien Morehouse, and two sons.